D1809124

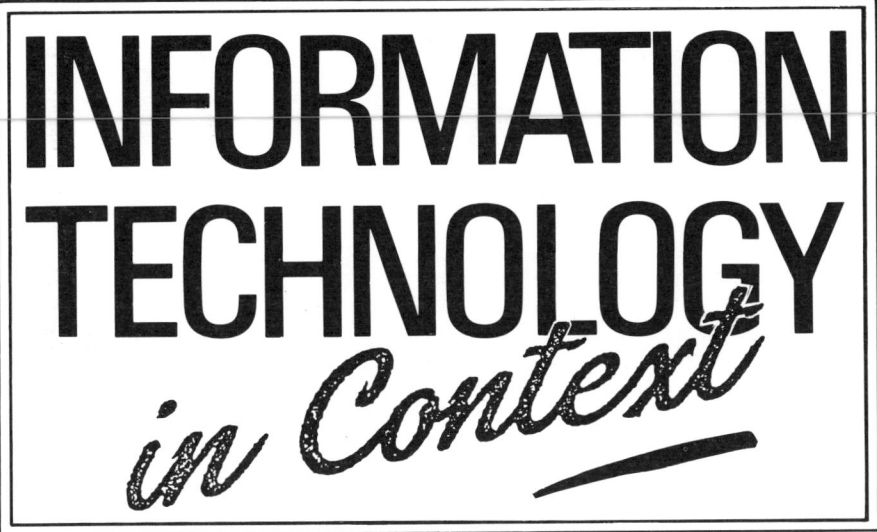

INFORMATION TECHNOLOGY *in Context*

JACKY GRIFFIN BOB DOLDEN

Hodder & Stoughton
LONDON SYDNEY AUCKLAND TORONTO

Publisher's Acknowledgements

The following companies, institutions and individuals have given permission to reproduce photographs in this book:
Barclays Bank plc (ix), British Telecom (85), C. Itol Electronics Co. Ltd (93, middle), EMI Records UK (132), Epson (UK) Ltd (92), Hewlett Packard Ltd (93, top), IBM UK Ltd (11, 21, bottom, 61, 117), IBS (154), Lloyds Bank plc (58), Live Aid (152), Metropolitan Police (viii, 36, top, 46, bottom right, 49), NCR Ltd (13), Nottingham County Council (46), Racal-Milgo Ltd (80), Sally and Richard Greenhill (42, 45), Science Photo Library (79, bottom, 128, bottom right, 129, bottom). Stukeley Computer Services (151), Vincent Martinelli (47, 128, bottom left, 129, top), Virgin Records (xi, bottom), W.H. Smith Group plc (156).

The publishers would like to thank the following for permission to use the photographs making up the cover:
Access – Lloyds Bank plc, Barclaycard, British Telecommunications plc, Citroen, National Westminster Bank plc, Scotcade.

The publishers would also like to thank the following for their help in the production of this book:
Alleyn's School, Dulwich, Ashton Tate, Croydon Police Station, Darton House School for the Blind, Ford Motor Co., Gateway Supermarkets, Girobank, Kent County Library, J. Sainsbury plc, Record Trade Centre.

© 1990 Jacky Griffin and Bob Dolden

First published in Great Britain 1990

British Library Cataloguing in Publication Data
Griffin, Jacky
 Information Technology in context.—(GCSE computer studies through applications).
 1. Computer sciences
 I. Title   II. Dolden, Bob
 004

ISBN 0 340 49322 4

All rights reserved. No part of this publication may be reproduced or transmitted in any form or by any means, electronically or mechanically, including photocopying, recording or any information storage or retrieval system, without either the prior permission in writing from the publisher or a licence permitting restricted copying. In the United Kingdom such licences are issued by the Copyright Licensing Agency, 33–34 Alfred Place, London WC1E 7DP

Typeset in Gill Sans by Wearside Tradespools, Fulwell, Sunderland
Printed and bound in Great Britain for the educational publishing division of Hodder and Stoughton Limited, Mill Road, Dunton Green, Sevenoaks, Kent by St Edmundsbury Press, Bury St Edmunds, Suffolk

Contents

Introduction for teachers

Information Technology in Context is concerned with pupils developing their IT capabilities and learning and applying problem-solving skills. It is designed to help teachers and students to learn about IT using stimulating, active and exciting methods.

It leaves behind more traditional approaches of teaching in a dry, abstract way, and instead involves real people, situations and activities in the world of computers. It adopts the strategy of a spiral curriculum, where topics are introduced several times, from different aspects and at different levels, so that students gradually build up a real understanding of IT concepts. Ideas from recent research findings as well as from practical experience have been incorporated in order to make the subject interesting and relevant to *all* students. It avoids all unnecessary links with mathematical and technical concepts, and instead builds upon students' general knowledge.

Each chapter of the book uses an application of IT as a vehicle for introducing, reinforcing or completing IT concepts. A variety of questions is included throughout the chapter to encourage practical activities including discussion, investigation, problem-solving and group work. The questions are often open-ended and may have no single correct answer, but many equally valid alternative ones. The questions and activities at the end of each chapter draw ideas together and generalize topics in a wider context. The applications have been chosen to reflect the interests of students, their suitability as teaching vehicles and to cover the range of types of application expected in IT and computing courses. Each application is chosen as an example of its type, and should not be seen as a generalization. For example, the Crest Supermarket chain used in the first chapter is not intended to be a model for other supermarkets. Knowledge of other supermarket systems which students may bring to the classroom can be used to highlight the similarities of and differences between systems.

This book is designed to be used as a teaching book for courses in Information Technology and Computer Studies. All the topics on all the current GCSE Computer Studies syllabuses can be covered using this book. It is suitable for a wide range of students, since the book has been carefully written to ensure a suitable level of readability. New vocabulary is introduced naturally, with context rather than formal definitions providing the meanings. The open-ended nature of many of the questions makes it possible for them to be answered at different levels.

Project work is an essential part of GCSE and many other courses. The precise format of the project work required for syllabuses varies, but always follows the idea of students 'using computers sensibly to produce solutions to appropriate problems' (GCSE National Criteria for Computer Studies). The activities in this book encourage this approach.

Many of the end-of-chapter software activities could be developed into suitable projects. Most of them are capable of being made into projects at a variety of levels of complexity, so that they may be attempted by students of different abilities.

Concepts are rarely covered entirely in one section of the book. More often, they are built up over a number of chapters. They are introduced at first at a superficial level, and are carefully developed throughout the book. Consequently, it is important to follow through the book in the order in which it is laid out. This is not intended to limit the styles and strategies that teachers use in the classroom, but to provide stimuli and opportunity for teachers to use a wide variety of methods and activities. In addition to following this book, students would need to learn how to use a range of software, for example, word processors, data retrieval packages and spreadsheets.

Information Technology in Context is designed to be used in the classroom. It is expected that other resources will be available at times, for example, reference books and computers. But the most important resource in the classroom is the teacher, who can use his or her professional skills to develop the cues provided in this book. Many of these cues are given in the form of questions which are introduced throughout the text.

The questions can be used in a variety of ways. They can be used as the starting points for class or group discussions or investigations. Many questions can also provide stimuli for written work. Teachers may like to combine these activities, for example with individual written work following on from periods of discussion.

In many cases, there are many possible answers to a question. Sometimes, no one answer is more 'correct' than any other. The purpose of the questions is often to raise issues, and to provide stimuli to encourage students to think about problems and the ways they can be solved. Teachers will need to react sensitively to the answers given by students, and to avoid directing students towards particular ideas or solutions. Students should be able to answer many of the questions at a level appropriate to their achievement. Teachers should also be aware that the level of answer is relative to the position of the question in the book. Early questions will require limited detail and expect little in the way of background knowledge of computing, whereas later ones should make use of accumulated knowledge and understanding. Because of the way that concepts are built up, and the way that the questions are used, it is best if students attempt all the questions which are incorporated into the text.

The general questions at the end of each chapter have different roles from the other questions. Some of the general questions expand concepts into other application areas, whereas some draw ideas together. Others provide ideas for further depth of work, including projects. It is not necessary for students to attempt all of these questions, nor is the order in which these questions are attempted important, as long as they are used in relation to the appropriate chapter.

These are examples of ways of using some of the questions in the book:

Question: What could Patricia do if someone wants to buy an item which doesn't have a price label? (page 1)

Many answers would be valuable here, and would probably be best considered in some form of discussion. Advantages and disadvantages of the suggested solutions should also be considered. For example, it may be suggested that Patricia should leave the till to go and look for the price on the shelf. Does this solve the problem? Does it raise any other problems?

How might the customers queuing for Patricia's till react?

It is not expected that students will know what actually happens in this situation in any particular supermarket. The crucial points are that the students realize that unlabelled items present a problem, and that somehow a way must be found of dealing with the problem. Further, they should appreciate that there are many possible solutions, each with pros and cons.

The discussion could be followed by students preparing individual written answers.

Question: The STOCK file is kept on a magnetic storage medium. Why could this not be a magnetic tape? (page 7)

At the point at which this question is raised, students have not been 'taught' that magnetic tape can only be used for serial access of data. They do know that the STOCK file needs to be accessed and amended very quickly – in real-time. The analogy of data files on magnetic tape to music recorded on cassette tape could be made. Students are likely to appreciate the problems involved in quickly finding a specific part of a specific song on a cassette recording. Where appropriate, new ideas should be linked to existing knowledge in this way.

Question: Which things were looked up from the STOCK file? Which were worked out by the computer? Which were keyed in by the POS operator? (page 10)

This question refers to the items printed on a till receipt. This is much more of a traditional, closed type of question, where students can find the answers from the preceding text, and there is little scope for variation or alternatives.

General question: This is an example of a data capture form. It is used to collect information from people applying to join a swimming club.

NAME _____

ADDRESS _____

AGE ____

HOW FAR CAN YOU SWIM? ____

WHAT SORT OF SWIMMING DO YOU DO? ____

WHICH NIGHT CAN YOU COME TO THE CLUB? ____

If you had to fill in this form can you think of any problems you might have? Do you think the club will always get the sort of answers they are expecting? What else might they need to know that they have not asked? Could they have worded the questions more clearly? Could they have given instructions on the form?

Design a better data capture form for the swimming club. (page 28)

This question comes at the end of the first chapter, where data capture forms have been considered in the context of their use for collecting data for the STOCK file. This question aims to put data capture forms into another context, so that the more general principles involved in their design will emerge. The design in terms of its artistic merit is of secondary importance to the functionality of the form. The question includes a number of prompts to raise some of the issues involved, but of course the teacher and/or students could raise others.

General question: You have spent some time studying the computer system installed into Crest Supermarkets. Do you have any suggestions for changes or improvements to it? (page 28)

This provides the opportunity for an overall look at the whole system. It also encourages a deeper investigation. Again, there may be additional prompts that the teacher could include, or this question could be used as a challenge to a student who has already grasped the main concepts and who is capable of working through this alone. It would also be suitable for collaborative work for a small group of students.

Software activity: The Crest Supermarket decides to use a VDU terminal as a changing display of special offers. Using a viewdata program, design some special offer pages, and link them together into a display. (page 29)

Obviously this question does not attempt to teach the use of a particular viewdata package. In view of the range of software available in schools, it is not appropriate to include activities relating to particular programs. This software activity, like the others, provides an opportunity for linking the practical computer-based work with the rest of the course. It could be done as an individual or group task or even as a class project. The level of sophistication of the activity is dependent on many factors, such as the ability and interests of the students and the way the teacher organizes the computer-based work; but it would be possible for most students to develop this, and any of the other software activities, into GCSE project work at an appropriate level.

▷ What this book covers

The format of the book makes it difficult to describe exactly what is covered in each chapter, since many concepts are developed over a number of chapters. This section tries to give a summary and an overall picture of each chapter, to assist in lesson and course planning.

Bazaar Computers

This initial chapter introduces many topics and concepts which are developed throughout the book. The scene is set in a particular supermarket, but widens to include other types of retail situations. Considerations needed for systems analysis and design form an important part of this chapter. There are illustrations of the need for data security, and for back-up systems to overcome system failure. Examples are given showing why data needs to be coded and how this can be done, and this leads on to methods of data storage. Relevant hardware is considered throughout the chapter, together with a wide range of input media.

Keywords for each section:

The story so far . . .
automatic re-ordering, barcode, codes, file, laser scanner, POS, parallel running, pilot study, printer, program, terminal, testing, VDU

Keeping track
barcodes, direct access, field, file, key-field, magnetic storage medium, magnetic tape, on-line, POS, record, real-time, search, update

Coding information
barcodes, check digit, codes, file, light pen, POS operator

Putting the stock on file
barcodes, bubble memory, cassette tape, codes, data capture, field, file, magnetic tape encoder, magnetic disk, non-volatile memory, network, on-line, price look-up, program, server, sort, terminal, update, VDU, validation, verification, volatile memory

Following instructions
barcodes, flow diagram, POS, truth table

Taking stock
automatic re-ordering, barcodes, batch processing, cassette tape, codes, file, Kimball tag, machine readable, magnetic tape, magnetic disk, magnetic strip, mark sense form, optical mark reader, optical character reader, on-line, POS, real-time, system flow chart, update

Designing the system
barcode, data capture, documentation, feasibility study, file, implementation, mainframe, software packages, program, programmer, programming languages, systems design, testing

General questions and Software activities
batch processing, codes, data capture, data collection, errors, feasibility study, file, input, logic diagram, merging, network printer, POS, real-time, server, system failure, terminal, testing, transaction file, truth table, update, VDU, validate

The Computer Force

The scene for this chapter is computer use within the Metropolitan Police. Following on from a discussion of the computer control of traffic lights, more general ideas on control technology, representation of algorithms and modular approaches to programming are developed. The police use of databases leads into issues of computer and data security, as well as social and personal implications of computer use.

Keywords for each section:

The story so far . . .
communication, mainframe

The Camberwell incident
codes, communication, flow chart, password, terminal, VDU

Helping with inquiries
communication, field, file, magnetic storage medium, record, search

Patterns of incidents
content addressable file store (CAFS), disk controller, file, flow chart, free text retrieval, full structure indexing, indexing, record, real-time, search

Spreading the word
communication, file, printer, real-time, terminal, updating, verify

Traffic incidents
control, dry run, flow chart, procedures, program, pseudo-code, sensors

Lock up your data!
back-up, central processor unit, communication processors, computer fraud, error reports, file, password, security, terminal, VDU

General questions and Software activities
algorithm, computer fraud, control, file, hard copy, output, pre-printed stationery, pseudo-code, security, terminal, updating, VDU

Money Power

This chapter examines the ways that computers are used in a range of financial applications. Computer use is looked at from different points of view to encourage pupils to consider the pros and cons of computerization A number of modes of data processing are introduced, and an algorithmic approach to problem solving is developed, mainly through examination of the function of an automatic cash dispenser. Issues relating to error detection are also covered.

Keywords for each section:

The story so far . . .
file, record

Clearing the cheque
code, field, file, flow chart, machine readable, magnetic ink character recognition, magnetic tape, master file, sort, terminal, transaction file, update, verify

Checking for mistakes
errors, modulo check, record, turn-around document, update, validation

Cash around the clock
field, file, magnetic storage medium, operating system, PIN, restricted keyboard, terminal, time-slice, time-sharing

What the customer sees
analyst programmer, character set, input, pilot, programmer, program, restricted keyboard, terminal, testing, touch-sensitive screens, user-interface

The money program
algorithm, input, PIN, procedures

Banking on TV
Ceefax, code, computer fraud, EFT, EFTPOS, errors, hard copy, interactive system, network, Oracle, packet switching, Prestel, printer, security, teletext, VDU

General questions and Software activities
ASCII, batch processing, character set, code, communication, direct access,

errors, file, flow chart, interactive, machine readable, on-line, off-line, software package, program, records, serial access, time-share, user-interface

Volumes of Computers

The uses made of information technology in libraries form the background for this chapter. Files and file structures, methods of processing and operation, and information retrieval, including communications and access of remote data bases, are the major areas covered.

Keywords for each section:

The story so far . . .
analog, ASCII, barcode, batch processing, baud, bit, block gap, buffer, byte, cassette tape, character set, code, digital, field, file, flow chart, K, Kilobyte, magnetic tape, tape reader, memory, modem, parity bit, parity check, records, signal, sort, update

Deciding on the system
assembler, barcode, BASIC, cassette tape, COBOL, code, compiler, documentation, file, FORTRAN, high level language, input, interpreter, investigation, low level language, machine code, magnetic type, object code, output, programmer, program, program modules, programming language, program library, source program, systems analyst, testing, translator, update

Where are the books?
error report, field, file, flow chart, input, magnetic tape, master file, output, pre-printed stationery, printer, sort, transaction file, update, validation

Dear Borrower . . .
batch processing, bit, buffer, CPU, central processor unit, computer operator, Data Protection Act, error message, error report, field, file, graphics, log, magnetic backing store, magnetic tape, magnetic disk, memory, microfiche, network, on-line, operating system, operator's console, output, password, peripherals, printers, program, record, security, serial access, serial file, signal, sort, terminal, update, utility

At the computer centre
batch processing, CPU, communication file, front-end processor, multi-access, multiplexer, on-line, operating system, real-time, systems analyst, terminal, time-share, time-slice, update

Making the system better
Blaise, Ceefax, field, file, index, interactive system, inverted file, key word, logic diagram, modem, network, Oracle, Prestel, record, SIR, search, teletext, terminal, truth table

General questions and Software activities
barcode, bugs, cassette tape, coded information, computer operator, direct access, documentation, errors, feasibility study, file, flow chart, implementation, input, local area network, magnetic media, network, object program, operating system, peripherals, procedures, programmer, SIR, sort, source

Computer Washing

This chapter is set around the design and manufacture of a washing machine. It develops earlier ideas relating to control technology, algorithms and programming. Systems analysis and related problems are discussed. The chapter also looks at low level programming, the function of the CPU, and the component parts of a computer. Sensible approaches to decisions about the appropriateness of computerized solutions are also encouraged.

Keywords for each section:

The story so far . . .
data collection, input, investigation

The washing programmes
algorithm, code, flow chart, program

The design
arithmetic and logic unit, analog, analog to digital converter, assembly language, BASIC, bit, bug, chip, compile, control, control unit, digital, electro-mechanical control, electronic displays, high level language, input, interpreter, low level language, machine code, memory, memory map, microcontroller, microprocessor, object code, output, port, program, programmer, program errors, RAM, ROM, sensors, testing, translation, transmission errors

Inside the machine
assembler, bit, chip, control unit, fetch–execute cycle, instruction register, instruction set, machine code, memory location, microcontroller, port, program, program counter, translator

What's going on?
baud rate, bit, display processor, fluorescent display, graphics display, input, LED, microelectronic components, microcontroller, parity, port, program, pulse train, serial interface, serial port, transmission error

Getting it clean—removing the bugs
bug, debug, microcontroller, program, programmer, testing

What could go wrong?
back-up memory, electrical pulses, flow chart, microcontroller, output, sensors

General questions and Software activities
algorithm, arithmetic and logic unit, applications, bit, CPU, chip, computer configuration, control application, control unit, flow chart, input, microprocessor output, software packages, pre-printed stationery, programming, simulations

Computer Disks

Although some new topics are covered, this chapter mainly functions as a consolidation and revision section. The scene is set in a record company, and looks at some of the plans and decisions which have to be made. Much of the previous content of the book is developed, including systems analysis and design, hardware considerations, applications software, methods of processing and implications of computer use.

Keywords for each section:

The story so far . . .
computer bureau, data processing department, investigation, mainframe, programmer, programming, program

Can computers help?
graphical output, hard copy, input, output, program

Paying the musicians
code, computer bureau, data capture, field, file, flow chart, in-house, input, investigation, software package, program, validation, verification

Records around the world
applications package, BASIC, COBOL, communication, database, dBase III+, feasibility study, file, flow chart, high level languages, implementation, software package, programmer, routine, testing, utility

Sharing information
Data Protection Act, file, record locking, record, restricted data, security, terminal, update

Developing the system
CPU, buffer, file, graphical output, hand-held computer, hard copy, intelligent terminal, input, investigation, memory, mini computer, mouse, operating system, output, payroll, peripherals, pre-printed stationery, printer, program, security, terminal time-share

Compiling the charts
barcodes, cassette tape, code, communications, data collection, magnetic tape, network, Prestel, terminal

General questions and Software activities
applications, batch processing, communication, computer bureau, computer configuration, Data Protection Act, file, hard copy, on-line, peripherals, programmers, software package, systems analyst, systems diagram, systems flow chart, update

Acknowledgements

Wayne Shevlin at Virgin Records
David Buckle at Hotpoint PLC
Krysia Kmita
The Metropolitan Police
The British Market Research Bureau

Bazaar Computers

▷ *The story so far...*

Patricia Marley has worked in the Crest Supermarket in Dalton for 6 months. She started off sticking price labels on things, and checking and filling the shelves, but now she has moved on to working on the checkout. She has to key in the prices of all the things customers buy, take the money and give the correct change. She quite likes her job, but she hates it when things are brought to the checkout without prices marked on them, and she sometimes makes mistakes when she works out how much change to give.

I	**What could Patricia do if someone wants to buy an item which doesn't have a price label?**

Sylvia McFarland is the Checkout Supervisor at the Crest Supermarket. Her job is to make sure that there are no problems at the checkouts. This means that she has to organize the staff tea and lunch breaks, so that there are never too many people off at the same time. She has to try to make sure that the checkout operators don't make mistakes because this could upset customers, or lose money for the supermarket. She has to keep an eye on the checkout operators to make sure that they work hard, and are honest.

2	**What sort of mistakes could checkout operators make? Can you think of ways of preventing these mistakes?**
3	**If a checkout operator was dishonest, how could they cheat the supermarket? Can you think of ways of stopping the cheating?**

The barcode on a packet of Kenco coffee

This Crest Supermarket is one of a large chain of supermarkets. The directors of the chain are convinced that using computers would make the supermarkets more efficient.

The management staff at the Dalton Crest are sent on a course to explain to them how the computer will change the way that the supermarket is run. They then have to train the rest of the staff.

Sylvia is told that the checkout tills will be replaced by new ones called 'Point of Sale' or POS tills. The POS tills will be connected to the computer, but they will still look a lot like the old tills. Most of the items for sale in the supermarket will have special labels that these POS tills can read, so that the checkout operator will not have to key in the price.

They are called barcodes, because the bars of black and white are a code for information about the item.

A device on the POS till reads the code by shining a light beam on it, and detecting the pattern that is reflected back.

Sylvia expects that the code contains the price of the item, and she is surprised to be told that it doesn't. Every item has a different code, which contains information on where it was made, the manufacturer, the sort of

Here is the device which reads the barcodes

A point of sale terminal

thing it is, and its size, but not its price. 'But how is all that information any use at the till?' asks Sylvia. 'The checkout operator only needs to know how much to charge the customer!'

Sylvia is told that the computer keeps a file of the code numbers of all the items, together with their prices. When the code number has been read, the price can be found from the file. It can then be printed on the receipt, and added to the total cost of all the items.

```
CREST
SUPERMARKET

3*    0.35
1*    1.19
1*    0.55
1*    0.55
1*    0.55
      3.19 TL
```

4   Does this mean that they can stop sticking price labels on everything in the supermarket?

5   Which items cannot have a barcode stuck on them? How could these be dealt with at the checkout?

Sylvia quickly realizes that this new system will help to stop mistakes, and cheating by the checkout operators.

```
CREST SUPERMARKET
      DALTON

11:12:88

TILL NUMBER 5

MILK         0.35
ANDREX       1.19
TISSUES      0.55
TISSUES      0.55
TISSUES      0.55
  TOTAL      3.19
AMT TRD      5.00
  CHANGE     1.81

15:31

    THANK  YOU
```

6   What sort of mistakes and fiddles will be stopped? How will they be prevented?

7   Could any new sorts of mistakes or fiddles be introduced?

What about the customers? The supermarket must keep its customers happy, or else it won't make any money.

8   What difference will this new computer system make to the customer? Before you think about your answer, think about the time it takes to key in a price compared to the time it takes to pass an item over a light beam. And look at the two receipts. The first one is from the old system. The second one is the type that the new POS system will produce.

Ranjit Deer is in charge of all the shelf-filling workers. When he hears about the new system he first of all thinks 'Oh good! I won't have to get people to stick price labels on everything. That will save time in shelf filling.' Then he wonders if he will have to arrange for the barcodes to be stuck on to all the items. This worries him, because he is sure that mistakes will be made. To a human being, one barcode looks very much like another.

He is relieved to find that the barcodes are put on the goods by the manufacturers, because all the manufacturers and all the supermarkets use the same kind of barcodes. But he is very surprised to find that he must continue to have price labels stuck on everything.

What's the price?

9   What's the point of sticking price labels on everything? The POS till finds out the price from the computer, so why must everything have a price label? Sylvia thinks it's important that everything has a price label. Why? Do you think it's necessary? What else could the supermarket do?

Donna Mandela is the manager of the grocery department. She has to make sure that the supermarket doesn't run out of grocery items.

10 Why is it important that the supermarket does not run out of things?

The chain has a very large central warehouse where it keeps stocks of most items sold in the supermarkets. Shops order items from the warehouse and deliveries are made twice a week. The warehouse space in the supermarket is very small, so they cannot have more stock than will fit on the shelves in the supermarket.

11 What sort of items could not be kept in the central warehouse?

Donna has to be very careful to always have enough of everything, but not too much. She is pleased to hear that, when the computer system is installed, she will be able to send in orders and receive goods from the central warehouse every day. In fact some items will be ordered automatically by the computer. Donna needs to decide the smallest amount of the item that they need to have. Once the stocks falls beneath that amount, the computer could transmit an order to the warehouse. The information is transmitted from the supermarket's computer terminal via telephone lines to a terminal with a printer at the warehouse.

12 What sort of items could be ordered automatically, and what could not? Think about things like washing powder, bread, baked beans, lettuces, ice cream and salad cream.

13 Why should the terminal in the shop have a VDU? Why should the one in the warehouse have a printer?

It takes a lot of time to find out just how many tins of beans or packets of yoghurt are left in the shop. Someone from Donna's department has to go round every day counting the number of items left on the shelf. The computer system will be able to keep an automatic record of the number of items left. Every time an item is sold, it will take one away from the total number of those items. Every time an order is received, the number of items is added to the total. This is not a fool-proof system of stock control.

14 How could this system go wrong? What could happen to make the number of items left on the shelf different from the number on the computer file? When the computer system is installed will it still be necessary to do the visual stock-checks?

Leela Ramdeen is the Manager of the Dalton Crest Supermarket. She is responsible for the overall running of the shop, and most importantly, she must ensure that the shop makes as much profit as possible. She does this

Why is it important to know what is in stock?

by making sure that as much as possible is sold, and that as little as possible is wasted. She knows that the success of her shop is watched very carefully by her bosses, the directors of the chain.

She has been told that the computer system will help her to sell more goods, because the shop will run out of items less often. Because the computer system covers the whole chain of shops, linking all the parts together, she knows that her bosses will be able to find out more detail more quickly about her shop's performance.

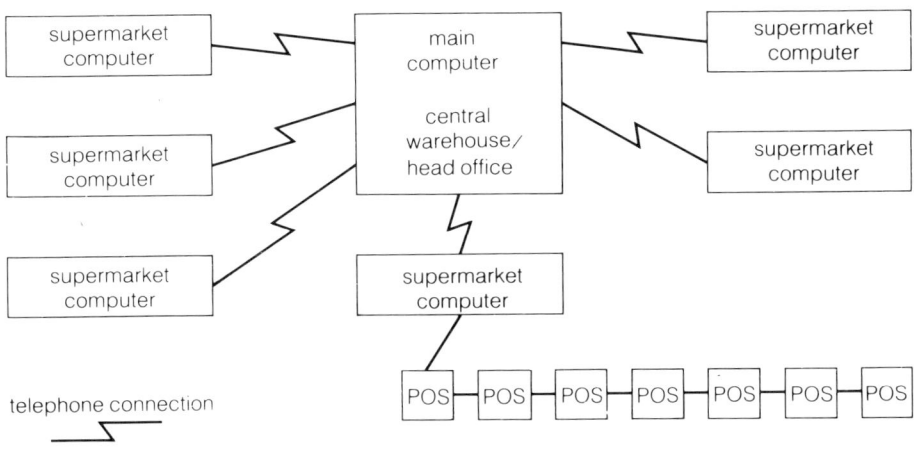

The computer system

Before the computer system is installed, a number of things must be done.

The staff are trained, so that they are prepared to work with the computer system. They are told how their jobs will change.

15 Do you think that all the staff need to be trained? Can you think of any who will not be affected? Which people will find that their work has a lot to do with the computer?

16 What training do you think Patricia needs? Does Sylvia need more training than Patricia?

The Crest directors want to be certain that the computer system works properly before it is installed in all their shops. They try it out in a small number of shops first. This is called doing a pilot study. They discovered from the pilot study that some changes needed to be made to the system before it was installed in the rest of the shops.

18 The rest of the shops were computerized one at a time. Why did they not computerize them all at the same time? Think about the training and other things that have to be organized for each supermarket.

In each supermarket, most of the computer equipment, or hardware, is installed first, in the offices at the back of the shop. But the POS tills are put in place last, when they are ready to be used.

19 Why would the POS tills be put in place so late? How could the
    computer system be checked if there are no POS tills being used
    with customers?

The computer system would be thoroughly tested. The hardware would
be checked and the programs (software) and the data would be checked
too. But even so, things could still go wrong. So for a while, the old system
of running the supermarket is still used, alongside the computer system.
That way, the computer system is tested, and compared with the old
system.
   But eventually, the old system is abandoned, and the computer system
takes over. It will be able to cope with any problems that may come up.
Or so everyone hopes!

▷ Keeping track

A customer buys a packet of creamed coconut. He takes it to Patricia's
checkout (Checkout Number 5), and Patricia passes the packet over the
barcode reader. The price of the packet is looked up in the STOCK file. It
is 68p. The number of packets of creamed coconut is reduced by one in
the STOCK file. The amount of money taken at Patricia's till is increased by
68p and this is recorded on the TILL5 file. The receipt is printed, and the
amount to be paid comes up on the display on the POS till. The customer
hands Patricia £1. Patricia keys in £1 as the amount tendered, and the
amount of change to be given is displayed. Patricia gives the change to the
customer. At the end of each day the stock levels are looked at by the
computer. If the number of packets has fallen below the minimum allowed
stock level, the computer transmits an order for a pre-set amount to the
warehouse.

1 Draw a diagram to show this sequence of events.

2 What information must be kept on the STOCK file about each type
   of stock item?

The STOCK file, like other files, is made up of records. A record contains
all the information on one stock item. Each piece of information is
contained in a field.

3 Draw a table to show the fields needed in the stock file, and give
   three example records.

STOCK FILE

	FIELD 1	FIELD 2	FIELD 3	FIELD 4	FIELD 5	etc.
Record 1						
Record 2						
Record 3						

4 The computer needs to be able to read off the prices of items very quickly. There is a large number of records and it would take too long for the computer to look through every one to find the right one. So the system has to use a direct access system to allow it to go straight to the relevant record.

Not every field in each record is searched, in any case. One particular field is looked at in each record, until the correct one is found. This field is called the key-field.

5 Which field is the key-field here?

Because the POS till is connected to the computer it is said to be on-line. Because the information on the price needs to be returned to the POS till very quickly, and because the STOCK file needs to be updated immediately, this needs to be a real-time system.

6 What could happen if the STOCK file was only updated at the end of each week? Would it be sufficient to update the STOCK file just at the end of each day?

7 The STOCK file is kept on a magnetic storage medium. Why could this not be magnetic tape?

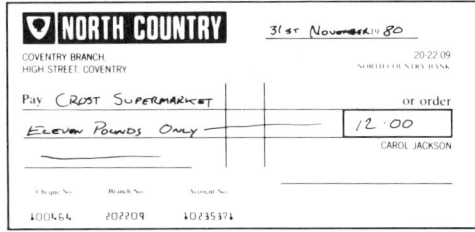

This cheque has not been signed. What other mistakes have been made in the way it has been filled out?

One Monday Patricia works all day on till number 5, except when she has her lunch and tea breaks. The till is not used during her tea breaks, but at lunch time Sylvia takes over. At the end of the day, two big mistakes are discovered. Firstly, a cheque has been accepted which has not been signed by the customer.

8 How could the computer system be used to find out who accepted the faulty cheque?

The second mistake is that the amount of money in the till does not agree with the total of the till receipts. The till is £5 short.

9 How could this mistake have happened? How could it be arranged so that it is possible to say who made the mistake? Why is it important to know who made the mistakes?

The computer system keeps a record of keying-in errors made by each operator. It also keeps a record of the number of items passing through each checkout, and the total amount of money taken at each checkout. This information is given to the manager every day.

10 Why are these reports useful to her?

Information on the activities at each POS till are kept in a separate file for each till. The files are called TILL1, TILL2, TILL3, etc.

> **11 What fields would be needed for these files? What would be the type and length of these fields?**

Show three sample records for one of these files.

POINT OF SALE FILE

	FIELD 1	FIELD 2	FIELD 3	FIELD 4	FIELD 5	etc.
Record 1						
Record 2						
Record 3						

▷ Coding information

The barcodes on the goods are made up of black and white bars which represent numbers. They can be read by a barcode reader. The numbers are also codes for information about each item. Each size and variety of goods has a different barcode. All 580 g cans of Heinz Baked Beans will have the same barcode. The barcode on 450 g cans of Heinz Baked Beans will be slightly different.

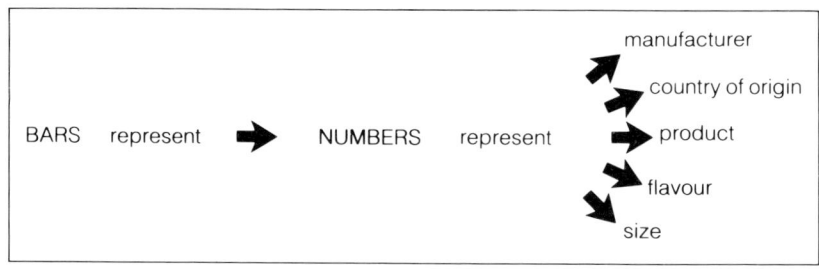

Example:
The barcode on an 8 ounce pack of Kenco Continental Strong Dark Roast Coffee shows these numbers:

5010275978664

The code for the country of origin, or the country where the item is packed, is 50. This means the UK.

10275 is the manufacturer's code. All Kenco products will have this number in their barcode.

97866 is the code for this particular size and type of coffee.

4 is used for checking.

Most barcodes have 13 digits, but they can sometimes have 11 or 8 digits instead. The last digit does not represent anything. It is used as a check to make sure that the barcode is read correctly. All the numbers in a barcode are combined together in a special way to give the last number. When the barcode is read by the scanner or light pen, the computer checks that the last digit matches with the other digits. If it doesn't, then it means that it has not been read properly. Usually, this causes the scanner to bleep, and the operator has to try to read it again.

This last digit is called a check digit. It is only there to check the other digits. Here is how the check digit in a barcode is worked out. (This looks complicated, but it is all done by the computer, remember!)

First 12 digits of barcode number:

5 0 1 0 2 7 5 9 7 8 6 6

Alternate numbers are added together.

* † * † * † * † * † * †
5 0 1 0 2 7 5 9 7 8 6 6

First, all the numbers marked † are added together:

$0 + 0 + 7 + 9 + 8 + 6 = 30$

This total is multiplied by 3:

$30 \times 3 = 90$

Second, all the numbers marked * are added together:

$5 + 1 + 2 + 5 + 7 + 6 = 26$

Then 90 and 26 are added:

$90 + 26 = 116$

Then, beginning with 116, count up until you reach a number ending in 0. This would be 120.

The check digit is $120 - 116 = 4$.

So the complete barcode is 5010275987664.

> **1   How does this help to check that the number is correct? Why is one total multiplied by a different number?**

Here is a list of other barcode numbers

5010275978657   5010033014344
3201560216115   5010033090928

> **2   Which one, do you think, is the barcode for a Lyons Apple and Blackcurrant pie?**
>
> **3   Which one is the barcode for another item made by Lyons?**
>
> **4   Which one is the barcode for something that was not made in the UK?**

The checkout operator has to find the barcode on each item.

> **5   Where do you think the barcode should be to make it easy to find? Should there be more than one copy of the barcode on each item? Where are barcodes usually put? Why do you think this is so?**

The barcode for an apricot pie made by Lyons in the UK. What part of the barcode tells us that the pie was made by Lyons?

```
CREST SUPERMARKET
      DALTON

11:12:88

TILL NUMBER 5

MILK          0.35
ANDREX        1.19
TISSUES       0.55
TISSUES       0.55
TISSUES       0.55
  TOTAL       3.19
AMT TRD       5.00
  CHANGE      1.81

15:31

  THANK YOU
```

This receipt was given to a customer after she paid for her shopping:

The receipt was produced by the till. It used the data in the barcode to find some of the information it needed, and it worked out some of the other items.

6   Which things were looked up from the STOCK file? Which were worked out by the computer? Which were keyed in by the POS operator?

7   Why do you think the till number, the date and the time are included on the receipt?

▷ Putting the stock on file

Fatima Carr works at Crest's Head Office. She will be responsible for setting up the first STOCK file. Each shop will be responsible for keeping its own STOCK file up-to-date, but they will all start off with the same one. Fatima, and her colleagues James and Shireen, will key in all the information about the several thousand different products that the supermarkets sell.

First of all, the data must be collected together. It needs to be written down, so that it can be read easily by Fatima, James and Shireen. Fatima designs a form that will hold all the necessary information about each product.

1   What should Fatima consider when she designs the form? What information has to be entered for every item? Which fields will Fatima be unable to complete in this first STOCK file?

2   Design a data capture form that you think would be helpful to Fatima and her colleagues.

Fatima designs a form . . .   . . . James prepares the relevant information . . .   . . . Shireen inputs it

The data is entered at a Magnetic Tape Encoder, which has a keyboard, VDU, tape drive and processor unit.

The data is keyed in at the keyboard. It is very important that no mistakes are made in entering this data.

3 What sort of mistakes could be made? What could happen if these mistakes were not noticed or corrected?

To prevent mistakes being made in entering the data, it is checked as much as possible.

After typing in each line, Shireen is requested to check what she has typed. She compares what she has typed, which appears on the screen, with what is written down. If they are the same she presses the Y key, and then begins to type in the next line. This checking is called verification.

4 What do you think should happen if the two lines are not the same? If the two lines are the same can you be sure that the data is correct?

5 Can you think of any other ways that the data could be verified?

The Tape Encoder does some checking as the data is typed in. It can be programmed to check the data to make sure that it is sensible, but it cannot be programmed to make sure that the data is correct. For example, the barcode numbers should always have 13 digits. The encoder can be programmed to count the digits, and warn the operator if they type in too many or too few digits. This is called a length check. The barcode number should be made up of numbers, not letters. The machine can check each figure as it is keyed in, and can be programmed to accept only numbers. This is called a type check. These kinds of checks are called validation checks.

6 What kind of validation checks could be made for each field in the STOCK file?

At the Dalton Supermarket, each section manager will be responsible for keeping the STOCK file up to date for their products. So Donna Mandela will be responsible for keeping the data on the grocery items up-to-date.

7 Some updating is done automatically by the computer. What updating is done in this way?

The file will need updating in other ways too.

8 What updating will be needed when new stock arrives from the warehouse?

Collecting data – why is it sometimes necessary to check stock levels by seeing what is on the shelves?

During the winter, Donna decides to keep a smaller stock of ice-cream in the shop.

> 9   What field will need to be changed for each sort of ice-cream they sell? Can you think of any other seasonal changes that Donna might want to make?

The price of Napolina tinned tomatoes is to be increased from 29p to 32p.

> 10   What must be done to make sure that the customer knows the new price? What must be done to make sure that the correct price is charged? Why should this be done when the shop is closed?

Donna discovers that packets of Mushroom Soup mix have not been selling very well, and there are 25 packets on the shelf. The 'Sell by' date on these packets is next Friday's date. Donna wants to sell these packets quickly.

> 11   Draw a diagram showing all the things she must do to encourage people to buy these packets.

Patricia Marley is having a party. She is going to buy the food and drink from the supermarket. If Patricia could change the prices on the STOCK file she could save herself a lot of money. Imagine if she reduced the price of a bottle of wine from £3.50 to 50p, then bought 10 bottles!

> 12   What could be done to make sure that unauthorised changes are not made to the STOCK file?

Some of the section managers at the Dalton Crest are nervous of using the computer. They are worried that they might press the wrong keys, and accidentally erase the STOCK file. Leela Ramdeen tells them that this cannot happen.

13 How could this sort of accident be prevented?

The section managers are not convinced. 'But no system is absolutely accident proof. What would happen if the STOCK file was erased?' asked Donna. 'Would the shop have to close down?'

14 Could the STOCK file be erased accidentally? How could it happen?

Leela explains that the system will be set up so that there will be back-up procedures in case something goes wrong. Normally, all the POS tills will be linked to the supermarket's computer. There the STOCK file is kept on disk, so that the prices can be looked up very quickly, and the STOCK file updated just as quickly.

If the main computer, or its files, can no longer be accessed by the POS terminals, then they can use a back-up copy of the price look-up part of the file. All of the POS tills are linked together in groups of six.

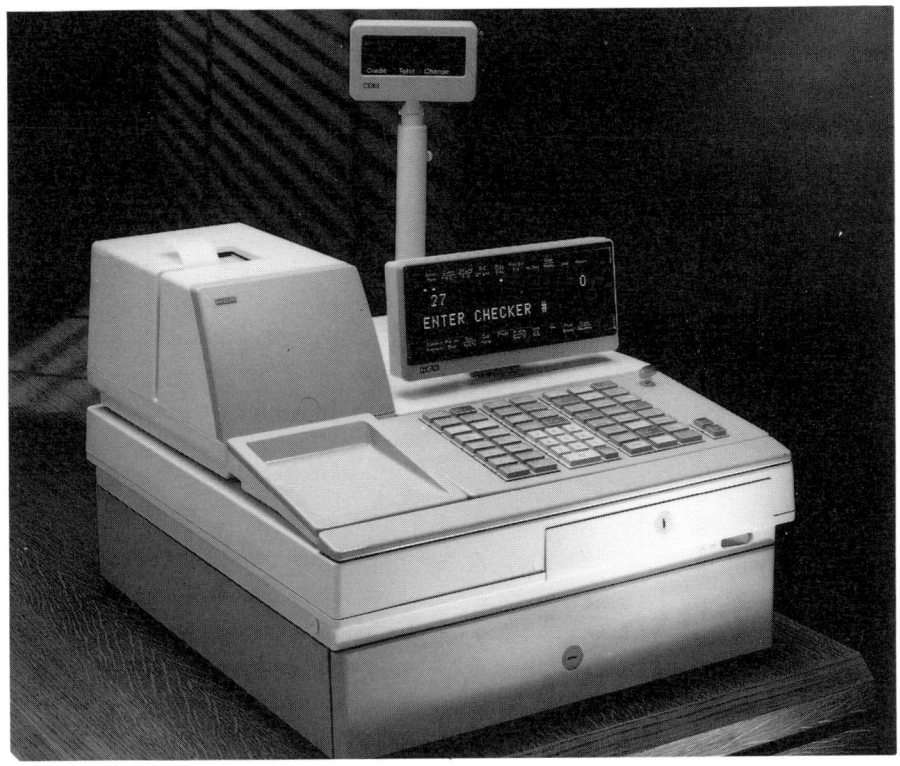

The POS till can never charge the wrong price – or can it?

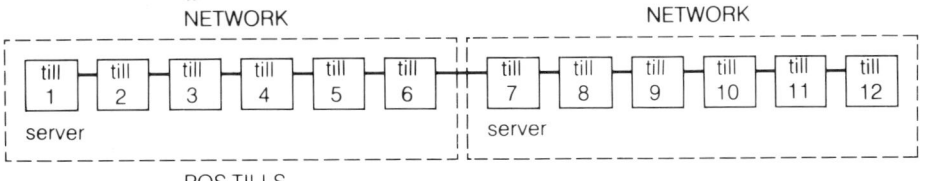

A Point of Sale network

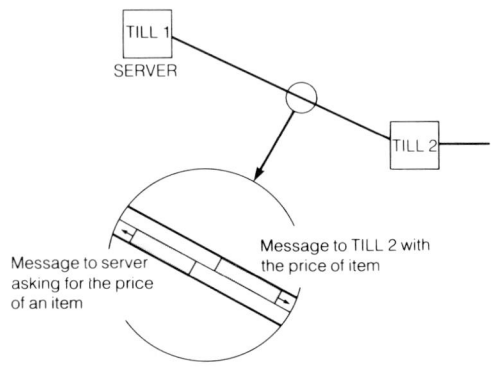

Message to server
asking for the price
of an item

Message to TILL 2 with
the price of item

Network communication

So tills numbered 1, 2, 3, 4, 5 and 6 are all linked, and so are tills numbered 7, 8, 9, 10, 11 and 12. One till in each group has some bubble memory, and on this is kept an up-to-date copy of a file containing the barcodes and the prices of all the supermarket's goods. So each group of POS tills operates like a network of computers. Each POS till can find the correct price from the server's price look-up file, held in bubble memory. The till sends the code of the item to the server; the price is looked up and sent back to the till.

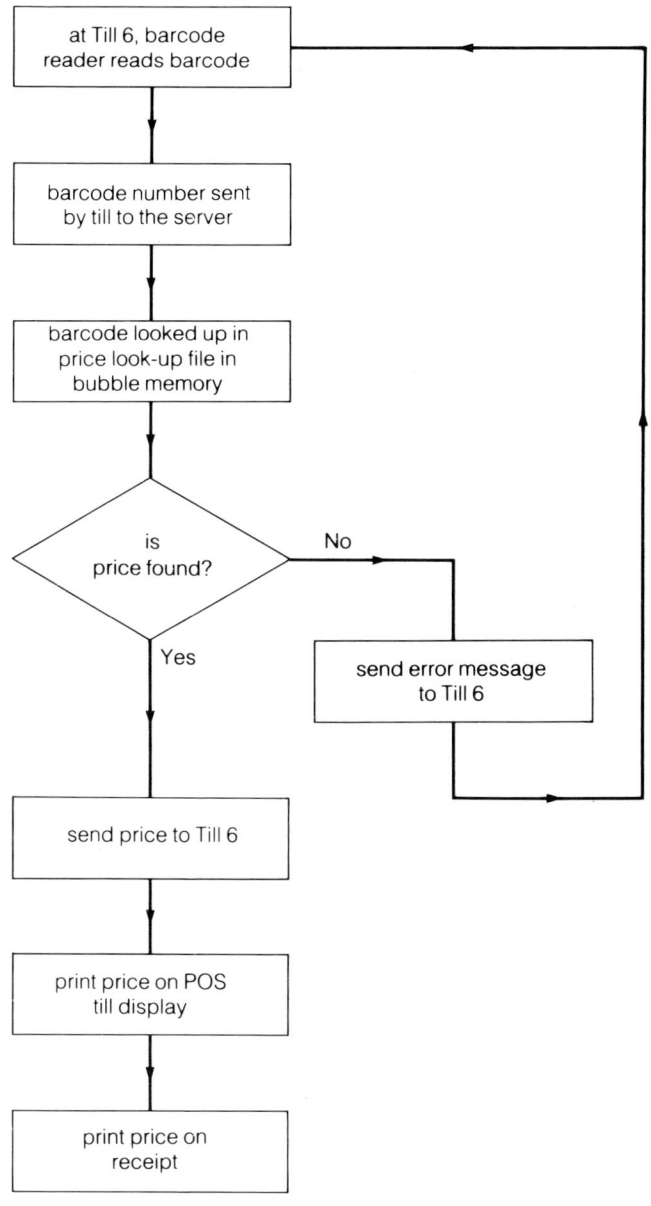

A flow chart of Point of Sale operation

So the shop would be able to stay open, serving customers as normal. But using this back-up method, some of the computer's other activities would not get done. Which ones?

15 Why do you think the price look-up is backed up so carefully?

Some of the other activities are backed up in a different way: for example, the stock levels. The items sold are recorded on a cassette tape at each POS till, so that the STOCK file can be updated when the shop's main computer comes on-line again.

16 What information would need to be recorded for each item sold?

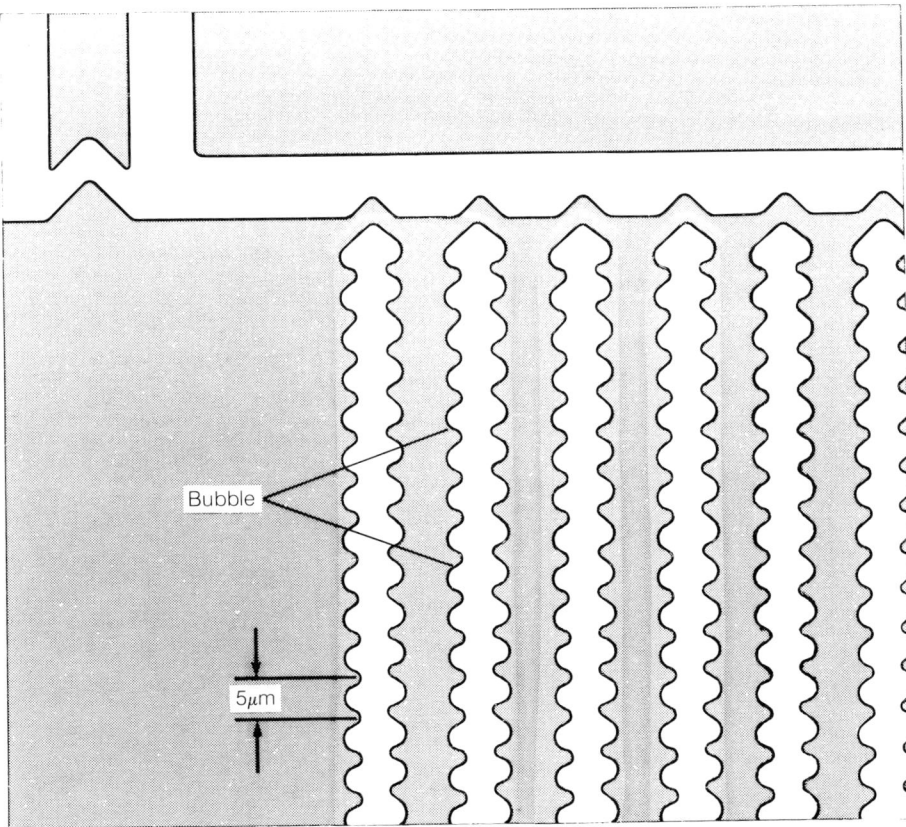

A bubble memory consists of a thin film of magnetic material covering a flat surface. By applying a magnetic field, bubbles can be made in this film. Bubbles are small cylindrical magnetic areas. Data can be represented and stored as chains of bubbles and gaps.

Bubble memory is used because it is non-volatile. This means that it still holds data even when the electricity supply is turned off.

17 Why is non-volatile memory important for storing the look-up file?

18 Are magnetic disks volatile or non-volatile? What about normal computer memory?

Bubble memory is used instead of disks because the data can be accessed much more quickly. The diagram on page 16 shows how the main STOCK file can be updated with the data from the cassette tapes.

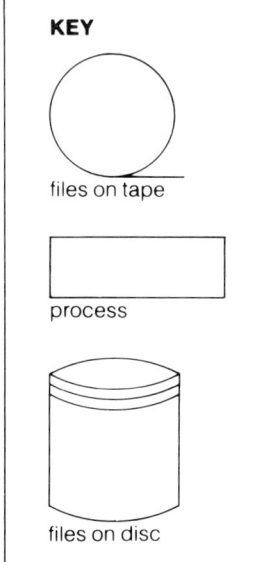

KEY

files on tape

process

files on disc

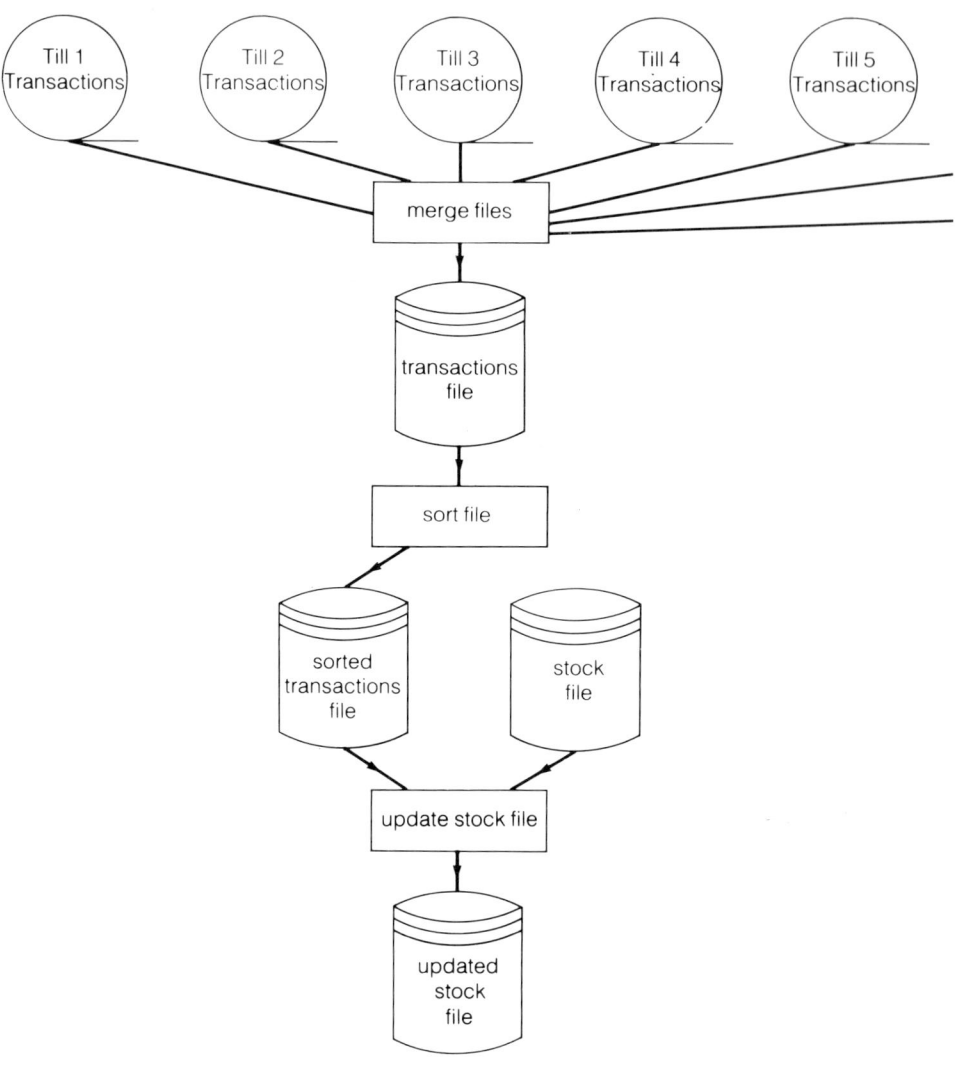

| Till 1 Transactions | Till 2 Transactions | Till 3 Transactions | Till 4 Transactions | Till 5 Transactions |

merge files

transactions file

sort file

sorted transactions file

stock file

update stock file

updated stock file

A systems flow chart showing sorting and updating of the stockfile

19 What happens first to all the data on the cassette tapes? Why do you think this is done?

20 Why does this collection of data need to be sorted? It could be sorted in many different ways, for example, in order of price. How could they decide which way to sort it?

▷ *Following instructions*

Surindra Patel has just been promoted from shelf filling to working on the checkout. She has been given some training, but Patricia has been asked to work with her for the first few days, in case she has any problems. Patricia is only too happy to be able to show off her knowledge, and she is keen to impress Surindra.

She decides to write down instructions for Surindra. She quickly realizes that it would take too long for Surindra to read through instructions every time she got stuck, so she tries to draw a diagram. This sort of diagram is called a flow diagram or flow chart. Can you follow the instructions? If you were stuck could you find out what to do next?

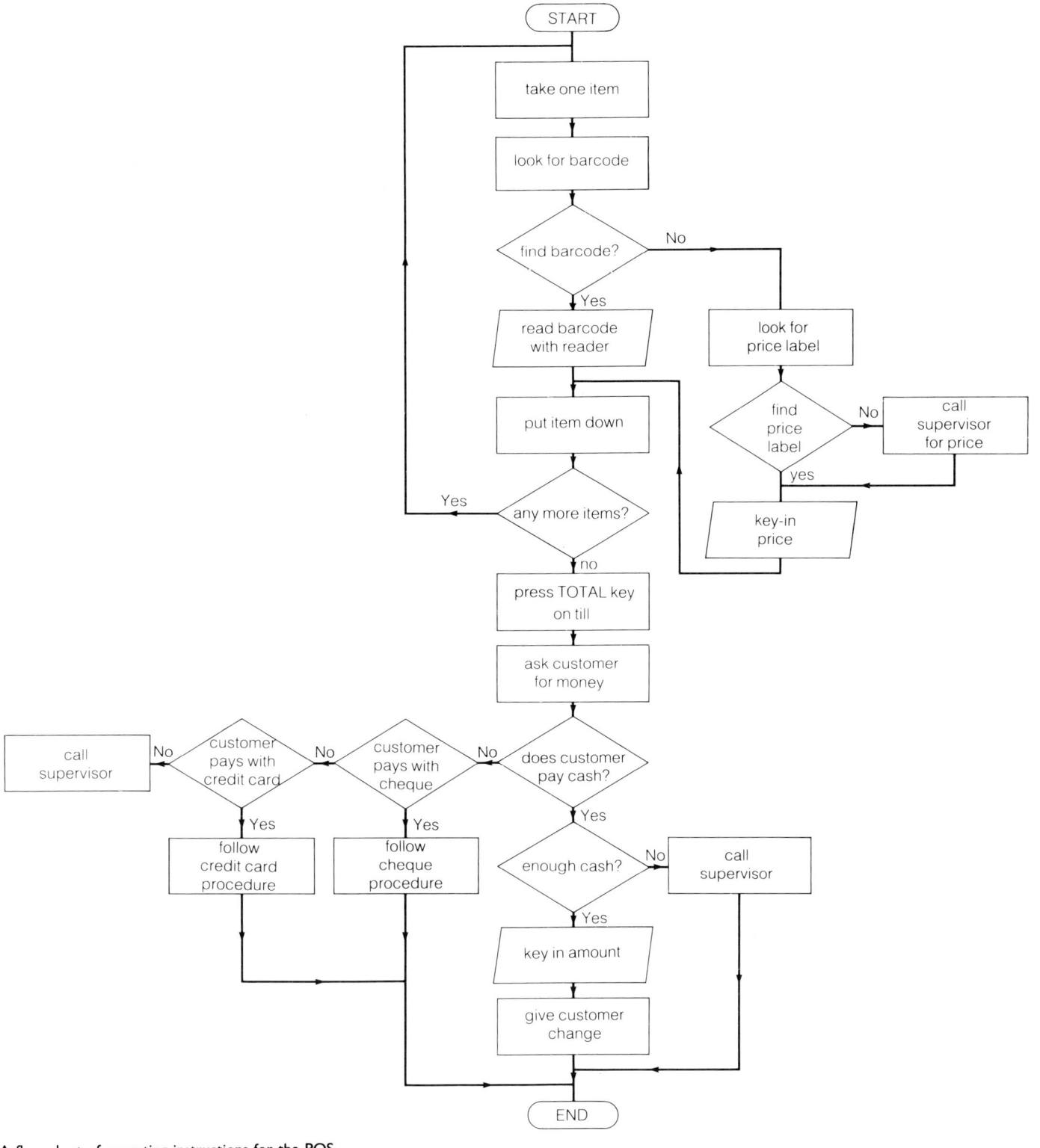

A flow chart of operating instructions for the POS

1 What do you do if an item doesn't have a barcode?

2 What if there's no barcode or price label?

3 If a customer pays cash, what do you do after you've checked that they have given you enough money?

Surindra is fairly happy with these instructions, but she finds sorting out payments a problem. There seem to be so many different ways to pay, and different things to check. She decides to try to devise a way of writing down these rules so that she can refer to them quickly.

First, she knows that there are three different ways to pay: with cash, by cheque, or with an Accard credit card. She feels happy dealing with cash, so concentrates on the other two ways.

So, she knows that if the customer is not paying cash, they must pay either by cheque or by Accard. She makes up a reference table. To make it smaller and quicker to read, she uses 1 to stand for 'Yes' and 0 to stand for 'No'.

4 Can you explain what this table means?

Next she thinks about a customer paying by cheque. If they pay by cheque, they must have a cheque and a cheque guarantee card.

But then Patricia reminds her that cheques are not that straightforward. There are other things to take into consideration. The customer must have a cheque card with the cheque, and the cheque must be filled in correctly, and the signature on the cheque must match the one on the card. Also, the cheque must be for less than £50, or the customer must provide proof of identity.

Cheque OR Accard

Cheque	Accard	OK?
0	0	0
0	1	1
1	0	1
1	1	1

Cheque AND Cheque Guarantee Card

Cheque	Cheque Guarantee Card	OK?
0	0	0
0	1	0
1	0	0
1	1	1

Truth tables for payment methods

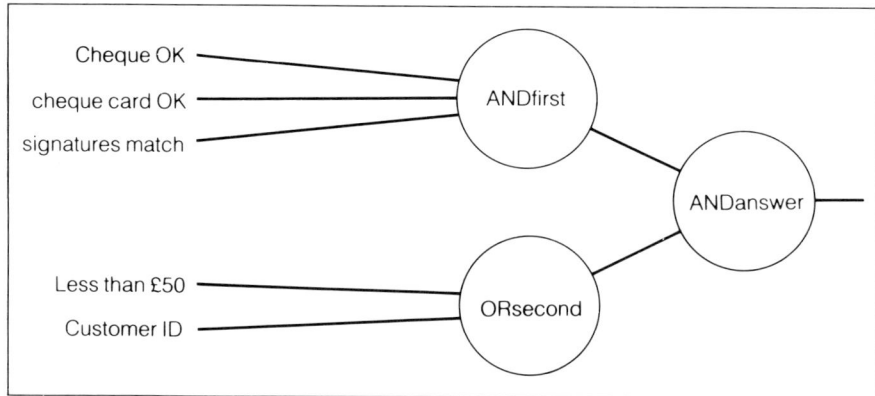

A logic chart for accepting a cheque

If the answer is 1 then the payment can be accepted. If the answer is 0 then it cannot.

5 Copy and complete the table on page 19 for all the different possible circumstances.

This type of table is sometimes called a truth table. Surindra thinks that these tables could be useful on other occasions.

(Cheque AND Card AND Signatures) AND (Less than £50 OR ID)

Cheque	Card	Sig.	first	Less £50	ID	second	answer
0	0	0	0	0	0	0	0
0	0	1		0	0		
0	1	0	0	0	0		
0	1	1		0	0		
1	0	0		0	0		
1	0	1		0	0		
1	1	0		0	0		
1	1	1	1	0	0	0	0
0	0	0	0	0	1	1	0
0	0	1		0	1		
0	1	0	0	0	1		
0	1	1		0	1		
1	0	0		0	1		
1	0	1		0	1		
1	1	0		0	1		
1	1	1		0	1		1
0	0	0	0	1	0	1	0
0	0	1		1	0		
0	1	0	0	1	0		
0	1	1		1	0		
1	0	0		1	0		
1	0	1		1	0		
1	1	0		1	0		
1	1	1		1	0		
0	0	0	0	1	1	1	0
0	0	1		1	1		
0	1	0	0	1	1		
0	1	1		1	1		
1	0	0		1	1		
1	0	1		1	1		
1	1	0		1	1		
1	1	1		1	1		

6   Can you think of another use for this sort of table? Draw up the table to show what can happen.

▷ Taking stock

Every week the supermarket carries out a manual stock check. Assistants from each department go round the supermarket counting the number of items on each shelf. The computer records all the items that are sold, and keeps the stock levels up-to-date.

1   So why do you think the shop bothers to do a manual stock check? How could there be differences between the stock level in the STOCK file, and the stock level actually in the shop?

The assistants record the number of items on a special form.

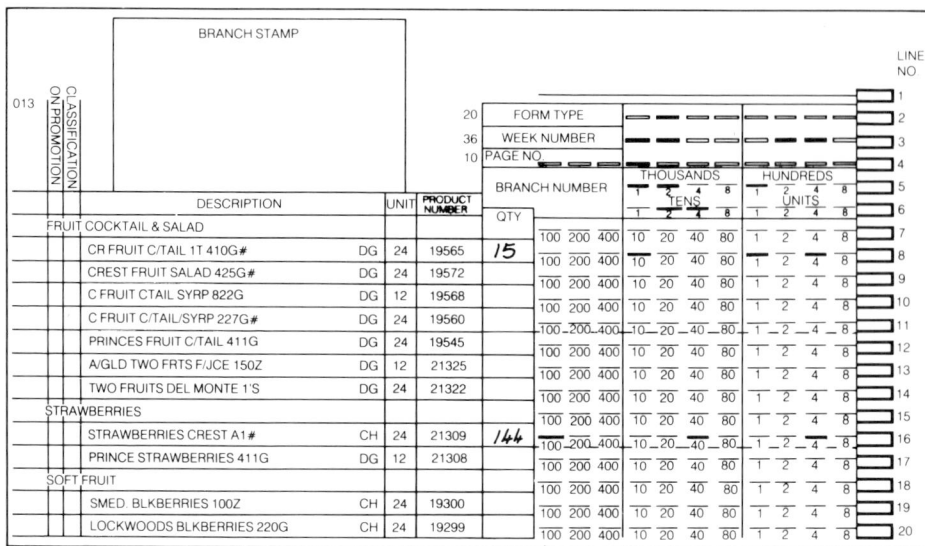

A mark sense data collection form

These marks must be drawn very carefully with a pencil. They are read by a device which shines light on the form and then detects the pattern of light reflected back. The bar marks do not reflect light back, but the white paper does, so the device can tell where the marks are.

The device, called an optical mark reader (OMR), can only read the marks on the form, not the other writing. The meaning of the line depends on its position. A line in a certain place means, for example, 20 tins of Crest fruit cocktail.

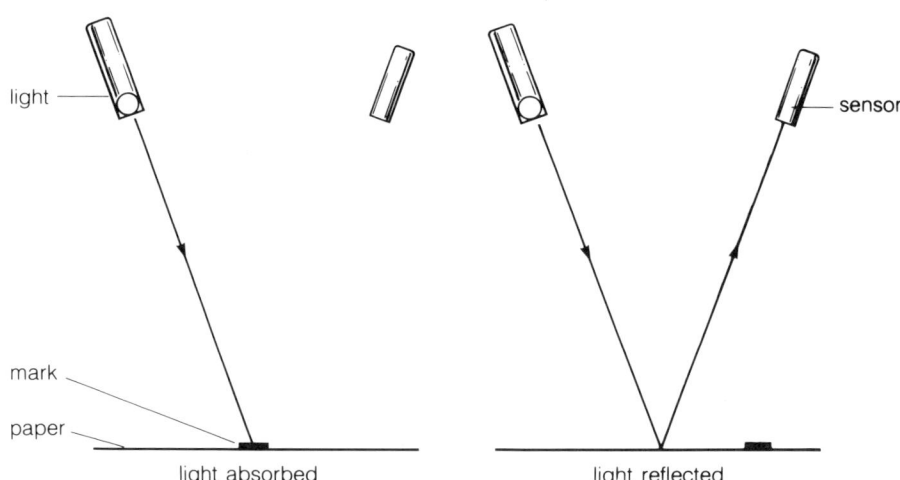

The operation of an optical mark reader

2   Why do they use a special form like this? Why doesn't the assistant just write down the name and number of each item on a piece of paper? Why is the number of items recorded twice, in two different ways?

3 What do you think the stock totals are used for? Who would make use of them?

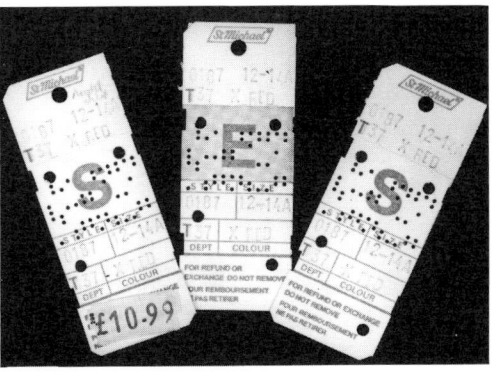

Other shops use different ways of checking their stock levels, and of stock control. Down the road from the Crest Supermarket is the Baby Togs shop, which sells clothes and other things for babies and small children. All of their items for sale have a tag on them.

Like the Crest Supermarket, Baby Togs is one of a chain of shops. They also have a central warehouse. But they do not have POS tills. They have tills where the assistant has to key-in the price of an article. The till works out the total cost of all the items bought by each customer, and the total amount of money that should be in the till at the end of the day. So, these tills do not help the shop to keep track of its stock levels.

When an item is sold, the assistant removes the Kimball tag and puts it on the pile, so the pile of Kimball tags shows how many things have been sold. More than that, the pattern of holes on the tag is a code for some information about the item; for example, what the item is, what size it is and what colour it is. The price is printed on the tags.

Some Kimball tags

4 Why is the price printed on the tags?

5 Why is the price not coded into dots on the tag?

The Baby Togs chain does have a computer at its head office. At the end of every working day, each Baby Togs branch sends all its Kimball Tags to Head Office. The data on the tags is read by a computer with a special device. This device shines a light beam at each tag. A light-sensitive plate on the other side of the tag can detect the pattern of holes, because the light only comes through the holes. The pattern of light is then coded as a series of digits, and is stored on magnetic tape. This data is used to prepare reports on each shop. The reports show how many of each item the shop has sold.

The data is also used by the central warehouse. They know that some items will need to be sent to a shop, if its stock level falls below a certain level. For example, the Dalton branch sells a lot of terry nappies. When they have only six packs left, they know that they have only about two days supply left. The warehouse knows this too. And they know when the shop has sold all but six packs. So the shop doesn't need to order from the warehouse. The warehouse will send a supply of terry nappies automatically.

stock sold

minimum stock level reached

new stock ordered

new stock arrives – new increased stock level

The automatic ordering cycle

6 What other items can you think of that could be ordered automatically, like the terry nappies? What kind of things should the shop order themselves?

7 Do the Baby Togs shops need to do any manual stock checks?

The stock file at Baby Togs' head office contains data on the stock at all the Baby Togs shops.

8 How could this file be organized? Would it be better to store the file on magnetic tape or on magnetic disk?

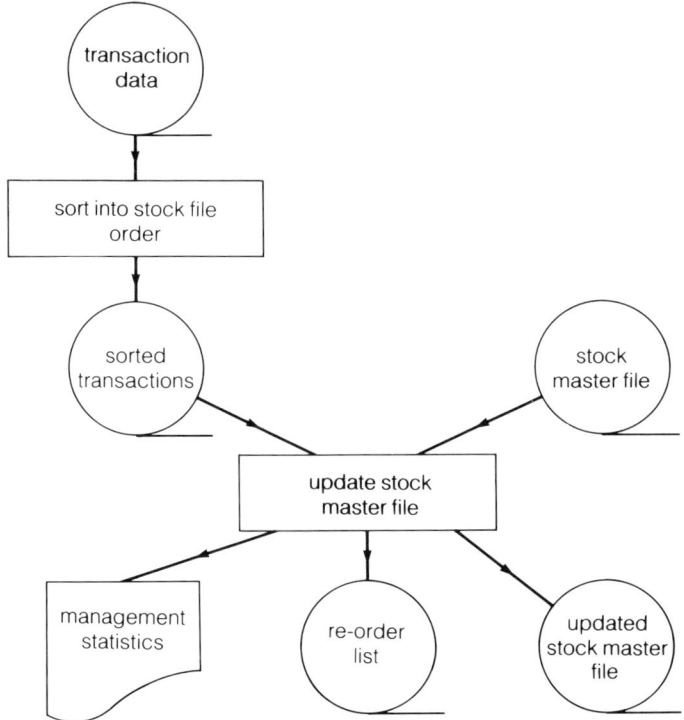

A systems flow chart showing how the file could be updated

9 What is the transaction data? Why is the transaction data sorted? What do you think management statistics are?

The data must be read from the Kimball tags.

10 Draw a systems flow chart to show how this could be done. Show what would happen with damaged tags that could not be read by machine.
    The transaction data could also include details of goods received at the warehouse. Show this on your flow chart too.

Surindra's friend, Alvin, works at Baby Togs. He got into trouble in his first week. He was asked to get the Kimball tags ready for sending to Head Office. He put all the tags in neat stacks of 10, then stapled them together.

Kimball tags, barcodes and mark sense forms are all called machine readable because the data on them can be read by a machine of some sort. Other shops use different sorts of machine readable tags. Beany's Shoe Store uses tags with bar marks.

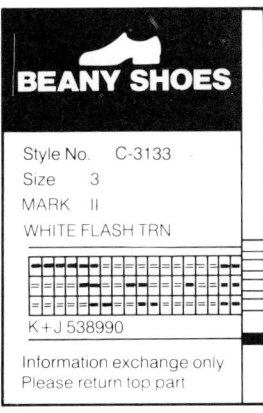

Some Beany's Shoe Store OMR tags

The marks are read by an optical mark reader (OMR). The data coded in the marks is decoded. The meaning of a bar depends on its size, and on its position.

Chandra and Avis fashion shops use tags with special writing. This writing can be read by an optical character reader (OCR). Light is shone on each character. The pattern of reflected light is compared with a set of stored patterns, to see which character it is. The characters used in this way are designed so that no two look much alike. This makes it easier to tell them apart. There are some advanced devices which can read more normal sorts of writing.

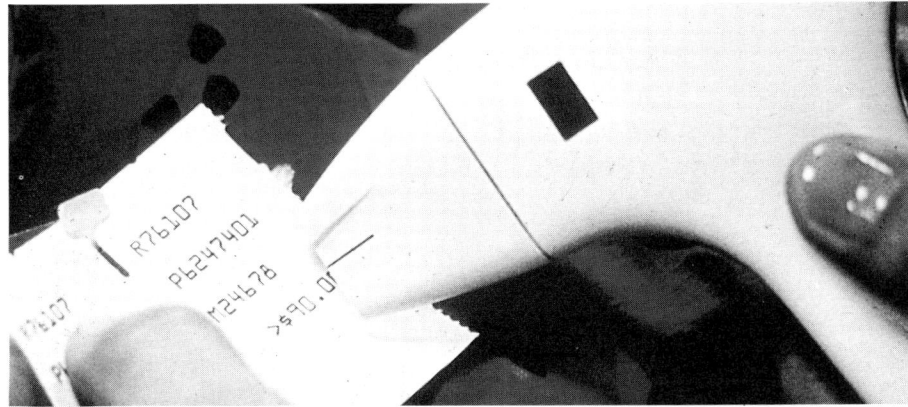

An optical character reader

Searl's Department Store uses tags with a magnetic strip. Data is recorded on the strip in a similar way to the recording of music on the cassette tapes. The information is stored on the tape as patterns of magnetic blobs.

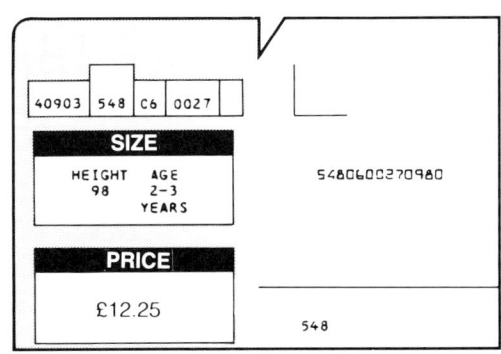

A Chandra and Avis fashion shop OCR tag

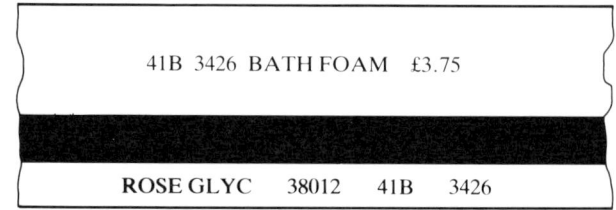

A Searl's department store tag with magnetic strip

The same data is recorded twice on each tag. Once in machine readable form, and once in human readable form.

12 Why do you think this is done? Which tags do not need to record the information twice?

The shops use these tags because, at some point, the data on them will be read by a machine and used by a computer. Some of the shops have on-line, real-time systems, like Crest Supermarkets. Others, like Baby Togs, have a batch processing system, where all the data is processed together, perhaps at the end of the day. With batch processing, the STOCK file will be updated with many transactions in one go, long after the transactions actually took place.

13 Can you think of any problems that may arise from using this method, instead of updating the file immediately in real-time?

▷ Designing the system

When Crest Supermarkets first thought that they might install a computer system, they decided that they should get some expert help. They went to a firm of Information Technology Consultants called 'Practical Solutions'. This firm will look in detail at an organization like Crest. They try to discover whether or not computers, or other forms of new technology, would improve the way the organization runs. They see if it would help them to make more money, or to become more efficient. Of course, Practical Solutions charge quite a lot of money for their services. They have to employ people who know a lot about businesses, and a lot about computers.

Sharon Baker and Adnan Yateem run Practical Solutions. The directors of Crest Supermarkets asked them to make a feasibility study of the Crest organization. Sharon and Adnan had to find out how the Crest Supermarkets were organized, and then consider if computers could help them. They reported back to the Crest directors and told them that they thought that the business could be improved and gave them some idea of the sort of costs and changes that would be involved.

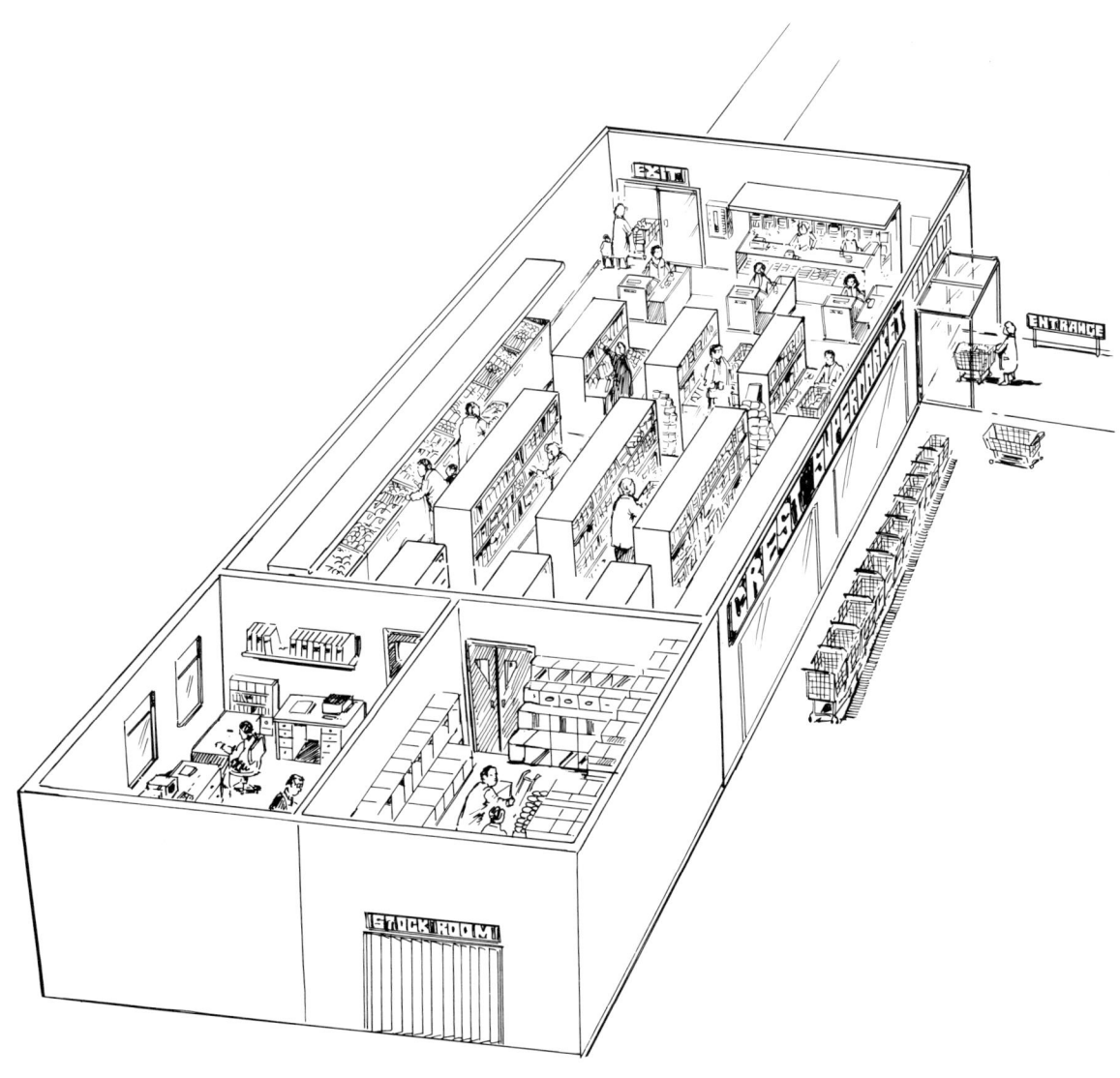

How can the system be improved? In which parts of the store would a computer be useful?

The Crest directors decided that computers would be a help. The next stage was to get Sharon and Adnan to make a very detailed study of each part of the Crest organization.

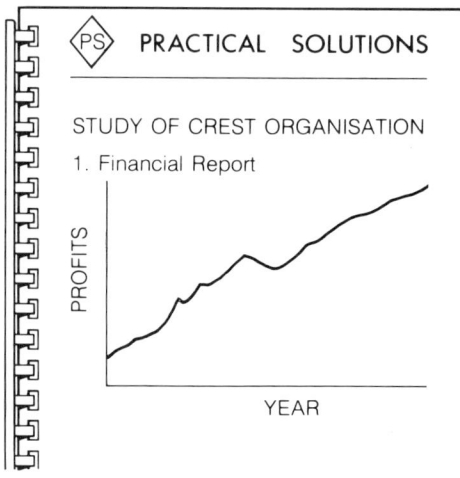

PRACTICAL SOLUTIONS

STUDY OF CREST ORGANISATION

1. Financial Report

What sort of information should be contained in this report?

1   How do you think Adnan and Sharon found out everything about the way the Crest supermarkets are run? Do you think the Crest directors know everything that goes on in their shops? Who did Sharon and Adnan need to talk to?

Sharon and Adnan produced a lot of tables and diagrams that showed how all the parts of the Crest organization worked, from the checkout operators to the warehouses and the financial reports. They looked at all the information that was used and needed by each part of the organization. All this was discussed with the Crest directors and checked to make sure it was correct.

The next stage was to plan the new system. This would need to be based on the old system, but would also include improvements. Some improvements would only be possible because computers were being used, but others were improvements that could have been made anyway. The systems plan had to be very detailed and very precise. It included things like:

▶ the designs for the data capture documents and the till receipts,

▶ details of all the files that would be needed and how they should be structured,

▶ details of all the processing,

▶ the type and amount of hardware that was required.

2   What other information would be needed at this stage? What other planning would need to be done? How would Sharon and Adnan prepare their report so that the Crest directors could understand it?

When the systems design had been agreed, the next step was to plan the software. The systems design was tailored to Crest's way of working, so it was not possible for software to be bought. The software packages that were for sale were not quite right, and would have needed to be changed a lot. Sharon and Adnan decided that it would be better to have the software specially written, then it would be *exactly* what they wanted. The programs were written by a company called Spring Software. They employ about twenty programmers, who can write programs in several different programming languages.

The programs had to be thoroughly tested, to make sure that they did what they were supposed to. Documentation was produced which explained what the programs did, and how they could be used. Some of this documentation was for the programmers to use, in case the program went wrong, or needed to be changed. The rest of the documentation was for the people who would use the programs, so that they would know how they worked, and what files they used.

3   What sort of documentation would the programmers need? Who would write the documentation?

4 Who would need the 'user's' documentation? What would need to be included? Who would write this documentation?

5 What should happen to the documentation if a program is changed in some way? How could the writers make it easier to change the documentation?

The next stage in the whole process was the implementation of the system. This involves installing the equipment and testing the system.

6 Why are mainframe and mini computers used, and not just microcomputers?

The whole operation of installing a computer system, from the first idea to the working system, can be shown on a diagram like the one on the right.

7 So you can see that this can be a never ending process. Why do you think it never ends?

The Crest computer system

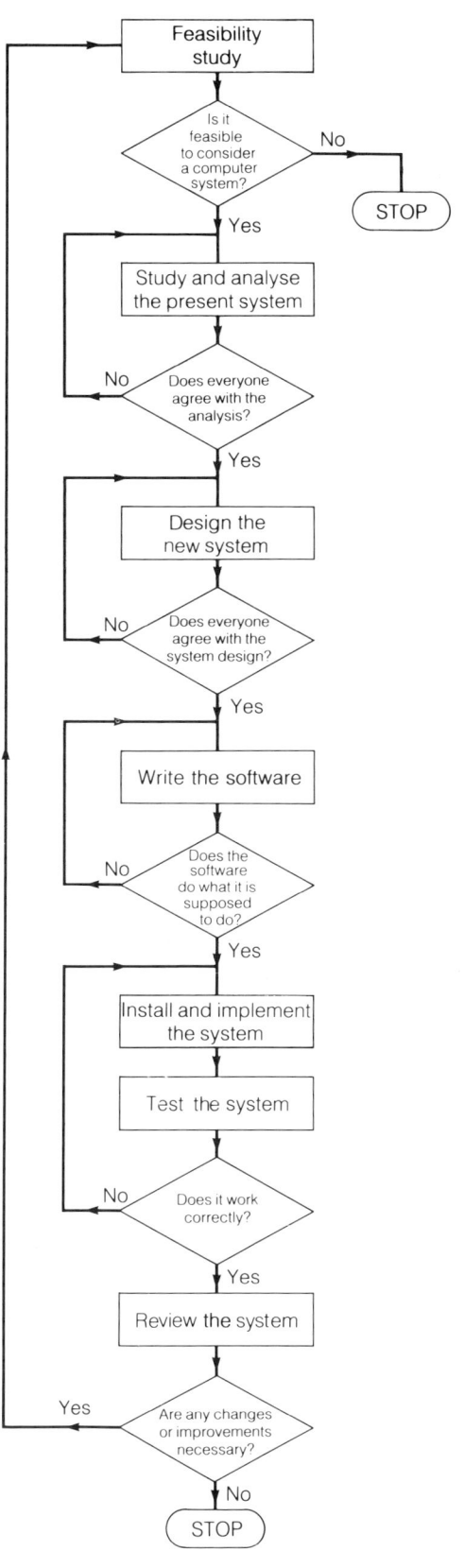

A flow diagram of the operation of installing a computer system

▷ General questions

1 The changeover to a computerized system should have made the supermarket more efficient. Because of the differences in the way the shop operates, it could be necessary to make changes to the layout of the shop. For example, customers go through the checkouts more quickly. And frequent deliveries mean that the shop can carry less stock. What changes would you make to the layout of the shop?

2 Data files can be held on magnetic tape or magnetic disks. Processing can be real-time or batch. Put ticks or crosses in the boxes in the diagram to show what kind of storage can be used for these two types of processing.

	Batch processing	Real-time processing
Magnetic tape	A	B
Magnetic disk	C	D

What combination of backing store and processing (A, B, C or D) is used in each of these examples:
a in normal operation, updating the stock file of the Crest POS system as goods are sold?
b after a system failure, when the POS tills have been keeping their own transaction files, merging these files together?
c after a system failure, updating the STOCK file with the merged transaction files?

3 This is an example of a data capture form. It is used to collect information from people applying to join a swimming club.

NAME

ADDRESS

AGE

HOW FAR CAN YOU SWIM?

WHAT SORT OF SWIMMING DO YOU DO?

WHICH NIGHT CAN YOU COME TO THE CLUB?

If you had to fill in this form can you think of any problems you might have? Do you think the club will always get the sort of answers they are expecting? What else might they need to know that they have not asked? Could they have worded the questions more clearly? Could they have given instructions on the form?

Design a better data capture form for the swimming club.

4 Why is it so important to check data that is being entered into the computer?

Validation checks ensure that only 'sensible' data is accepted. What sort of validation checks could be made on a date, such as 12/3/89?

Validation will only find some errors. Errors that pass the validation stage should be detected when the data is processed.

If the barcode reader reads the code off an item that is not stocked by the shop it will pass the validation stage, but what will happen when the price is looked up?

If, during testing of the system, the computer gives the wrong prices for items at the POS terminals, what might be the cause of the error?

5 You have spent some time studying the computer system installed into Crest Supermarkets. Do you have any suggestions for changes and improvements to it?

6 The central warehouse receives daily orders from the supermarkets via the computer terminal. The warehouse has to assemble the orders and arrange to have them delivered. How could the computer help in these tasks?

7 A TV company is producing a quiz game, testing people's knowledge of cars and driving. They are very fussy about the type of people they will accept as contestants on the show.

They want people who own a car, or who drive someone else's regularly, and they want people to have been driving for at least two years. They will allow people without these qualifications, if they have passed the Advanced Driving Test. All contestants must be between 21 and 55 years of age, and they will not accept anyone who has any motoring convictions.

Complete the logic diagram, which shows the way contestants are accepted. Put OR, AND or NOT into each of the circles to make the diagram correct.

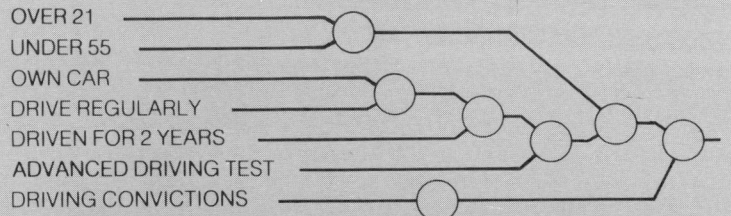

OVER 21
UNDER 55
OWN CAR
DRIVE REGULARLY
DRIVEN FOR 2 YEARS
ADVANCED DRIVING TEST
DRIVING CONVICTIONS

Logic diagram to show the way contestants are accepted

Draw up a truth table for all the different inputs. Use your truth table to find out whether or not these people would make suitable contestants:

a   Jyotna, age 23. Drives a taxi for a living. Passed her test when she was 19. Has a clean driving licence, but has not passed her Advanced Driving Test.

b   William, age 42. Has passed his Advanced Driving Test, and has been driving regularly for 20 years. Had a 2-year ban for a 'drink–driving' offence in 1983–85.

c   Would any drivers you know be suitable contestants?

8   One school has a computer lab with 12 separate computers, 6 disk drives and 1 printer. Another school has a computer lab with 12 computers networked together with a network server, sharing one disk drive and one printer between them.
    What do you think are the advantages and disadvantages of each school's computer equipment?

9   Do you think a computer could help in the running of a small grocery shop? Do you think it would be worth it in terms of cost and usefulness?

10 Imagine that your school tuck shop is considering using a computer to help keep its records and stock in order. Carry out a feasibility study to see if a computer would be worthwhile.

▷ Software activities

1   Design and create a stock file for a school's tuck shop. Update the file as goods are sold and bought in. Check stock levels for each item.

2   Employers need to keep information about their staff. What would employers use this information for? What information might they need? Design a staff information file, and enter details of the staff of the Crest Supermarket.

3   Each week, every member of staff at the Crest Supermarket is given a letter outlining their duties and times at work for the following week. Design the format of the letter. Use a word processing program to produce one or more of these letters.

4   The Crest Supermarket decides to use a VDU terminal as a changing display of special offers. Using a viewdata program, design some special offer pages, and link them together into a display.

The Computer Force

▷ *The story so far . . .*

Daily News

POLICE USE COMPUTER TO FIND MURDERER

HOME NEWS

POLICE HELICOPTER CHASE FOILS ROBBERY

BOMB ALERT AT AIRPORT

People

BRAVERY AWARD FOR WPC

POLICE WARN OF TRAFFIC CHAOS

BRIXTON GAZETTE

TRAFFIC CHAOS AFTER TANKER SPILLAGE

INTERNATIONAL NEWS

VIOLENT CRIME ON THE INCREASE

The Post

MISSING TEENAGERS FOUND DEAD

– POLICE ISSUE PHOTOFIT OF MAN THEY WANT TO QUESTION.

THE HERALD

DRUG RAIDS: 21 CHARGED

POLICE WARN OF BOGUS GASMEN

Each of these headlines is somehow connected with police work. The police force has a very wide range of duties.

> **1   Use the headlines, and any other resources, to make a list of all the different police activities you can think of. Then try to group the activities together under different headings.**

The duties of the police force are laid down by the government. The Home Office is the government department which controls the police. The police are grouped into police forces, each covering a geographical area. For example, the force covering the London area is the Metropolitan Police Force.

The Metropolitan Police District covers an enormous area. It includes crowded inner-city areas, as well as calm suburbs, and even villages, fields and forests. The amount of police work of all types is increasing, and the police forces have realized that they must make use of new technology to help them. All police forces have, or are in the process of installing, computer equipment. Also, there is a central computer available to all police forces. This is called the Police National Computer. This computer is situated at Hendon in North London.

Two of the main features of police work are communication and information processing.

Communication is important because information must flow quickly through the police organizations, so that action can be taken quickly when it is needed. For example, if a car is seen racing away from a bank robbery, the car's registration number needs to be given to the police headquarters quickly. Then this information has to be given to all police in the area so that the car can be stopped. If a burglar is seen in a house, a quick response from the police could result in the burglar being caught in the act. Also, solving one crime may prevent other crimes by the same criminal.

Information processing is also important. The police need to be able to look at large quantities of evidence, to try to see patterns and to select the important and relevant parts. For example, in a murder inquiry, the police may ask for help from the public. They may be given vast quantities of information, and they need to sort it out and select the most useful parts.

> **2   Why do you think that a lot of police work could be helped by the use of computers?**
>
> **3   Is there any police work where you think computers could not help?**

The Police National Computer holds large amounts of information. It holds:

▶ details of all vehicles and vehicle owners in Britain,

▶ information on stolen and suspect vehicles,

▶ a list of all people with criminal records,

▶ a list of all people wanted by the police,

▶ a list of all people who have been reported missing,

▶ a wide range of other information to help the police with their work.

4 Where do you think the police get all this information? How accurate do you think it is? Are some types of information likely to be more reliable than others?

'The car went that way!' What questions might the policeman ask the witness?

This information is kept to help the police solve crimes. For example, imagine this situation. A security firm's van is robbed of £200 000, and one of the guards is seriously wounded. There was a witness to the incident, who was able to give some information to the police. The witness gave a brief description of the two robbers and of the type and colour of their get-away car.

5   How could the Police National Computer help in this case? What information might it be able to find that could help the police?

The Central Command Complex for the Metropolitan Police is at New Scotland Yard. This is where the main computer is housed. A mainframe computer is at the heart of the computer system. It is a very powerful computer, which can handle 95% of all transactions in less than 1.25 seconds.

6   Why is the speed of operation so important for the police force?

The Metropolitan Area is divided into 75 Divisions. Each has a Divisional Control Centre, linked to the Central Command Complex. The local Police Stations are all linked to their Divisional Control Centre.

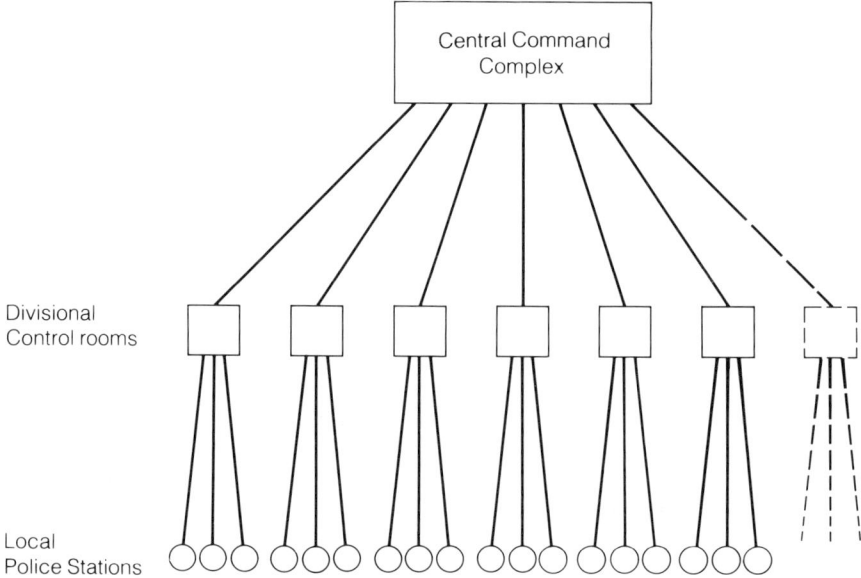

The structure of the Metropolitan Police Force

The Central Command Complex has been specially designed so that police officers can work comfortably and efficiently with the computers.

7   Both the computer and the workers must be able to work efficiently. What factors were important in designing the Central Command Complex?

What are the men taking from the house?

Rebecca Walters lives in Camberwell Grove, London. She sees a van pull up at her neighbour's house. Two men and a woman get out and go round to the back of the house. Her interest is aroused because she knows that her neighbours have gone away on holiday. So she decides to keep a look out. A short time later the men return to the van carrying a large object. Rebecca can't make out what it is. She decides to call the police.

Rebecca telephones 999 and gets through to the telephone operator who asks her which service she requires: police, ambulance or fire brigade. She asks for the police and is put through to the Central Command Complex at New Scotland Yard. This is where all 999 calls to the police are received in the Metropolitan Police region. Up to four hundred 999 calls can be handled at the same time.

Rebecca is suspicious so she dials 999 to alert the police

Communicators answer 999 calls 24 hours a day

The call is taken by Joe Blenman who is the 'Communicator'. The communicators each have a computer terminal which is linked to the Metropolitan Police computer. When Joe starts work, he has to key in his coded password.

1   Why does Joe have to use his password?

It is Joe's job to find out the reason for the call, and to key some of the details into the computer. He enters Rebecca's address and also details of

What are the advantages of inputting the information straight into the computer, rather than writing it down first?

why she is making the call. The VDU display is designed to remind Joe of all the information he needs to find out from the caller.

2 Can you think of any other 'prompts' that would appear on the VDU to remind Joe to ask all the necessary questions?

3 Some of the information is typed in a coded form. Why is it coded? What types of information could be coded? What types are difficult to code?

Joe tells Rebecca that a car will soon be on its way.

4 The communicators have an important job. What sort of training do you think a communicator needs?

5 All communicators are trained police officers. Do you think that it is necessary for the communicators to be police officers?

Joe must pass the information from Rebecca's call to a 'despatcher'. The computer allocates the call to Monica Wilson, who is free. And so the information is sent on to her. It is now up to Monica to decide what to do next. She decides to get a car straight on to the scene before passing the information on to the Divisional Control Centre.

The police need to be able to respond very quickly to urgent calls for help

Police officers must inform their Divisional Centre of their whereabouts, and what they are doing. This information is then transmitted to Central Command Complex. So Monica can find out from the computer which car is available in Rebecca's area. While Monica is radioing the car she also uses the computer to contact the Divisional Control Centre.

> **6 Draw a flow chart to show all the steps Monica must take in dealing with this 999 call.**

At the Divisional Control Centre they have an overall picture of their area. Each Controller knows what sections of the police force are being used. He or she can request support for the patrol car, if necessary. They could use more cars, or foot patrol officers, or the CID or other specialist units. In this case the Controller decides that no back up is needed at the moment.

Rebecca's call is dealt with in seconds, and a patrol car is soon on its way to her.

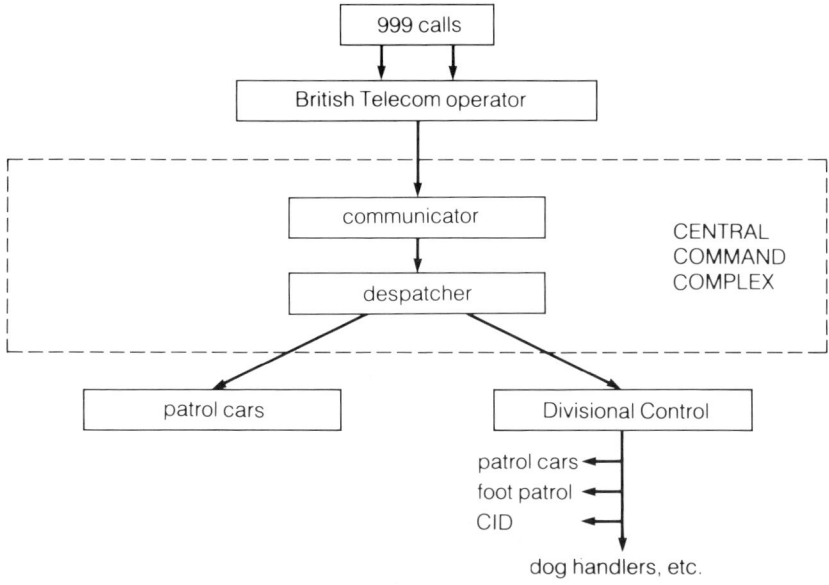

> **7 What other specialist units do the police have?**

The local police car, Papa 5, arrives at Rebecca's house. Unfortunately, they are too late. The van has gone. Luckily, Rebecca took a note of the van's registration number. The police investigate the neighbour's house, and find that a rear window has been forced and the house seems to have been ransacked. They have arrived too late to prevent the burglary, but hopefully they may be able to catch the thieves with the information Rebecca has given them.

Monica gave Rebecca's call a high priority, which meant it was dealt with before other calls which had already been received.

> **8 Why do you think Rebecca's call was given a high priority? Can you think of a call that would have been a higher priority? Can you think of a call that would have been a lower priority?**

Monica contacts the police car by radio

Communications room at a local police station

Some calls, like Rebecca's, are dealt with directly from Central Command Complex. Others are referred straight away to the Divisional Control Centre, who may pass them on to a particular police station.

9   For each of these calls, say whether you think it would be dealt with by:
    Central Command Complex,
    Divisional Control Centre, or
    a local Police Station.
    a A call saying that a bomb has just exploded in the centre of London.
    b A call from an old man saying that he has lost his dog.
    c A call from a driver saying that another car has driven into the back of her's.
    d A call from a shop asking for help with a suspected shoplifter.

▷ Helping with inquiries

A young man, out walking his dog, sees two women carrying a TV from the back of a house to a car. He stops to let the dog sniff round a lamp post. He remembers that he needs to get some milk at the shop, and makes a quick note of this on his shopping list. One of the two women shouts, 'He's rumbled us Chris. He's got the car number. Let's go!' The two women jump into the front of the car and drive off at high speed. The young man is rather surprised, but then realizes that the women must be burglars. In a great panic, he scribbles down the car's registration number, then dashes to the nearest public callbox and dials 999.

Things are not always as they seem. Is this a burglary or two women loading up their car?

The young man is panicking . . .
. . . but Joe is specially trained to deal with this enabling him to find out all the information he needs to know.

When he gets through to Joe, the communicator, he is in a dreadful state. 'I could have been killed,' he screams to the police officer. 'They know what I look like! They might come back for me!' Joe tries to calm him down, but the young man is nearly hysterical. Joe needs to know where the man is calling from. He asks for the phone number of the callbox, but the young man can't find it. 'Where is the callbox?' asks the communicator. All the young man will say is 'Ealing. By the pub. You know, the pub near the allotments.'

This is not enough detail for Joe to give to the despatcher, but Joe can identify the exact location of the callbox using the Computerized Gazetteer. This is a record of all the information about the area covered by the Metropolitan Police. Every street, every public telephone, public building, school, park, pub and more is recorded. It holds local 'unofficial' knowledge of the area. For example, it will hold local names of places that are different from the official names. The gazetteer does not hold private telephone numbers and addresses. This means that callers from private addresses need to give accurate information about their location.

1 Why do you think the gazetteer does not list private addresses and telephone numbers?

2 Private addresses and telephone numbers are kept on computer file by British Telecom. They will not allow the police to have access to their files. Do you think this is right? What do you think British Telecom use this information for?

3 How do you think the gazetteer can be kept up-to-date?

Joe uses the gazetteer to find where in Ealing there is a callbox by a pub and some allotments. He is able to give the despatcher the young man's location, and a patrol car is sent to him. By the time it arrives, he has calmed down, and has remembered that he has the car's registration number. From their patrol car, the police officers contact their Divisional Control Centre by radio. They give the Divisional Controller the car's registration number and a brief description of the women. This information is radioed to other patrol cars and foot patrols in the area.

The Divisional Control Centre also logs on to the Police National Computer to see what they can find out from the car's registration number. The computer searches through its files and finds that the car has been reported stolen.

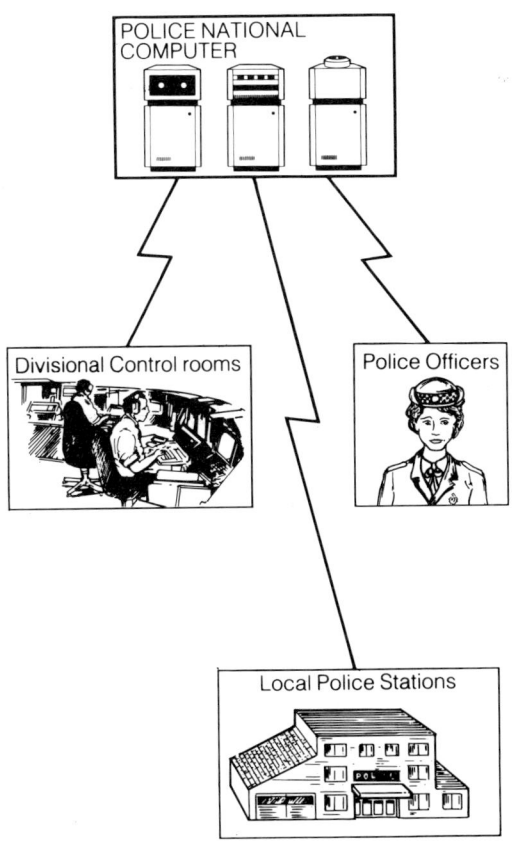

4   What information needs to be recorded on each vehicle? Design the structure of one record in the file, showing the type and length of each field.

5   What kind of magnetic storage medium will the file be stored on? Why?

A patrol car sees the car waiting at a set of traffic lights. Without too much difficulty the two women are detained. Some of the items found in the car were similar to items that had been reported stolen earlier that day. The two women give their names to the police. These are radioed to the Divisional Control. The Police National Computer is used to check on the names. There are records for women with these names. Both records show previous convictions for theft.

6   Can the police be sure that the information in the computer file relates to the two women in the car?

7   How could the police find out whether or not these two women are the same as the ones detailed in the police file?

8   What information needs to be recorded about each convicted criminal in the police file?

9   The police also keep information on suspected criminals. Do you think this information should be used in the same way as information on convicted criminals? Why do you think the police keep information on suspects?

▷ *Patterns of incidents*

Where's the car gone? It was parked here.

Patricia McDonald has been out for a meal at her local Indian restaurant with some friends to celebrate passing her driving test. When Patricia and her friends come out of the restaurant they find that her car has been stolen. Patricia phones 999 to tell the police. Joe Blenman passes this call on to Monica who decides that this is a situation for the Divisional Control to deal with. It turns out that this is the fifth car to go missing in the past four hours.

The Divisional Control know how many cars have been stolen by using the Incident Information System. Details of every incident are recorded. These details include the time, location and type of incident. So the police can, for example, observe patterns in types of crimes, and increases in types of crimes. They can plot the locations of crimes on the gazetteer to see if there are any patterns there.

Then they can decide on what action to take. In the case of Patricia's car, it is possible that the car thieves are already identified, and may even be caught by the time Patricia discovers her loss.

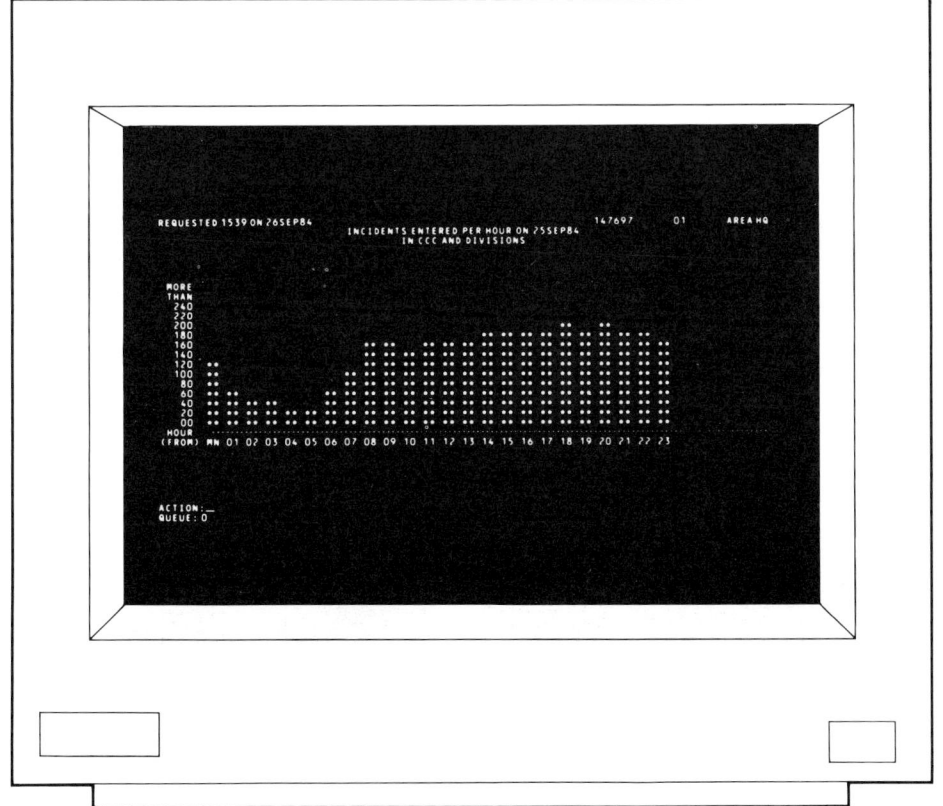

Using the Incident Information System to find patterns in crime. Why might this be useful?

1   What information needs to be recorded for every incident?

2   When should the information be entered in to the Incident Information System? Should the information be checked first?

The data on the file is used in different ways. It is used to detect patterns of crimes and to decide on how best to allocate duties to police officers.

3 Can you think of any other uses for this information?

The police use the Incident Information System to help them answer questions about the organization of the police. They can find the answers to questions like:

▶ which area of the division has the highest number of reported burglaries?

▶ what has happened on an officer's home beat while she has been on leave?

▶ where could we make the best use of the Accident Prevention Unit?

4 Can you think of any other questions the Incident Information System could help the police to answer?

All police officers are instructed to enter details of all incidents into the Incident Information System.

5 What could happen if they did not enter some incidents?

The Incident Information System file is used to provide information, and it must be able to do this very rapidly. So it works in real-time. The system used for searching the file must be capable of very fast searches through large amounts of data. Both the hardware and the software must be chosen with this in mind.

One hardware feature used by police forces is the Content Addressable File Store System (called CAFS for short) which was designed by the computer company ICL. In this system the contents of every record in the file can be searched for any combination of letters or numbers. Other police forces use disk controllers specially designed for fast access.

Different software techniques are also used. For example, a system of Full Structure Indexing can be used. In this system the software makes an index containing every word used in every record in the file, together with an indication of where the record is. This enables all records containing a particular word to be found very quickly.

```
INDEX          LOCATION
silver         308, 729, 146
silworth       516
simpkins       978, 103
singer         103, 426, 911, 325
singles        421, 705, 466
```

Part of a file index

6 Draw a flow chart to show the steps involved in finding all the records containing the word 'arson'.

7 Draw a flow chart to show the steps involved in finding all the records containing the word 'arson' AND the word 'petrol'.

More powerful systems enable records to be searched not just for words, but for groups of words or just groups of letters. These are called Free Text Retrieval Systems.

Collecting detailed information about each crime is a very important part of police work

Amin Nadir arrives home to find that his flat has been burgled. The whole place is in a mess. Cupboards and drawers have been emptied all over the floor. He calls the police, but as this is not a priority call it takes a while for them to arrive. They explain to Amin that there are so many burglaries that there is little chance of finding the thieves. They suggest ways that Amin might make his flat more secure to discourage other burglars.

Amin is very upset to hear all this. He is even more upset when he discovers that some very valuable items are missing. When his grandmother died, she left him an unusual gold watch, and a pair of antique silver candlesticks in the shape of trumpets. Amin insured these items, because they were so valuable, but he is still upset because of their sentimental value.

The police are a little more encouraging. If the thieves try to sell the items they would be easy to spot, because they are so unusual.

The police officers make a report of the burglary to the Incident Information System. At Scotland Yard, the details of all stolen items are compiled into a list. The list is stored on computer and is sent to all police stations. It is sent via telephone lines to a terminal at each station. The terminals have high speed printers attached, so the lost property list is received at the station as a printed document.

> 1 Why do the terminals have printers? Why is the lost property list printed out?
>
> 2 What use could police stations make of the lost property list? How could they use it to help Amin get his stolen property back?

The system used to deal with communications which are not urgent is called the Message Switching System.

> 3 Can you think of any other messages which could be sent using this system?

High speed printers ensure that all police stations have copies of lists of stolen items in the shortest time possible

To help the Metropolitan Police plan their work, they keep details of future events that they will be involved in in any way. So, for example, details of events such as the Notting Hill Carnival or the intended visit of a dignitary such as the President of Zambia are recorded. Details are kept on events up to 18 months ahead.

An event like the Notting Hill Carnival requires a lot of forward planning. What sort of problems would this cause?

4   Do you think it is necessary for this sort of information to be kept so far in advance?

5   Can you think of any other future events that the police would need to know about?

6   What details need to be kept of each event?

The file containing this information is called the diary. A department at New Scotland Yard called the Public Order Branch co-ordinates the information. They must first agree to the event taking place. Then they verify the details and key them in. It is important that this file is kept up-to-date. Updating is done in real-time.

7   Think of an example where information would need to be deleted from the diary.

8   Think of an example where information would need to be amended in the diary.

Messages concerning the diary are sent between Public Order Branch and the Divisional Control Centres using the Message Switching System.

9   What messages could be sent from Divisional Control Centres to Public Order Branch?

10   What messages could be sent from Public Order Branch to Divisional Control Centres?

▷ Traffic incidents

This has been a very busy evening in Wembley. There was a rock concert at Wembley Stadium, and a concert at Wembley Arena. It is now 11 p.m. and both events are finishing. A number of police have been sent to supervise the cars and pedestrians leaving the area, but it is possible to do more than this to speed up the clearing of the area. The traffic lights can be made to help.

A computer was first used to control traffic signals in the centre of London in 1967. Since then, the Area Traffic Control has been extended. Every set of traffic lights and every pelican crossing is linked to computer.

The program for each set of lights is very simple, but it is the way that all the lights have to fit into an overall plan which makes the computer essential in the operation. The program for one set of lights could be something like the one shown on the right. This program is written in pseudo-code. It is similar to a number of computer programming languages, but not exactly the same as any of them.

The waiting periods are very important.

> **1   Do you think the waiting times are reasonable in this program? If not, what do you think they should be?**

We can now look at a situation where there are two traffic lights.

There is a very narrow bridge which can take only single file traffic, as shown below. At each end of the bridge is a set of traffic lights. So there is a set at the north end, and a set at the south end.

Our 1LIGHT program can be modified so that it can be used to control both sets of lights. When you refer to a light on the north side use the word NORTH. In the same way, use the word SOUTH for the lights on the south side. For example, to set the north lights to show green, use

GO NORTH

```
PROGRAM 1LIGHT

REPEAT FOREVER
     STOPLIGHT
     WAIT 50
     READYLIGHT
     WAIT 4
     GOLIGHT
     WAIT 50
     WARNLIGHT
     WAIT 4
ENDREPEAT

END


PROC STOPLIGHT
     SWITCH ON RED
     SWITCH OFF AMBER
     SWITCH OFF GREEN
ENDPROC

PROC GOLIGHT
     SWITCH OFF RED
     SWITCH OFF AMBER
     SWITCH ON GREEN
ENDPROC

PROC READYLIGHT
     SWITCH ON RED
     SWITCH ON AMBER
     SWITCH OFF GREEN
ENDPROC

PROC WARNLIGHT
     SWITCH OFF RED
     SWITCH ON AMBER
     SWITCH OFF GREEN
ENDPROC
```

Here is a flow chart to show the stages in this system:

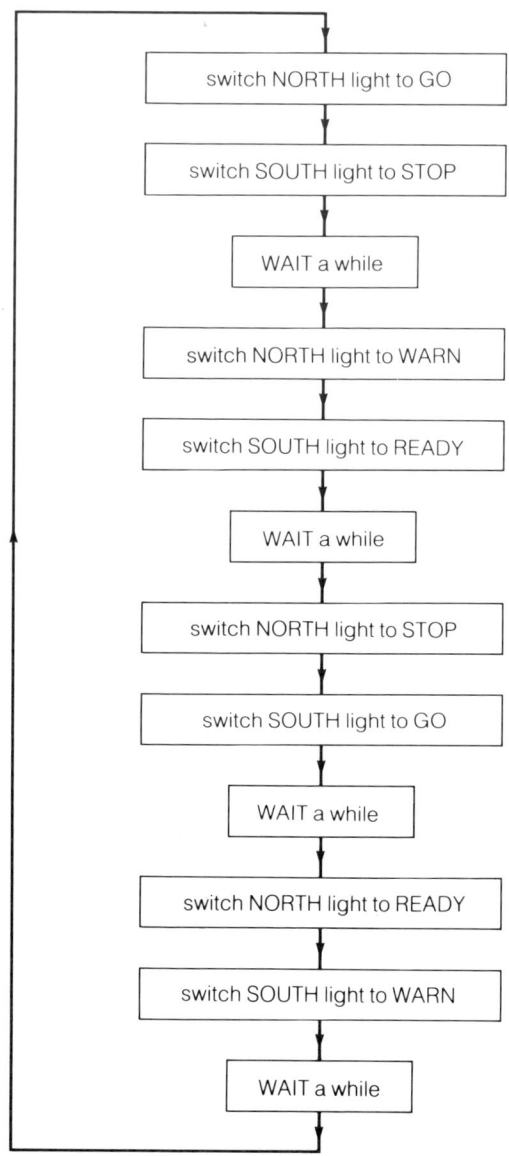

switch NORTH light to GO

switch SOUTH light to STOP

WAIT a while

switch NORTH light to WARN

switch SOUTH light to READY

WAIT a while

switch NORTH light to STOP

switch SOUTH light to GO

WAIT a while

switch NORTH light to READY

switch SOUTH light to WARN

WAIT a while

2 Write a program using the flow chart and the same pseudo-code
   and procedures to control both sets of lights.

3 The bridge is quite long. Using the stages in the flow chart, can you
   be sure that there will not be vehicles meeting head-on on the
   bridge?

4 Amend the flow chart and the program to allow for the traffic in one direction to cross before the traffic in the other direction starts.

This is a map of a cross roads. There are traffic lights at the north, south, east and west of the junction.

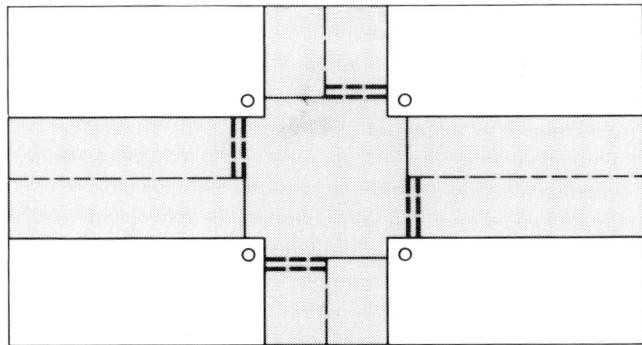

5 Write a pseudo-code program to control the four sets of lights. Swap your program with someone else. Dry run each other's programs to see if they work.

In areas with very heavy traffic, using traffic lights to control the flow is essential to avoid congestion

If an area is congested with traffic, like Wembley, the traffic lights in the area can be controlled to increase the flow of traffic out of the congested area. The lights will stay green for longer on the roads leading out of Wembley. This is controlled by computer, because if you change the flow of traffic in one area, there will be a 'knock on' effect in surrounding areas. The calculations to work out the timing changes needed at every set of lights are done rapidly by computer.

Traffic lights are set up to keep traffic in the city flowing as smoothly as possible. The amount of traffic using roads at all times of the day and night is recorded. This information is collected by sensors on the road. They detect when a vehicle drives over, and this data is recorded by the computer.

The traffic sensor can be seen in front of the car shown in the picture

A

The computer is programmed to calculate the best arrangement of traffic lights, so that motorists are kept waiting for the minimum length of time. Normally, traffic lights work to a routine planned according to the usual traffic flow on that road at that time of day. For example, look at the junction on the left.

There is about four times more traffic on road A than on road B. So road A should have green lights for much longer than road B. But it may not be as simple as that. Conditions further down one or both of the roads, or at the next junction, could affect the light sequence here.

6   What conditions may exist which mean that road A does not have green lights for much longer than road B?

Even when the best decision has been made, incidents happen which mean that changes need to be made to the 'normal' set-up.

7   What sort of incidents could cause a change in the usual traffic light routine?

Information about incidents can be sent to Traffic Control in a number of ways. For example, a police officer could radio in to say that there had been an accident. Or information could come from one of the traffic cameras which are placed high up on buildings overlooking major junctions. Or the data from the road sensors could be used.

A traffic camera

The traffic controller could use information from a traffic camera like the one on the left.

8 How could information about an incident be discovered from data sent by road sensors?

Look again at the junction of the quiet road and the busier road. At night the lights for the busier road will be left on green, and the lights on the other road on red. When the sensor detects a car on the quieter road, it will start the sequence to change the lights.

This program shows what happens when something drives over the sensor:

```
REPEAT FOREVER
        READ SENSOR
        WHILE OUTPUTFROM SENSOR IS 0 DO
                GO NORTH
                GO SOUTH
                STOP EAST
                STOP WEST
        ENDWHILE
        WARN NORTH
        WARN SOUTH
        READY EAST
        READY WEST
        WAIT 4
        STOP NORTH
        STOP SOUTH
        GO EAST
        GO WEST
        WAIT 30
        READY NORTH
        READY SOUTH
        WARN EAST
        WARN WEST
        WAIT 4
ENDREPEAT
```

9 What could happen if cars came along the north–south road at a rate of one every 15 seconds, and cars came along the east–west road once every 50 seconds?

10 How could you change the program to make sure that the lights were on green for the busier road more than for the quieter road?

A Pelican crossing is a pedestrian crossing controlled by traffic lights. The vehicles have to obey the traffic lights. The pedestrians have to obey red and green lights telling them when to go and when to wait.

The sequence of lights at a pelican crossing lets people cross the road safely but only stops the flow of traffic for a short time. What is the sequence of lights?

How have pelican crossings been designed to help blind people cross the road?

11　Many people have red–green colour blindness, which means that they can't tell the difference between red and green. How could a colour blind person tell the difference between the red stop signal and the green go signal?

12　What is used so that blind pedestrians know when it is safe to cross?

13　Work out the sequence of lights for a pelican crossing. Then, using the pseudo-code and the procedures, write a program to control a set of lights at a pelican crossing.

▷ Lock up your data!

When the computer systems for the police were being designed, there were two important points that the designers had to consider: security and reliability. The information held in the police files is very sensitive. In the wrong hands, some of this information could be dangerous too, because it could help people to commit crimes.

1　Can you think of an example of information on police files which could be dangerous in the wrong hands?

2　Can you think of an example of information on police files which should only be known by the police?

If information on police files was altered unofficially, it could hinder the police, and perhaps make it easier for someone to commit a crime.

3　Can you think of any other problems that may arise if information was changed unofficially?

4　Can you think of information which could be changed in order to help a criminal to commit a crime?

5　Can you think of any other cases where it would be harmful if the police files contained inaccurate information?

6　Can the police be sure that all the information that they put on the files is absolutely accurate?

The system must be designed so that no unauthorized users can gain access to the information. Apart from authorized police officers, no one should be able to use, remove, change or add to the information on the files.

So, the security system must be very tight. The computer and files for the Metropolitan Police are held at New Scotland Yard. No one may enter

The foyer at New Scotland Yard – why is security so important here?

New Scotland Yard without a pass, or official permission. All visitors are vetted before they are admitted, and they must be accompanied by a police officer at all times during their visit.

> 7 Do you think that this security measure is just to restrict access to the computer and its files? What other reasons are there for restricting access to this building?

There are further security measures to prevent unauthorized users from entering the computer rooms.

> 8 Do you think that all police officers should have access to the computer system?
>
> 9 What other security measures could be taken to make sure that only authorized people can enter the computer rooms?

Before accessing information on the computer, the user has to enter his or her password.

> 10 When a password is keyed in, what would you expect to see on the VDU?

More passwords are needed before the user can make any changes to any information.

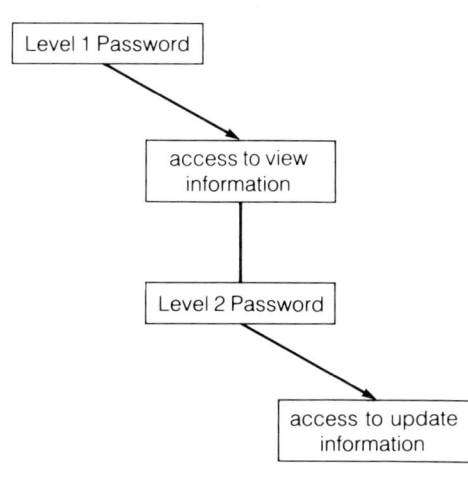

11 Why do you think there are different levels of passwords?

The efficiency of the police depends a lot on their computer systems.

12 Can you think of things that the police would find difficult or impossible to do without the computer system?

So, if the computer systems stop working, then the police work will suffer. The computer equipment is carefully looked after. The maintenance manager tries to sort out problems before they affect the operation of the system. To do this, all users have to make an error report if anything goes wrong, or behaves unusually.

13 Why do you think the officers have to make error reports?

So that there is very little chance of the computer system breaking down, a lot of the hardware is duplicated. In all police forces, the computer system will have at least two central processors. The Metropolitan Police have four central processors. If one breaks down, the others can take over.

There will be several banks of disk drives too. All the computer files are backed up, and the back-up copies are kept up-to-date. The central processors are accessed by terminals. These are connected to the computers by communication processors. Again, these are duplicated in case of breakdown.

A lot of hardware is duplicated so that the system can operate without stopping. If the system is operating without any equipment breakdowns all the available hardware is still used. So, for example, all the central processors will be used.

14 Why do you think the system is designed like this? What advantage will it be to use all this extra hardware?

One of the ways of reducing errors and breakdowns is to make sure that all the staff are trained in using the computer equipment. Many police officers find their work has changed considerably with the introduction of computers; for example, the police officers who work as communicators and despatchers. Others will find that the way they work changes very little.

15 Can you think of types of police work that will not change very much?

Many police officers may be worried about computers.

16 Why do you think this is so?

17 What could be done to help the police officers accept the computerized systems?

Many members of the public may also be worried about the police using computers.

> **18** What worries may they have? Do you think there are grounds for their worries? Do you think that the police computer systems should be changed because of these fears?

▷ *General questions*

1 Some of the information kept by the police should not be seen or changed by unauthorized people. Why is it important to make sure that unauthorized people do not gain access to some information?

Do you think that people should be able to look at information about them on police files?

Make a list of the different ways of ensuring that only authorized people can get access to the computer terminals and to the data files. Give an example of where each one is used.

2 The information kept by the police needs to be up-to-date. Give an example of information that needs to be updated immediately. What would happen if it was not kept up-to-date? Can you think of examples from other situations where information must not be allowed to get out-of-date? What types of processing are most suitable for updating this sort of data? Which type of processing could not be used?

3 Computer output can be hard copy, or paper or microfilm. Or it can be displayed on the VDU screen. Make lists of the advantages and disadvantages of each type. Give an example of output that is best on paper. Give another example of output which is best on the screen. What other forms of output can you think of?

4 Traffic lights can be controlled by computer. Many other machines and devices can also be computer controlled. For example, some cars are built by computer controlled robots. Find out about other computer controlled machines, and make a list of some examples.

5 Draw up a table summarizing all the ways that the police use computers. For each one, say whether you think the computer has improved the system, made it worse, or made no change.

6 How do you think the police will make use of computers in the future?

7 When motorists are convicted of certain motoring offences, they are awarded a number of 'points'. If they get 10 points within three years, they are automatically disqualified from driving. Their driving convictions are recorded on a computer file.

Design the file structure for this file.

Draw a diagram showing how the data could be checked to see if a convicted motorist has reached 10 points.

A set of instructions on how to solve a problem is called an algorithm. Algorithms can be written in any form. The diagram you have just drawn is an algorithm.

Write a pseudo-code program to implement your algorithm.

8 The police are increasing their use of computers. How do you think this will affect the lives of these groups of people: police officers, criminals, the victims of crimes, the general public?

1 Construct a pelican crossing using Lego or other materials. Use a control logo language to control the light sequence.

2 The Police National Computer keeps a file of information about vehicles. What is it used for? Design the file structure, and create a small file of vehicles on your computer. Interrogate the file to see if cars matching certain descriptions can be found.

3 People apply to the police for permission to hold meetings or demonstrations in public places. The police send out letters to tell them whether they can or not. The details are printed out by the computer on pre-printed stationery. Use a word processor to design the letter. Show one before it has the details completed, and one with some example details included.

4 The police want the public to understand what they do. They sometimes have exhibitions and open days so that people can visit and find out. They could use their computer to give information. Use a viewdata program to set up an information file about the work of the police force.

Money Power

▷ *The story so far . . .*

Carol and Yasmin share a small, rented flat in Coventry. It's quite near to the fashion shop they both work at, 'Hers & His'. Carol works as a sales assistant and Yasmin as a clerk in the office.

The manager of the shop tells all the staff that the company wants to change the way they pay them. Instead of paying them in cash, they want to pay their wages directly into their bank accounts.

Yasmin has had a bank account for over a year. Carol has always liked to hang on to the cash, although she does put some money into her National Savings Account at the Post Office. 'I can't see why they want to change the system,' says Carol. 'The manager says it will be better for everyone, but how will I ever know how much money I've got?'

1 Why do you think the company want to stop paying its workers in cash?

Yasmin tries to convince Carol that she will be better off with her money paid straight into the bank. 'You don't have to carry money round with you. You can pay for things with cheques,' says Yasmin. 'And it's easy to keep track of your money and what you spend.'

2 Can you think of any other reasons why Yasmin prefers to keep her money in the bank?

Carol wants to know more about bank accounts, so Yasmin tells her about hers. Her account is with the North Country Bank. When she opened her account they gave her a cheque book. Each cheque has her name and her account number on it. She is the only person who can use these cheques. She uses them to pay for things and to take cash out of her account.

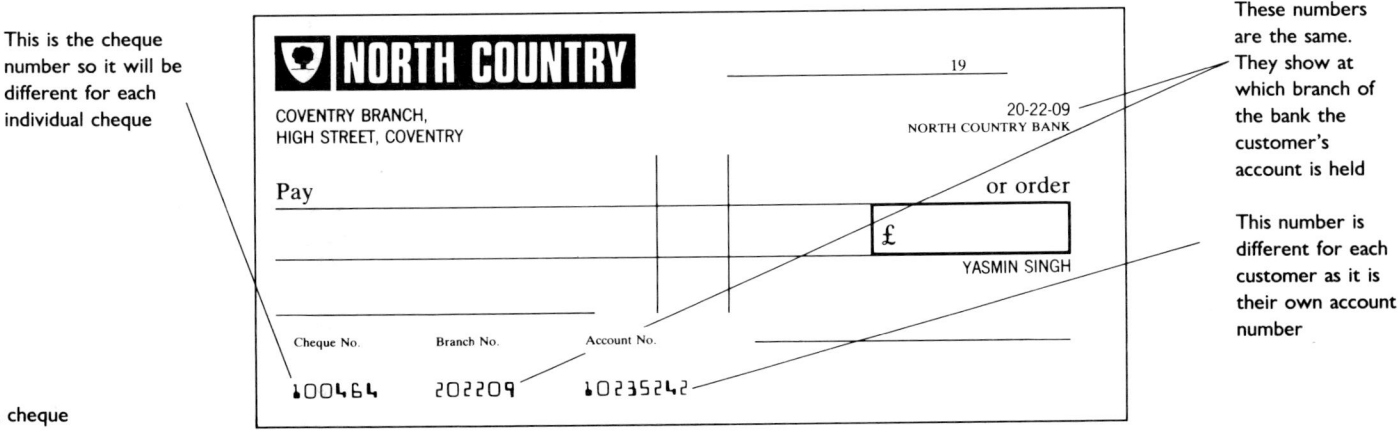

This is the cheque number so it will be different for each individual cheque

These numbers are the same. They show at which branch of the bank the customer's account is held

This number is different for each customer as it is their own account number

A cheque

3 **What does Yasmin have to write on the cheque when she uses one to pay for something?**

'OK, I see how you take money out of your account. How do you put it in?' Carol wants to know. 'You just take it to the bank and give it to them!' says Yasmin. The bank needs to know which account money is to be paid into, so they ask customers to use paying-in forms.

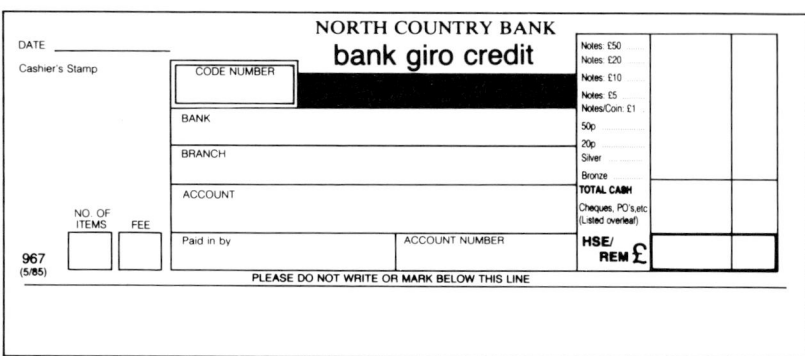

This is a paying-in slip. How should Yasmin fill it in if she wants to put a £10 note and a cheque for £5 into her account?

4 **What information has to be included on a paying-in slip? Why do you think the bank needs all this information?**

Banks are worried that cheques might be forged. Cheques are printed on special paper which has a pattern printed on it underneath the writing.

5 **Why do cheques have patterns printed on them?**

6 **Why don't the banks take the same trouble with the paying-in slips?**

'Well, it all seems very easy,' says Carol. 'But how do you know how much money you've got in your account?'

'I keep a record of every cheque, and everything I pay in, in my cheque book. And just to make sure, the bank sends me a statement of my account every month. It shows every transaction, that is, everything that has been paid in, and everything that has been taken out.'

Date	Cheque No.	Transaction Details	Amount	Balance
20/9/87	100125	Marks & Spencer PLC	42-99	346-87
26/9/87	100126	United Dairies (Milk)	4-20	342-67
30/9/87	100127	Lexley Garage (Petrol)	10-00	332-67
6/10/87	100128	J. Sainsbury	31-43	301-24
10/10/87	100129	D. Ashfield (Rent)	120-00	181-24

Carol needs to keep a record of her cheques. What will happen if she forgets to do this?

```
YASMIN SINGH                                                    1005L

                                                  CHEQUE
▼  NORTH COUNTRY                    STATEMENT OF ACCOUNT

COVENTRY MAIN BRANCH, HIGH STREET, COVENTRY              10235242

   2100      YASMIN SINGH
   G027      53B ALBANY STREET                          11 OCT 88
   01730     COVENTRY
   2/2                                                  1988/      3
```

DETAILS	PAYMENTS	RECEIPTS	DATE	BALANCE
BALANCE FORWARD			1 OCT	346.87
100126	4.20		1 OCT	342.67
100127	10.00		4 OCT	332.67
100128	31.43		11 OCT	301.24

```
ABBREVIATIONS:   DIV Dividend   STO Standing Order   BGC Bank Giro Credit   DDR Direct Debit   DR Overdrawn Balances
```

A bank statement – this tells the customer exactly how much money they have in their account

'What happens if you pay by cheque but you haven't got any money left in your account?' asks Carol.

'The bank could refuse to accept the cheque. They could send it back to me. And the bank manager would not be very pleased.'

'Well, I'm surprised that shops let people pay by cheque in that case. They could end up with a lot of dud cheques.'

'Most shops won't accept cheques on their own. If you have shown the bank that you can be responsible, and do not write cheques when you haven't got enough money in your account, then the bank will guarantee to pay the amount of the cheque. So the shopkeepers don't have to worry.'

'But how do they know which customers' cheques are guaranteed to be paid?'

'That's easy. They have cheque guarantee cards. The shopkeeper has to check that the details on the cheque and the cheque card match. Then they write the cheque card number on the back of the cheque, so the bank knows it has to pay up.'

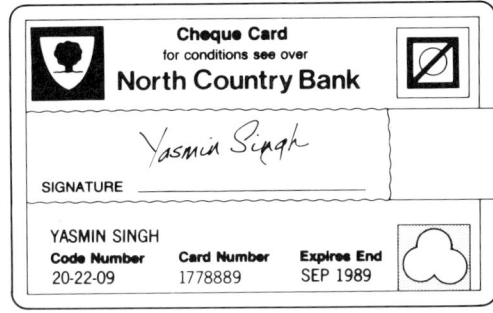

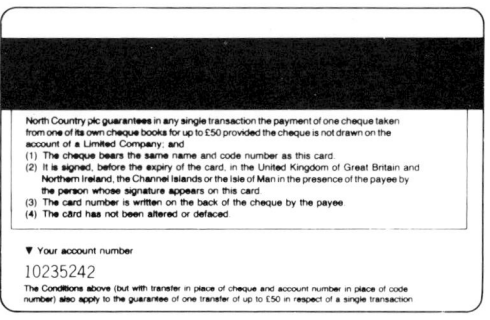

A cheque card

7   How do you think the bank will decide which customers it will give cheque guarantee cards to?

8   How do you think the banks stop customers who misuse the cards, by writing cheques even when they have no money left in their accounts?

'One last question. What happens if you run out of cash, and the bank is closed? You can't pay for everything by cheque!'

9   What sort of things are difficult to pay for by cheque?

'My bank has lots of cash machines, which can be used 24 hours a day. I have another card, a cash card, which I can use to get money.'

A cash dispenser – automatic teller machine (ATM)

'I just put the card in the machine, key in my personal identification number, and follow the instructions. I can find out how much money is in my account, withdraw money, or even pay money in.

'The cash machine is connected by telephone lines to the bank's computer. So it can look up my record in the file to see how much money I've got. It won't allow me to take out more money than I've got. When I take money out, it deducts the amount from my balance.

'It is very important that your cash card does not fall into someone else's hands.'

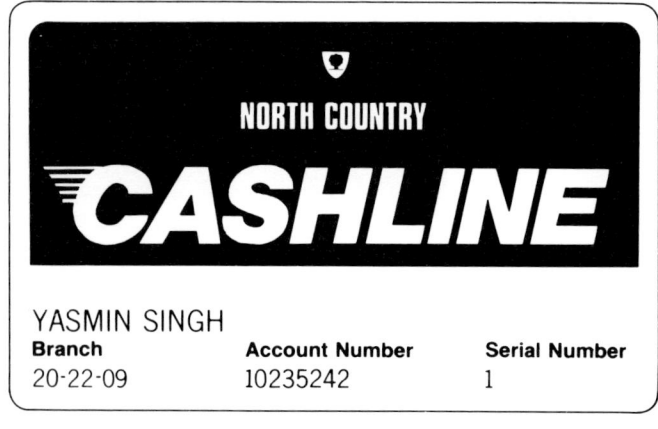

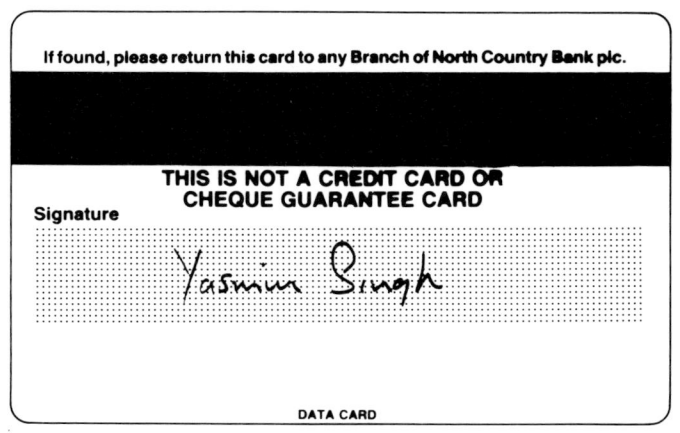

A cash card – each one has its own personal identification number

Could Yasmin's cash card be used by someone else?

Carol is, at last, convinced. She opens a bank account with the North Country Bank too.

▷ *Clearing the cheque*

Carol gets a cheque book, with her account number on each cheque.

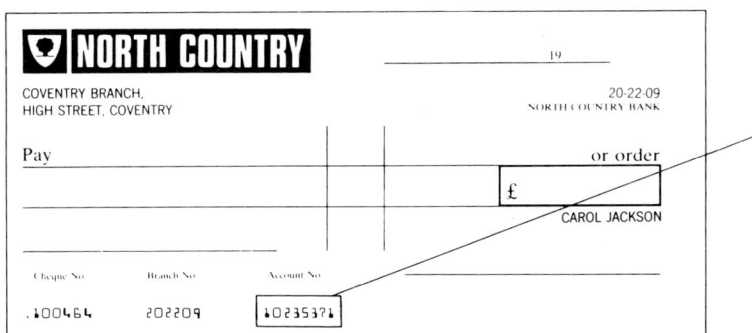

NORTH COUNTRY

COVENTRY BRANCH,
HIGH STREET, COVENTRY

20-22-09
NORTH COUNTRY BANK

19

Pay _____ or order

£

CAROL JACKSON

Cheque No   Branch No   Account No

⑈⑆⑆⑈⑈⑈   ⑆⑈⑆⑆⑈⑈   ⑈⑆⑆⑆⑈⑈⑈⑈

⑈⑆⑆⑆⑈⑈⑈⑈

MICR characters are printed in special ink which enables them to be read by a machine. Can you think of any other instances where special ink is used?

Carol notices that there is some unusual writing at the bottom of the cheques. Yasmin explains that some details are coded as numbers. These numbers are written in special machine-readable writing. This is so that the information on the cheque can be read quickly and accurately by a machine. This particular type of machine-readable writing is called MICR, which is short for magnetic ink character recognition. This is because the characters are printed with a special sort of ink. This ink contains very small particles of iron, which can be magnetized. The reader detects which character it is reading by the size of the magnetized area.

'But why do the cheques have to be read by a machine?' asks Carol.

The data on the cheque is processed by computer. If banks did not use computers, they would not be able to operate in the way that they do now. There are just too many customers, and too much money. Without computers, there just would not be the time to keep all the records up-to-date. And it would cost a lot of money to employ extra people to do this work.

1   What differences would there be if banks did not use computers?

Carol has made an appointment at the optician's to have her eyes tested. The optician tells her that she should wear glasses. She chooses some spectacle frames, but the optician doesn't have the ones she likes in her size. The optician says she will have to order them; they will be ready in about two weeks. Carol pays £15 deposit by cheque.

2   The optician doesn't ask Carol for her cheque guarantee card. Why not? What other payments could she make without a cheque card? How would the 'sellers' make sure that they would not lose money?

The optician pays all the takings into her bank, the Barland Bank, at the end of the day. Some of the money is cash, some cheques. The optician fills in a paying-in slip for all the money. Then the bank takes over.

The cash is counted and checked against the total on the paying-in slip. The cheques are all checked too. With the cash payments, the amount will have to be credited (added to) the optician's balance. For each cheque, money will have to be transferred from the customer's bank account to the optician's bank account. This is called clearing the cheques, and this is how it's done.

At the bank, a clerk types the amount of each cheque onto the bottom of the cheque, using magnetic ink and the special characters.

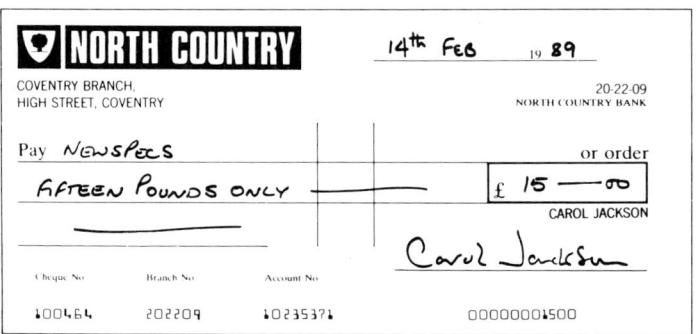

Why has the value of the cheque been typed in MICR characters under the signature?

| 3 | How could the clerk verify the amount typed in? |

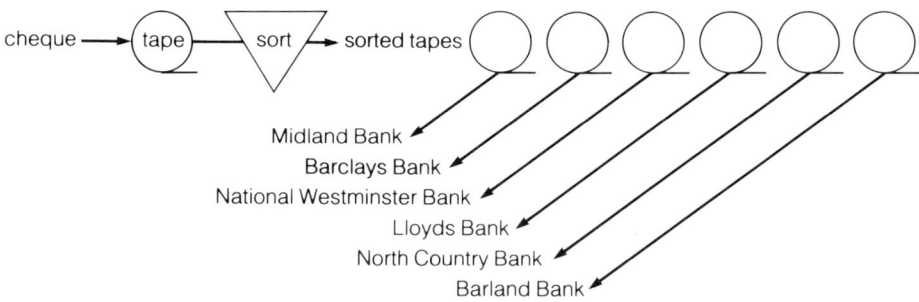

Clearing the cheque

The Banks Automated Clearing System

The bank then sends all the cheques to the Banks Automated Clearing System. The figures printed in magnetic ink are read from each cheque, and recorded on magnetic tape. The data is sorted by bank, so that all the data for the North Country Bank is put together. Then a separate tape is made for each bank. Each tape is sent to the Computer Centre for that bank, so the North Country tape, with the data from Carol's cheque, is sent to the North Country Bank Computer Centre.

All the cheques are sorted out, so that all the cheques from each branch of each bank are put together. So Carol's cheque is put with all the other cheques from her bank. The cheques are then sent to the bank.

All the paying-in slips are sent to the Computer Centre of the bank the money is to be paid in to. So the optician's paying-in slip goes to the

Barland Bank Computer Centre. Here the information on the slips is typed in at a terminal and saved on magnetic tape.

So each Computer Centre has two tapes containing details of transactions. One of amounts to be added to accounts, the other of amounts to be deducted. This data is merged to form one transaction file.

This transaction file is used to update the Master file containing data on all the bank's accounts. This file is called the ACCOUNTS file.

A record is kept of the amounts paid from each bank to every other bank. The banks can then see how much money they need to transfer from one to another to settle up the differences. For example, if £3m has been added to North Country from Barland, but only £2m has been added to Barland from North Country, then North Country will have to pay another £1m to Barland.

4   Draw a large flow diagram to show all the stages involved in clearing the cheques and updating the banks' ACCOUNTS files.

The banks keep the data on each customer in the CUSTOMER file.

5   Why don't they keep all the information on the customers and the accounts in the same file?

6   What data will be kept on each customer in the CUSTOMER file? What do you think the structure of this file is? Show the type and length of each field.

7   What data will be recorded for each account on the bank's master ACCOUNTS file? What do you think the structure of this file is? Show the type and length of each field. How would this file be sorted?

8   What data will need to be recorded for each transaction? Draw a diagram to show a possible structure for this file. Show the type and length of each field. Why would this file need to be sorted? What field would it be sorted on before it was used to update the master file?

All the file updating is done overnight.

9   Why do you think this is so? What is this type of processing called?

▷ Checking for mistakes

Carol and Yasmin have decided to each open a Girobank account to keep their payments for the rent of the flat and bills separate from their own money.

Yasmin decides that it is about time that one of them pays the electricity bill for the flat.

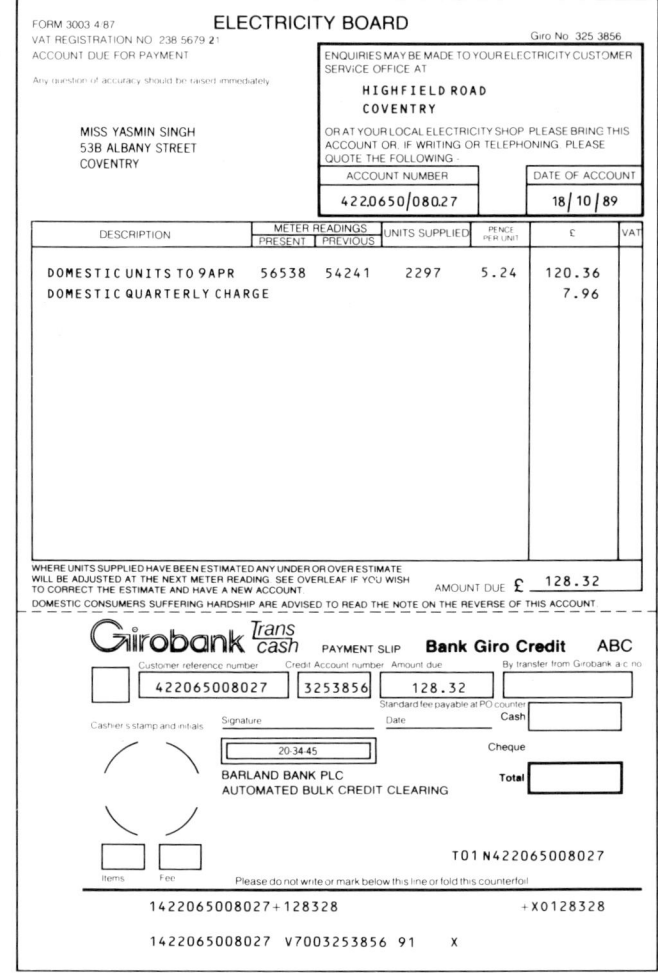

In what different ways could Yasmin pay this electricity bill?

She will pay it by transfer from her Giro account. Carol will pay her share to Yasmin later. Yasmin needs to fill in her account number on the bill's counterfoil. She finds her account number on her cheque book.

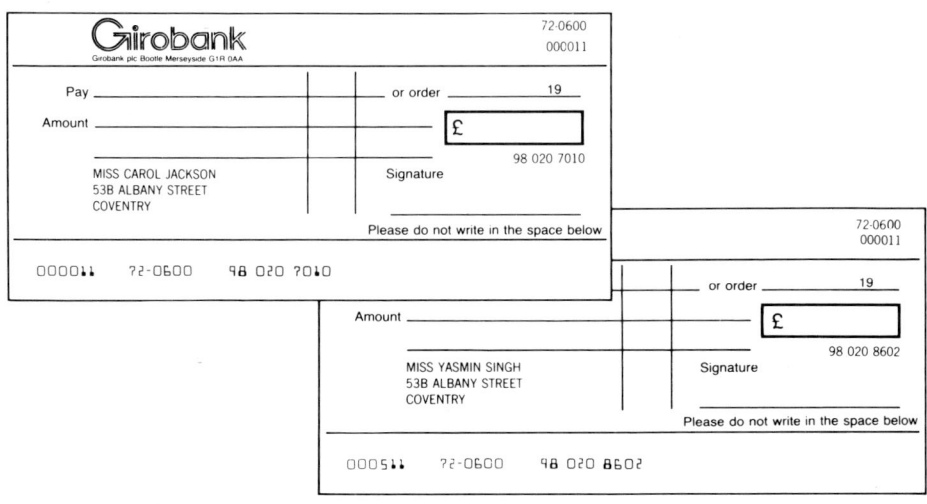

Carol's and Yasmin's Giro cheques

Next she signs the slip, and puts the date on it. She sends it to the bank in the post. The bank deducts the amount from her account and pays it to the Electricity Board's account. The counterfoil is called a turn-around document because the Electricity Board will get it returned to them. They will use the information on it to update their records, so that they know which customers have paid their bills.

An optical character recognition reader

> **I** Can you see the Electricity Board's account number, and the amount owed printed in OCR (optical character recognition) digits on the bill's counterfoil? What do you think the extra characters are for?

By mistake, Yasmin picked up Carol's cheque book, and wrote Carol's account number down on the counterfoil.

> **2** Do you think the £128.32 will be deducted from Carol's account, or from Yasmin's account?

The bank does do some checks to try to make sure that money is deducted from the correct account. For example, the computer does a validation check on all handwritten account numbers to see if there are the correct number of digits. It also does a weighted modulo check. This is designed to find two types of errors:

▶ transcription errors, where numbers have been written down incorrectly, for example, writing down a 7 instead of a 1;

▶ transposition errors, where the right numbers are in the wrong order, for example 134 instead of 143.

The weighted modulo check works like this:

Carol's account number is 98 020 8602.
Each digit is multiplied by a different number. The first digit is multiplied by 9, the second by 8, the third by 7, and so on, like this:

9	8	0	2	0	8	6	0	2
×	×	×	×	×	×	×	×	×
9	8	7	6	5	4	3	2	1
=	=	=	=	=	=	=	=	=
81	64	0	12	0	32	18	0	2

All these answers are added together. The total is 209.
   When this number is divided by 11, there is no remainder, which means that this is a valid number. If there is a remainder, then the number cannot be a valid account number, which means that there has been a mistake.

> **3** If an account number is invalid, it will be discovered anyway when the computer tries to deduct money from an account that does not exist. So why does the bank use this weighted modulo 11 process?

Yasmin's mistake of writing down Carol's account number will not be found out by this check, as both account numbers are real and valid.

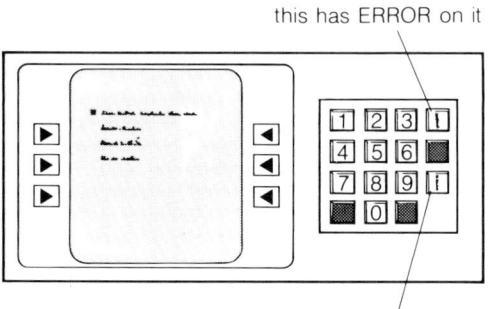

this has ERROR on it

this has ENTER on it

What other banking services are sometimes provided by cash dispensing machines?

4   What other checks might the bank do to stop the payment being made from Carol's account without her approval? These checks are not usually done. Why not?

▷ Cash around the clock

Carol runs out of cash after a hectic shopping trip on her day off. Luckily, she has still got some money in her account, and she now has a cash card which she can use at one of the North Country Bank's cash machines.

The cash machine has a small, restricted keyboard. It has keys for numbers, and for functions like 'withdraw cash' and 'enter'.

I   Why do you think a keyboard like this is used? Why don't they use a keyboard with separate keys for each letter and each digit?

Carol inserts her card, and keys in her personal identification number (PIN). Her PIN number is only valid when used with her card. She couldn't use her PIN with anyone else's card, nor could she use her card with another PIN.

2   Carol is advised to keep her card in a safe place, and to memorize her PIN and not keep a written record of it. Why?

The cash dispenser is really a computer terminal. It is connected to the computer by telephone lines.

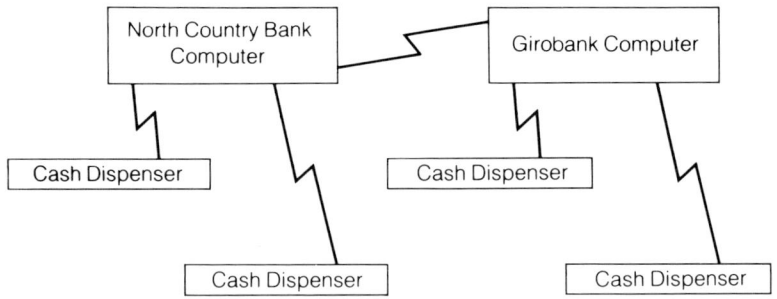

Communication links to cash dispensers

3   What kind of processing is needed to make sure that Carol's card is checked as fast as possible?

4   The file containing details of customer accounts is stored on a magnetic medium. What sort of magnetic medium must the file be stored on? Why?

5   You have already designed a file structure for the ACCOUNTS file. What other field(s) is needed to cope with the cash machines?

Many of the bank's cash machines could be in use at the same time. The customer should not have to wait longer just because other people are using the computer too. The computer's operating system makes it seem that any user is the only user at that time.

It allocates each user a time slice. This means that the computer deals with each user in turn for a very short time. When it has dealt with the last user it starts again. But this all happens so quickly that each user cannot detect the time delay. If an unusually large number of cash machines is being used at the same time, then there may be a noticeable slowing down in the speed of response from the computer. This kind of operating system is called time-sharing.

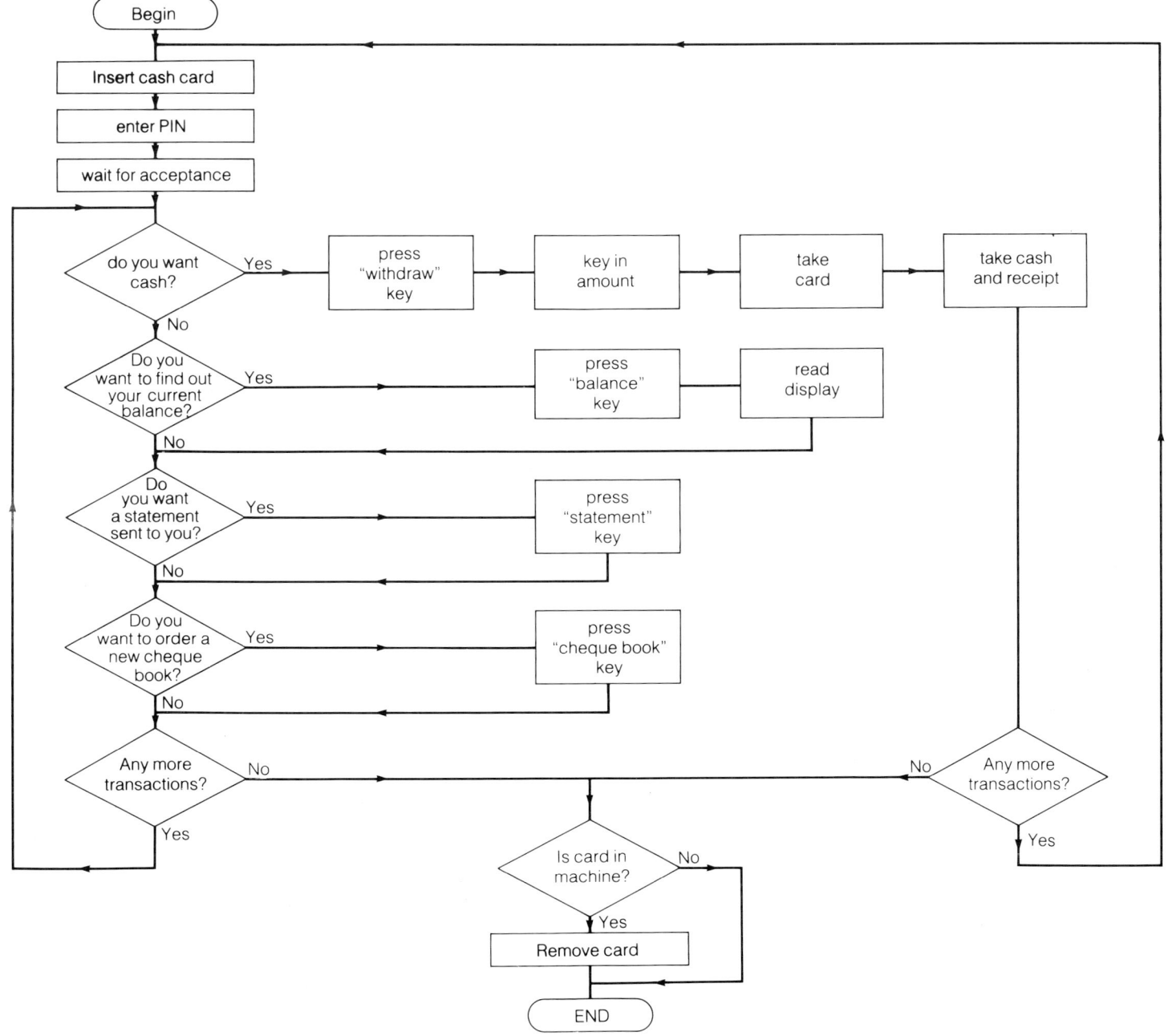

A flow diagram showing the steps that can be taken in obtaining service from a cash machine

> 6 When you withdraw money, what must you do before the cash will be released? Why do you think this is done?

> 7 If a customer wanted to order a new cheque book, and withdraw some cash, which would you advise them to do first?

▷ What the customer sees

The North Country Bank wants to pilot the use of computer terminals inside the banks. The bank wants customers to use these terminals to obtain a variety of services.

> I Why might customers prefer to use these terminals instead of going to a human teller?

It is decided to try these terminals out in a few branches. Before they can start they need to decide on the sort of terminals to have, and have suitable software to allow the customers to use the terminals.

The terminals could have normal typewriter keyboards, or they could have restricted keyboards like the cash machines. They could even use touch-sensitive screens for inputting data.

> 2 What advantages would a full keyboard offer? What advantages would a restricted keyboard offer? What advantages would there be in having a touch-sensitive screen? Can you think of any disadvantages for any of these methods of input? Which one would you recommend?

Rachel Varguesse, an analyst programmer, works in the computing section of the bank. She has been given the task of producing a trial program for testing on the terminals. She has been told that customers must only be able to access their own accounts. The things that the customer should be able to do at the terminal should include:

▶ find out how much money is in their account,

▶ list the amounts paid in and out of the account,

▶ obtain a printed statement,

▶ order a new cheque book.

Rachel is told that other services may be added later.

> 3 Can you think of any other services that might be considered?

Rachel decides that the services will be offered through a menu system, like this:

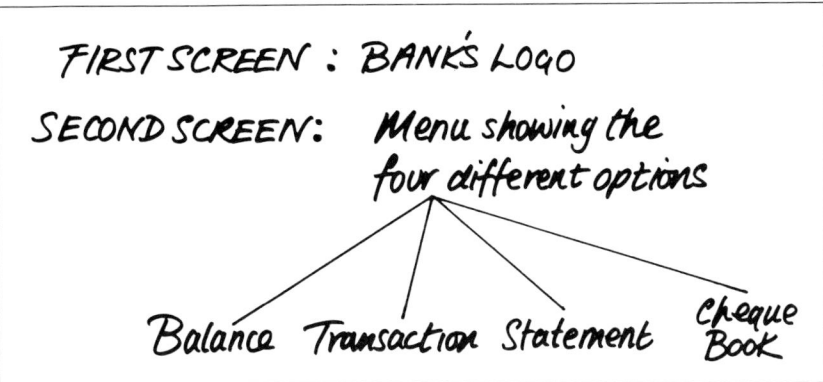

FIRST SCREEN : BANK'S LOGO

SECOND SCREEN : Menu showing the four different options

Balance   Transaction   Statement   Cheque Book

Rachel's sketch of the menu system

4   What other system could Rachel use for the user-interface? Why do you think she chose the menu system?

Rachel must give a lot of thought to the screen designs, so that the instructions will be easily understood, and easy to read.

5   It is always important that screen designs and instructions are clear and easy to understand. Why is it particularly important in this case?

The screen is monochrome, and it can display 12 rows of characters, with up to 20 characters in each row.

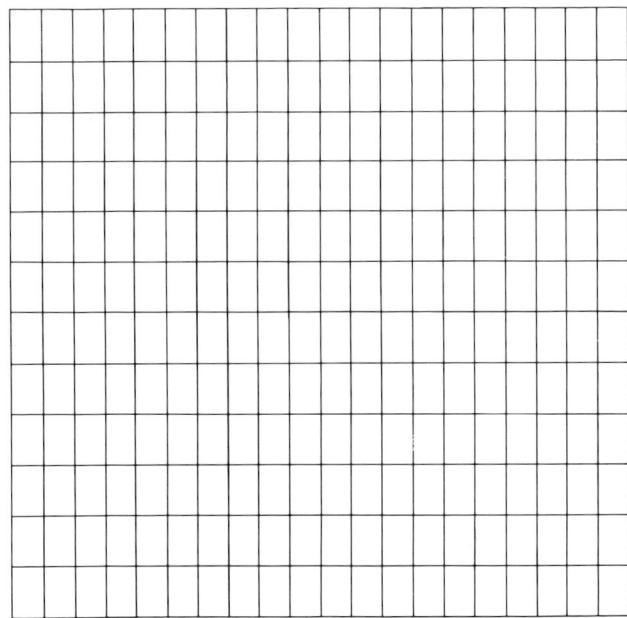

A cash dispenser screen layout

Rachel wants to make sure that all the characters on the screen are easy to read. She decides to design a set of characters for this purpose. On the screen, each character is made up from a pattern of dots. The dots all form a rectangle.

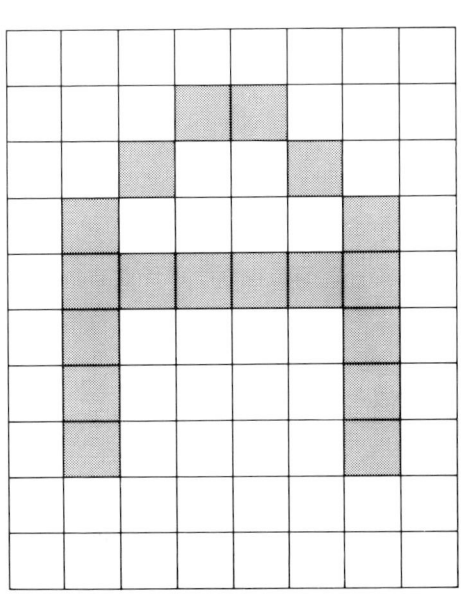

The design of a character

6 Use squared paper to experiment with some of your own designs for letters and digits. What other characters will Rachel need? Try designing some of these too. Try changing the character set of your computer to include your character designs.

7 Design the screen layout for the second screen display which lists the four different options. Remember that you will have to include instructions on what to type to select the chosen option.

8 Use a local viewdata system on a microcomputer to make your own menu system for the bank.

▷ The money program

Losing your cash card

A thief steals Yasmin's cash card from her handbag. Luckily she did not keep her PIN number written down. Because she has not needed to use it, she doesn't notice that the card is missing for a couple of days.

Meanwhile, the thief is trying to use the card to withdraw some money. He has had lots of goes, trying lots of different numbers. Eventually, he tries 1785, which is Yasmin's PIN. He finds out that she has got £218 in her account. He draws out £200.

When Yasmin goes to the bank to report her missing card, she discovers that it has been used to withdraw money from her account. She is furious, and complains bitterly to the bank manager. The bank manager passes on her complaint to Michael Sylvester, who is the head of the North Country Bank's Public Relations Department. His department has already received a number of similar complaints.

He discusses the problem with Maxine Simms, who is in charge of the Computing Department. They decide they must make some changes to the way the cash machines work. The software will be changed so that in future, users will only be able to try three different PIN numbers. If the third is incorrect, the machine will keep the card.

I How will this help to stop thieves withdrawing money with stolen cash cards?

The algorithm used for the software at the moment is this:

```
pin_ok = FALSE                              ;set starting values
card_entry                                  ;take in card
account_balance = account_file_lookup       ;find customer's balance
                                            ;for this account


repeat
     input_pin                              ;get valid PIN
until pin_ok
options
end

procedure card_entry
     clear_screen
     print at 4,13, "Next customer"
     print at 6,12, "Insert your card"
     wait_for_card                          ;wait until card put in
     card_pin = read_mag_stripe             ;get PIN from card
endprocedure

procedure input_pin
     clear_screen
     print at 4,8,"Please enter your"
     print at 6,8,"Personal Identification Number"
     print at 8,8,"and press the ENTER key"
     if input = card_pin then
          pin_ok = TRUE
     else
          print at 11,8,"PIN not correct, try again": pause
endprocedure

procedure options                           ;PIN entered ok
                                            ;allow withdrawal up to
                                            ;account_balance
                                            ;menu of services
                                            ;listing not available
endprocedure


procedure accounmt_file_lookup             ;find balance for the
                                            ;account
                                            ;listing not available
```

Algorithm for cash card machine

```
endprocedure
```

2 Show on diagrams on squared paper what the screen would look
   like in procedures card_entry and input_pin.

3 Change the algorithm so that the cash machine will only allow users
   three attempts at entering their PINs. After three goes the
   machine keeps the card.

4 Can you think of any way that this new system could be
   inconvenient for authorized users?

The bank needs to inform all card holders of this change in the operation
of the cash machine.

5 Use a word processing program to write this letter from the bank
   to the card holders. Explain what the change in operation is, and
   why it is for the customers' benefit.

One of the major banks allows customers to access their account details from home through Prestel. Prestel is a viewdata system with a remote database. This means that Prestel users can access information on a computer by means of telephone lines. Users also need a special VDU, or a TV with a special adaptor. They can also have a printer attached for taking hard copy of screen displays.

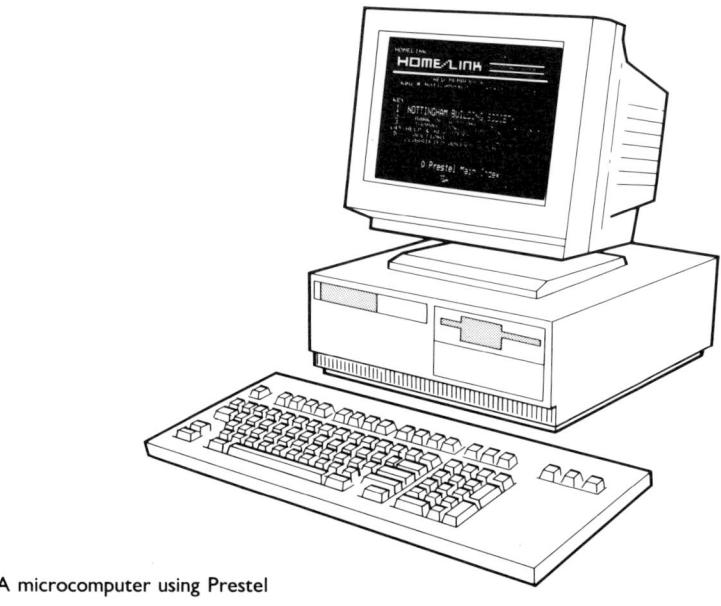

A microcomputer using Prestel

Information on the Prestel computer comes from a variety of sources, for example British Rail (train timetables) and universities (details of courses they offer).

The information is put onto pages. Some pages can be read by all Prestel users, while others are in 'Closed' areas which are only available if you pay an extra fee (for example, the share prices put up by the Stock Exchange) or if you belong to a particular group (travel agents, for example).

> **I   How does Prestel manage to restrict some parts of its database? How do travel agents get access to the data that is only to be used by travel agents?**

When you use Prestel, you have to pay for the use of the telephone line in the same way as you would if you made a normal phone call. You also have to pay for using the computer, at so much per minute. There is also a fee for some of the information pages, depending on whether the information provider wants to offer them for free or not. So, using Prestel can be an expensive business.

Prestel is different from the teletext systems that can be used by some TV sets. These systems, like Ceefax (on the BBC) and Oracle (on ITV) are broadcast with the TV signal, and not down telephone lines. They don't cost anything to access, other than the cost of the TV. But teletext is a one-way system. Information can be sent to the TV, but it cannot be sent from the TV.

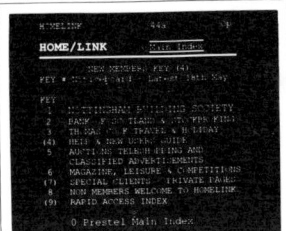 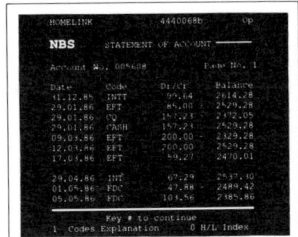 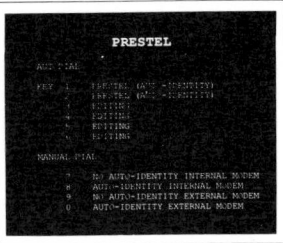

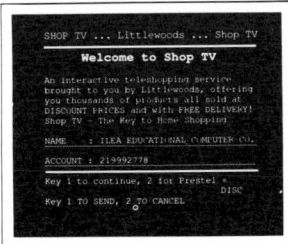 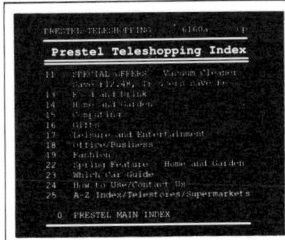 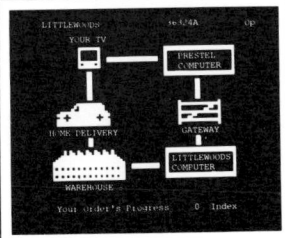

How can users access information from Prestel? Do they need any special equipment?

Prestel is a two-way interactive system. The users can send messages to the computer. This means that Prestel can offer services like Mailbox, where users can leave messages for other users, and teleshopping, where users can place orders for items. These items are sent by post and are paid for using credit cards. The user has only to give his or her name, address and credit card number.

Prestel can be used in this way for home banking. Users can send in requests for statements, and can ask for payments to be made from their account to other bank accounts.

2 Find out what other bank services are possible with Prestel.

3 What bank services are not possible with Prestel?

Yasmin is interested in this type of home banking. She thinks that it could save her a lot of time.

4 How could home banking save time for Yasmin?

But Yasmin also has two worries about this system: the cost and the security.

5 What extra costs will Yasmin have to pay if she uses a Prestel based home banking system?

There are thousands of people who have access to the Prestel computer. Yasmin is worried that some of them might try to get at her bank account.

6 Why is Yasmin worried that other people might get access to her account?

7 What do Prestel and the bank do to prevent users being able to access other people's accounts?

There is another way that money can be transferred from one place to another, using the telephone lines.

8 What does it mean to 'transfer money'? Does cash actually get moved from one place to another?

9 Why might people not want to move their cash from one place to another?

There is a system which allows banks to transfer large amounts of money to other banks. It is called Electronic Funds Transfer or EFT for short. The data (the amount of money, which bank it is from) are grouped into packets. Each packet also carries a code to indicate which bank it is going to. The packets are sent from one bank's computer to another bank's computer via computers called switching computers. These act a bit like telephone exchanges, sending the packets to the right places, but they also check the data for errors.

So, the banks' computers are linked together in a type of network called a packet switching network. Using a network called Swift, the EFT packet switching network covers banks in many parts of the world.

10 Why do you think banks prefer to use EFT than to send amounts of cash?

Banks are worried that using EFT will encourage fraud. For example, someone might find a way of accessing a bank's computer, and then transfer money to their own account. All banks have security measures designed to prevent this sort of thing happening.

11 What measures could the bank use to stop unauthorized people accessing their computers?

The bank's own employees must have access to the bank's computer.

12 What could be done to stop employees from committing 'computer fraud'?

Some people think that there have been a lot of cases of computer fraud in banks. But the banks claim that the amount of fraud is very small.

13 Can you think of any reason why the banks would not want their customers to know that computer fraud had been taking place?

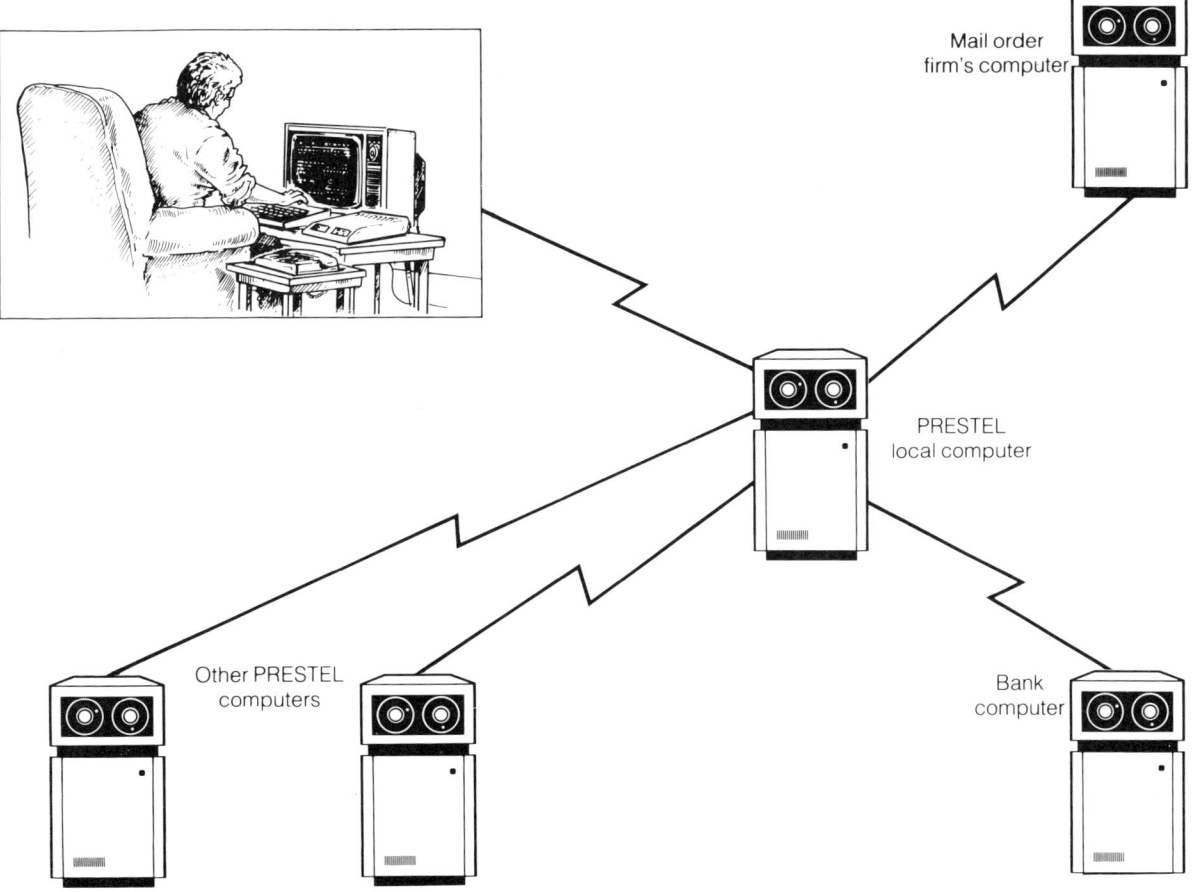

A packet switching network

The next stage in the use of EFT will be in shops where customers will not have to pay by cash, cheque or credit card. Instead, the shops will be linked to the banks' computers. Money to pay for the items will be transferred from the customer's bank account to the shop's bank account. This system is called EFTPOS, which stands for Electronic Funds Transfer at Point Of Sale.

14 How would this system be better for the customer?

15 How would it be better for the shops?

16 Can you think of any drawbacks to this system for the shops or the customers?

▷ General questions

1　Banks use computers for many different tasks. Make a list of all the tasks mentioned in this chapter, plus any others that you can find out.

2　Most organizations that are heavy users of computers would be unable to carry out their business if the computers broke down completely. What can banks and other organizations do to make sure that, as far as possible, they are never left without the computer power they need?

3　There is a lot of discussion about the possibility of banks being defrauded out of large amounts of money by thieves who use the computer system unlawfully. How might the computer system be used to defraud the banks? What can be done to prevent this happening?

4　There are many ways of paying for goods these days. Most of them do not involve the use of cash at all. Make a list of all the different ways you know of paying for things. Do you think there will ever be a time when cash is not used at all? Give some reasons for your answer.

5　Flow charts can be a convenient way of communicating instructions and other information. Draw a flow chart to show the stages you go through in travelling home from school.

6　These are different methods of processing data: time-sharing, interactive, batch, on-line, off-line. Two types of file access are serial and direct access. Put ticks or crosses in the boxes in this table to show the types of processing that can and cannot be done with serial or direct access files.

Now look at each box that you have ticked. Think of an example of that type of processing. Say which files are involved, and what medium they are stored on.

7　Sometimes methods of processing are combined. For example, with a cash machine, the bank's computer is using an interactive time-sharing system. For each type of processing shown in question 6, give an example where it is combined with another type.

8　The user-interface between the computer and the person is very important. What do you think are the main points to consider when designing the user-interface for a program?

9　Make a list of all the different types of machine-readable writing you know, together with an example of where each one is used. What are the advantages of using machine-readable writing on documents?

10　Many computer systems make use of telephone lines to allow communication between devices. Find out some examples of the use of telephone lines in computer systems.

METHODS OF FILE PROCESSING

	Time-sharing	Inter-active	Batch	On-line	Off-line
Serial					
Direct access					

1 Use a spreadsheet program to enter the accounts of your weekly income, spending and saving for the past four weeks. Use the spreadsheet to forecast your total income, expenditure and savings for the year if:
   a your income stays the same,
   b your income increases by £2 a week,
   c your income increases by 10%,
   d your income decreases by £1 a week.

2 Banks often need to write to customers. Make a list of all the different sorts of letters they send. The way the letters are set out and worded is very important. The bank does not want to upset or annoy their customers. Use a word processing program to design and produce some of these letters.

3 Banks need to keep records of information about their customers. What do they use this information for? What information do they need to keep? Design and create a sample bank's CUSTOMER file. Make some customer inquiries using your file. How does your computer system access the customer information that you have entered – is it by random or serial access? The bank's file contains records for many thousands of customers. What method of file access must this system use? Find out how the different information retrieval packages access data files on your computer system.

4 Banks offer a great variety of services. They want to make sure that all their customers know about these services. One way of advertising these services in a bank would be to create a viewdata system for people to use. They could follow through the pages to find out about the services they need. Design and implement a viewdata system for this purpose.

5 Most microcomputers use a group of characters called the ASCII character set. In this set, the letter A is coded as 65, letter B as 66, and so on. The computer you use at school, like most micros, probably uses a 10 × 8 set of dots to display each character.

ੳ u/o	ਅ a/e	ੲ i	ਸ s	ਹ h	ਕ k	ਖ kh
ਗ g	ਘ gh	ਙ ng	ਚ ch	ਛ chh	ਜ j	ਝ jh
ਞ nj	ਟ t	ਠ tth	ਡ d	ਢ dh	ਣ nh	ਤ t
ਥ th	ਦ d	ਧ dh	ਨ n	ਪ p	ਫ f	ਬ b
ਭ bh	ਮ m	ਯ ye	ਰ r	ਲ L	ਵ v/w	ੜ rh

The Punjabi alphabet

Use a piece of squared paper to show how some of the characters from the Panjabi alphabet might be displayed using 10 rows and 8 columns.

Investigate how to change the character set of your computer.

6 Banks take care to try to stop errors getting onto their computer files but from time to time things still go wrong. As you use spreadsheet and information processing packages you may find that you make some of these errors:

▶ entering a letter when a digit was expected (error detected by the validation process),

▶ mis-spelling a word and the package doesn't understand your spelling (syntax error),

▶ entering the wrong number or name and the package searches for the record but can't find it (error found during processing),

▶ entering the wrong formula and the package does what you have asked but the result is not what you wanted (logical error).

Give examples of the errors that you have found using spreadsheet and information processing packages.

Volumes of Computers

▷ The story so far...

No. 4763

Expires 31-7-96

FARADAY HIGH SCHOOL
LIBRARY
READER'S TICKET

Name *Kelvin Thompson*

Class *1 DF*

Kelvin's school library ticket

Kelvin Thompson is a member of two different libraries. He belongs to the school library. He often needs books to help him with his school work and the school library makes sure that there is a good selection of these books. But Kelvin's hobby is gardening, and the school library doesn't have many gardening books. So Kelvin also belongs to the Borough Council's library. This library has one main building and four smaller branches spread around the borough. Kelvin can use any of these and they all have a reasonable selection of gardening books.

Kelvin's school has one library for all the 800 pupils. There is one full-time librarian who looks after it. There are about 6000 books in the library. About 2000 are fiction books. Around 500 of the non-fiction books are for reference only, and cannot be taken out of the library. Every book has a different code number written inside it.

| 1 What do you think the code number is used for?

Every pupil is allowed to take out two books at a time, so they are all given two library tickets.

Every book that can be borrowed has a ticket stuck in it, and a page for stamping the date.

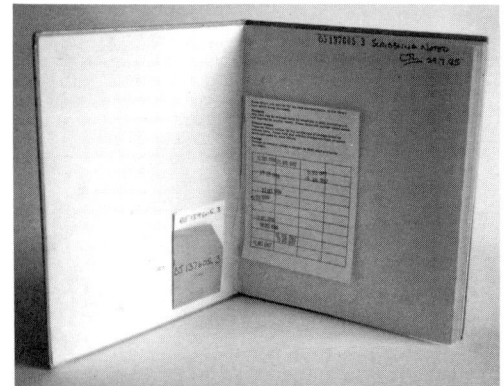

A school library book

When Kelvin wants to take a book out of the library, he first has to find the book he wants. Then he takes the book and one of his library tickets to the librarian. The librarian:

▶ stamps the book with the date it must be returned by (two weeks ahead, or the end of term, whichever is sooner),

▶ takes the card out of the book,

▶ puts the book card inside Kelvin's card,

▶ puts Kelvin's card in a box with all the other cards from books taken out that day. This box has a label on it which says when all these books should be returned.

The pupils cannot just take books from the library, they must first show them to the librarian with their library ticket

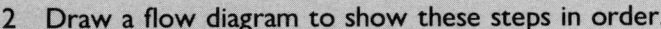

2   Draw a flow diagram to show these steps in order.

The book cards and the library members' cards are kept in long narrow boxes, just wide enough for one card. At the start of each day's work, the librarian puts a taller card with a date on it after the last card. The date is when all the books taken out today must be returned. At the end of the day, the librarian sorts out all the day's cards into book number order. When a book is returned, the librarian can look at the date stamped in it, and then can look for the card in the right section.

3   Why do you think the cards are sorted out into book number order?

When Kelvin takes a book back, he hands his book to the librarian. The librarian:

▶ looks at the last date in the book,

▶ looks for the tickets in the box labelled with this date,

▶ takes the book ticket and puts it back in the book, gives Kelvin his ticket back,

▶ puts the book on one side ready to put it back on the shelf.

4   Draw another flow diagram to show these steps in order.

Using this system the librarian knows:

5   that no-one takes out more than two books. How?

6   if a book is overdue. How?

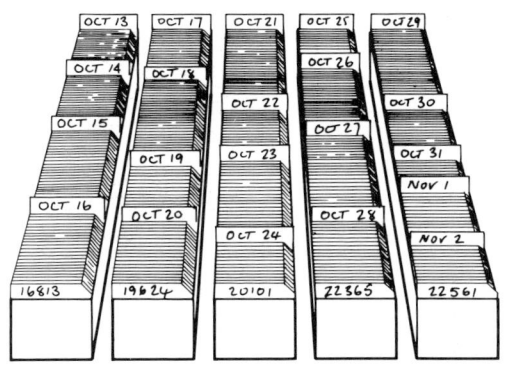

The library files

The librarian sends a note to students who have overdue books.

Who's lost this book?

7 Design a form that the librarian could use to remind students that they have overdue books. It must include all the information that the student and the librarian need.

There are some things that the librarian finds difficult to do using this library's system. For example, think about this situation.

Shirley Bond finds a book in the playground. She can tell that it's a library book, even though the date stamping page has been torn out. What other things could make Shirley think that the book belongs to the library? Shirley takes the book back to the library. The librarian needs to know who left the book in the playground.

8 Why does the librarian need to know this? It is possible, but not very easy to find out. How can this be done?

The library has more than one copy of some books. For example, it has two copies of *The Box of Delights* by John Masefield, because it is a very popular book.

9 If Shirley had found a copy of this book in the playground, how would the librarian find out who had borrowed that particular copy?

Sian Davies wants to find a book about electricity for her Physics project. She looks on the library shelves but can't find a suitable one. There may be other books that have already been taken out, so she goes to ask the librarian.

The librarian has three files of index cards. Each file has one card for every book in the library. One file is arranged in alphabetical order of the author's surname. Another file is arranged in order of subject. Every subject is given a code number and the books are arranged so that these numbers are in order. The third file has all the cards arranged with the book titles in alphabetical order.

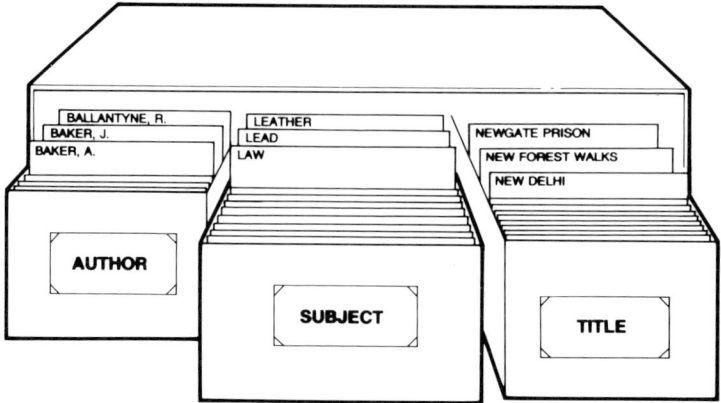

10 Which set of cards will the librarian use to find a book on electricity? Think of an example when each of the other two sets of cards would be used.

11 What information should be included on each card? Design the layout for each type of card.

The librarian finds the names of two books that might be suitable for Sian. Neither of the books is in the library at present. The librarian askes Sian if she would like to reserve them. This means that when the books are returned, the librarian will let Sian know. Then she will be able to take them out. The librarian sends a note to Sian telling her that a book has been returned.

12 How could this note be delivered to Sian in school? What needs to be written in the note so that Sian knows which book it is? Design a form for the librarian to use. The form should remind the librarian of all the information that is needed.

While carrying a pile of magazines to put them back on the shelf, the librarian accidently bumps into into a pupil and drops them. Unfortunately she is also carrying the box containing all the cards of books that are on loan which falls to the ground. The cards are all over the place. Many of the book cards have fallen out of the borrowers' tickets. The librarian says 'Oh dear', and thinks of the problems that this accident is going to cause in the library.

13 Will the librarian know who has overdue books?

14 Will the librarian still be able to lend books?

15 Will there be any problems when books are returned?

16 Will borrowers be able to keep books without the librarian knowing?

17 Will the librarian be able to reserve books?

18 What do you think the librarian should do to make the best of this situation?

The librarian has dropped the box containing all the cards of books that are on loan. This will cause her a lot of problems.

The librarian has to keep a list of information for all the books that are reserved. The name of the book needs to be kept.

19 What other information does the librarian need for each book?

Every time a book is returned the librarian must check to see whether or not it has been reserved.

20 When would be the best time to do this? Change your second flow diagram, from question 4 to show this extra step.

21 Make a list of all the documents (cards, tickets, etc.) that are used in this library system.

BOROUGH PUBLIC LIBRARIES

KELVIN THOMPSON

12 March 1987

This ticket must be shown every time a book is borrowed or renewed. Change of address must be notified immediately.

BOROUGH PUBLIC LIBRARIES

DO 121939 10

DO NOT FOLD

What advantages are there of using a barcode on a library card?

Librarians have to train for the job for several years.

> **22** **What do you think a librarian's job is all about? Do you think that their main activity is stamping books?**

Kelvin's library ticket for the Borough library is very different from the school library tickets. It has a barcode on it, similar to the ones on items for sale in supermarkets.

The cards inside the books are different too, but the books still have a page for the return date to be stamped, like the one below.

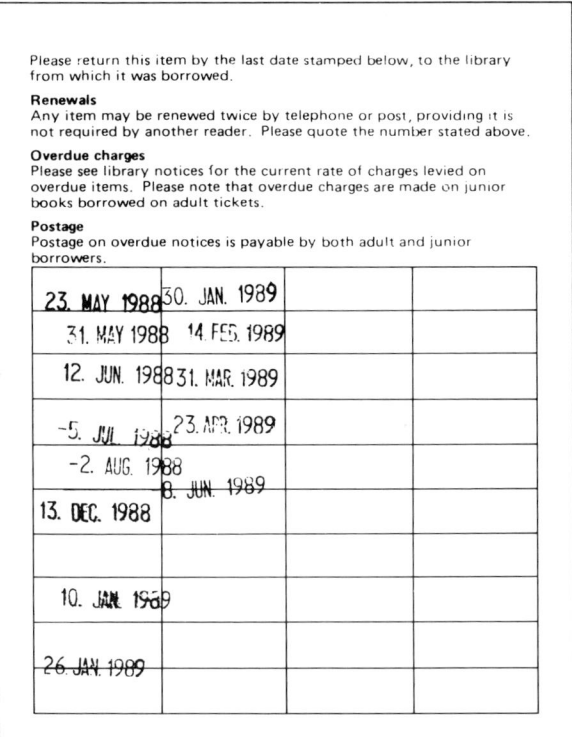

The Borough Library is much bigger than the school library. It has more than 100 000 books for lending and many thousands of books, magazines and periodicals in the reference libraries. If the book you want is at a different branch of the library, they will arrange to have it sent over to your local branch. So each branch needs to know which books are at every other branch.

The Borough Library uses a computer to help keep track of all its books, and to help to run the library efficiently. Like other Local Authority services, the library is paid for by money collected from the local businesses and residents. The Local Authority must provide the best possible service with the money that it is able to collect. The Chief Librarian would like to have a more sophisticated computer system, but it would cost more than the library can afford to spend.

23 What features of a computer system can be expensive? What do you think would be the differences between an expensive system and a cheaper one?

Kelvin finds it much quicker to take out and return books at the Borough Library. For a start, he only has one library ticket, even though he is allowed to take out up to four books at a time. Information relating to Kelvin is coded into the black and white bars which make up the barcode on his ticket. In fact the barcode only contains Kelvin's library membership number.

Every book in the library has its own unique code number. So, each of the library's three copies of *Lord of the Flies* has a different number.

24 Why does each copy of every book have a different number?

This number is coded into the black and white bars which make up the book's barcode.

When Kelvin takes out a book, he gives the book and his library card to an assistant. The assistant uses a light pen to read the barcode on Kelvin's ticket, then to read the barcode in the book. Kelvin is then given back the book and his ticket.

The barcode in a book

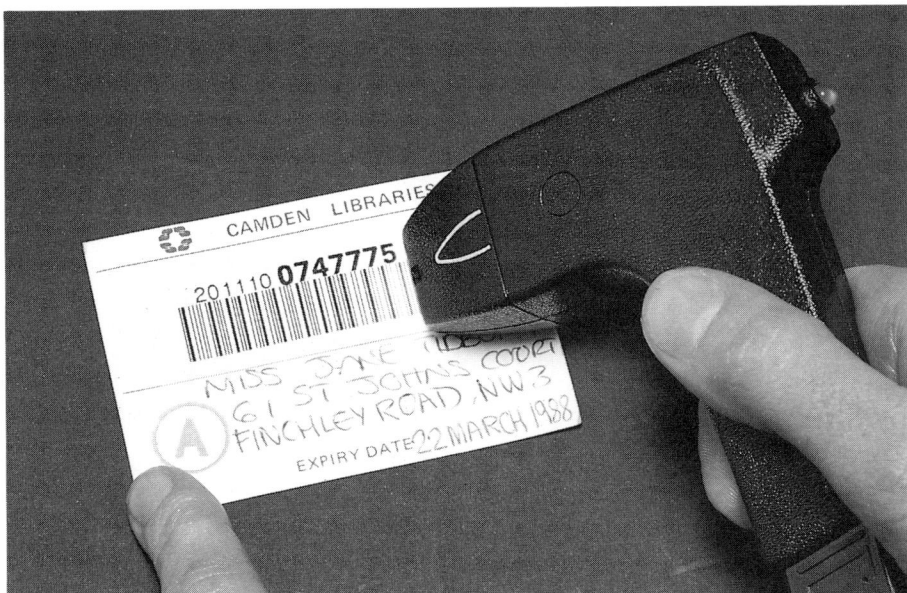

Does your local library use a light pen like this one?

When he returns a book, the same thing happens. The barcode in the book is read. The data from the barcodes is recorded on a cassette tape.

25 It is also necessary to record whether a book is being taken out or returned. How might this be done?

At the end of each working day, the data on the cassette tapes are transmitted to the library computer. Each branch library has a modem, which allows the data on the cassette tape to be sent along telephone lines.

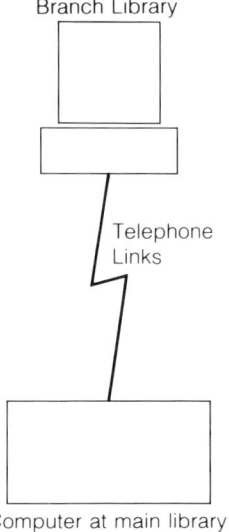

Branch Library

Telephone Links

Computer at main library

Transmission of data

Where else, apart from libraries, might modems be used?

At present, telephones carry sounds as analog signals. Data for the computer is in a digital form. The modem in the branch library converts the digital signal into analog. At the main library, where the computer is, there is another modem which converts the analog signal back to a digital signal.

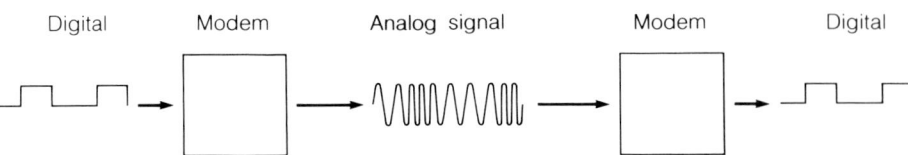

Digital   Modem   Analog signal   Modem   Digital

Inside the computer, characters like letters, numbers and punctuation marks are represented by a pattern of bits. A bit is something that can only be in one of two states. It can be on, or it can be off, like a light bulb. Bits are written down as 1s and 0s, where a 1 means on, and a 0 means off.

Every character is represented by a pattern of seven bits. The computer uses a standard set of codes called the ASCII (said like askey) character set. This is used by many other computers. In this set, the letter capital A is represented by this pattern of bits:

$$1\ 0\ 0\ 0\ 0\ 0\ 1$$

When the computer sends the signal for the letter A it sends the pattern:

on   off   off   off   off   off   on

The pattern for each letter is different. For example the pattern for C is:

on   off   off   off   off   on   on

An extra bit is sometimes added, for checking the first seven. This eighth bit called a parity bit. A parity bit can check for even or odd parity. If it is even parity, it means that the last bit will be a 1 only if it makes the total number of 1s an even number.

For example, all of these would be passed by an even parity check:

10000001	11000000	11110000
11001001	10101010	11111111

If it is odd parity, then the bit will be 1 only if there it makes the total number of 1s an odd number. For example, all of these would pass an odd parity check:

10000000	10010010	11000001
00011100	10110101	11101001

So, if there is a mistake somewhere, and some of the bits are sent or received wrongly, the parity bit may be used to discover the mistake.

26   Give an example of a mistake that would be discovered by a parity check. Give an example of one that would not be detected.

27   What do you think should happen if there is a mistake of this kind?

Each on and off is held for a fixed amount of time, so that the device receiving the character has time to read each bit. Some extra bits are also sent so that the modem knows when a character is about to be sent, and when it is finished. The sending and receiving computers, and the modem, must all be set up so that they know how many bits are to be sent for each character. The library system sends one extra bit at the start, then the character, then two more bits.

So the final signal sent by the computer for the letter A looks like this:

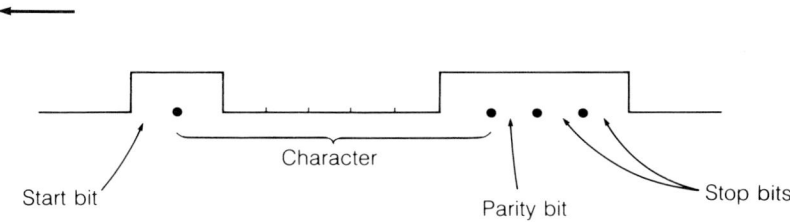

The representation of the letter A to be transmitted

The computer is set up to send signals to the modem at a certain rate. Each bit is left on, or off, for 1/330th of a second. This means that 30 characters are sent each second. The rate at which characters are sent along the wires from the computer to the modem is called the baud rate. The computer is capable of sending out the signal with the ons and offs much closer together, but the telephone system limits the speed. Using dedicated lines, that is lines that are just used for this and nothing else, a faster speed could be achieved.

The signal sent along the telephone lines from the modem has to travel quite a long way. The signal could get weaker, and there could also be interference on the line. To make loss or corruption of the signal less likely, it is modulated by the modem. At the receiving end, it is changed back to the computer signal.

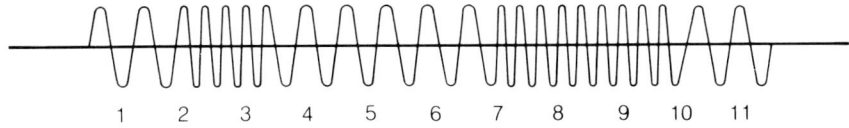

The analog signal for letter A

28   How has the modem changed the signal? Why do you think this makes it stronger?

29   Show how the modem would change the signal for the letter C.

The data that is sent is used to update the library files, which keep records on all books and on all the library members. Reminders for overdue books, and letters to say that reserved books are available, are all sent out from the main library.

The data files
The data files are kept on magnetic tape, as this is cheaper than disks, and anyway, the files are only updated once a day using batch processing. The smaller the files, the less storage space is needed, and the quicker the files can be updated. This makes it important not to waste space in a file. Sometimes data can be coded, so that a couple of digits or letters stand for several words.

> **30 What kind of information could be coded? What information would be difficult to code? Can you think of any disadvantages of using codes?**

First of all, there is a file which contains data on all the books in the library. This is called the BOOK file. What data does the library need on each book? It needs to know enough about the book so that:

▶ it can be replaced if it is lost,

▶ it can be found if only some information on it is known: for example, Kelvin might want to find all the books written by a particular gardening expert called Peter Seabrook,

▶ the librarian knows which subject area it is about,

▶ the librarian knows whether the book is in the library or out on loan.

> **31 Draw a diagram showing the format of one record in this file. Show the length and type of each field. Then show an example record for this book.**
>
> **32 How many characters are reserved for each record? If there are 100 000 books, how many characters would be in the whole file? (Multiply the size of one record by 100 000.) Memory space is usually measured in kilobytes, called K for short. One byte holds one character. One kilobyte holds 1024 characters. How many K are needed for this BOOK file? Use a calculator to divide the number of characters by 1024.**

The diagram shows how the file is stored on the tape.

> **33 1 K of the file can be stored on 1 cm of tape. How long must the tape be to hold the whole file?**

The tape actually has to be longer than this, because of the way the tape reader works. It starts the tape, then it reads a number of records, then it stops and those records are processed. Then it starts again. The data can only be read when the tape is moving at the correct speed. To allow for all

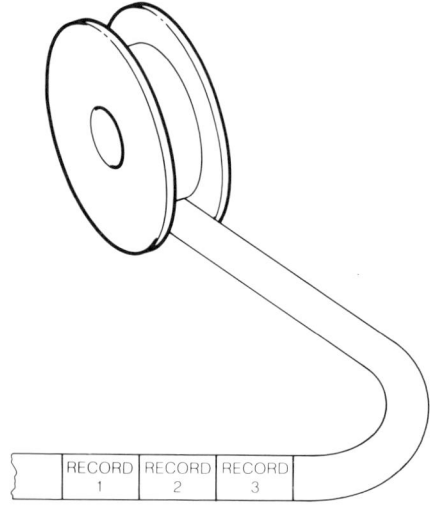

RECORD 1 | RECORD 2 | RECORD 3

Some data stored on magnetic tape

this stopping and starting, and to let the tape reader get up to the right speed each time, the data is arranged in blocks, with gaps in between. The gap is usually about 2 cm long.

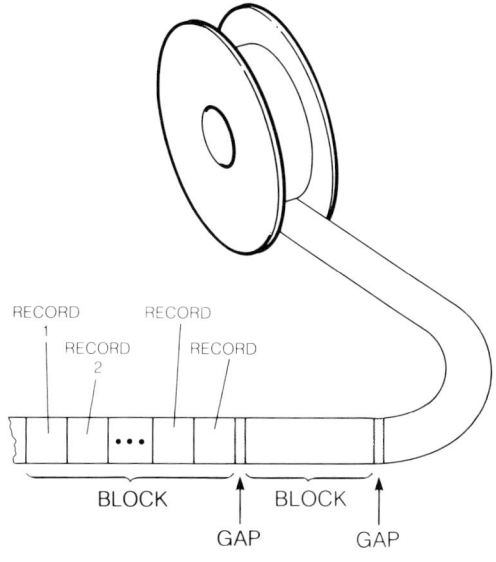

An inter block gap on magnetic tape

34 How much memory would the tape reader need if it read the tape in one go?

In fact, the tape reader has only 10 K of buffer memory for reading data.

35 How many records can be read at one go?

This is the number of records that makes up one block.

36 About how long is one block in cm?

The library also needs to keep data on all the library members. This file is called the MEMBERS file.

37 What data does it need on each member? The library needs to be able to:
▶ identify each member of the library,
▶ know where to send overdue letters,
▶ know whether members belong the Junior or Senior library.

38 Draw a diagram showing the format of one record in this field. Show the type and length of each field. Then show an example record, using information about yourself.

The library also needs to know which books are on loan to each member. The file which holds this data is the LOANS file. This file has one record for each book currently on loan.

39 What data about each borrowed book would need to be kept on this file?

40 Draw a diagram showing the format of one record in this file. Show the type and length of all the fields. Then give an example record, showing you as the borrower of this book.

There needs to be a record of all the books that library members have reserved. This is called the RESERVED file. There would be one record for each reserved book.

41 Draw a diagram showing the format of one record in this file. Show the type and length of each field.

▷ Deciding on the system

The Borough Library has not always had a computer system. At first it used a manual system similar to the one in the school library. The computer system was designed by systems analysts employed by the Local Authority.

> 1 Why do you think that the Local Authority needs to employ systems analysts? If they did not employ them, how could the library computer system have been designed?

The computer system was designed to suit a number of people. The Chief Librarian's needs were very important, as he is responsible for running the library. The other library workers were important too, as they have to work with the computer system. The Finance department had to be satisfied, because they had to find the money to pay for the system, and did not want to spend more than they needed to.

> 2 Who else should have been considered when the library computer system was designed?
>
> 3 Can you think of any ideas for the system which would be approved by the Librarians, but not by the Treasurer's Department? Can you think of any other ideas that some of the people would want, but others would not want?

The systems analysts spent some time investigating the library system before they started to design the computer system. But even when they thought they had come up with a good system design, they wanted to make sure that it would be easy to make changes to it in the future.

> 4 Why might the system need to be changed, even after it has been implemented?

By making sure that the system is well documented, it is easier to make changes. That means that the analysts wrote down in detail what each part of the system is designed to do. They needed to write down all the stages in the system, what files are used at each point, what comes up on the screen at each point and what has to be keyed in at each point.

> 5 Make a list of all the things that would need to be in the systems analyst's documentation, and say why each thing needs to be there.

When the computer system design was complete, programmers began to write the programs for each part of the system. The programmers were employed by the Local Authority. But the programs could have been written by programmers at a 'software house'. The Local Authority would have paid the software house, and the software house would have paid and employed the programmers.

> 6   Can you think of some advantages and disadvantages to the Local Authority of employing its own programmers? What are the advantages and disadvantages of paying the software house to write the programs?

The programmers wrote several programs, each to perform one part of the system.

> 7   Why did the programmers write several programs, rather than one long program?

Even small programs are divided into smaller sections or modules. When the modules have all been written and tested, they are joined together to make the complete program. For example, the program which reads the book's barcode and stores it on cassette tape could be divided into a number of parts:

▶ to read the barcode,

▶ to check the barcode reading,

▶ to store the data on cassette.

> 8   Why do you think it is better to divide programs into smaller sections before starting to write them?

The programmers are all writing different parts of the same system. It is very important that someone organizes the prorgammers' work, to make sure that nothing is left out and nothing is done more than once. This is the job of the programmers' Team Leader. The leader also organizes the testing of the programs, and the linking up of some smaller programs or modules into larger programs.

> 9   Programs have to be tested to make sure that they work, and to make sure that they work properly. How could you check that a computer program was producing accurate output?

Different programs and modules are written in different languages, according to which is most appropriate. This decision is often made by the team leader, who then has to allocate modules to programmers who can use the necessary language. The team leader tries to give easier modules to those who have less experience, leaving the complex work for the more experienced programmers.

> 10   What skills do you think are important for a good team leader? Design a newspaper advertisement for a team leader's job.

TELEPHONE OPERATORS

We currently have vacancies for Full time Day Operators at our Directory Assistance Centre in Streatham, 136 High Road, London SW16 1BL.

Full time day operators work 41 hours per week and must be available to work some Saturdays and Bank Holidays.

Applicants should have a clear speaking voice, good hearing and spelling and have the ability to deal tactfully with our customers. No experience is necessary as full training will be given.

Applicants should be aged between 16-58 years (we welcome applications from mature persons).

Starting salary is up to £7,489 p.a. (inclusive of London allowance) rising to £8,065 p.a.

For further details please contact the Recruitment Manager on 01-769 0855.

British
TELECOM

British Telecom is an Equal Opportunities Employer.

Here is an advertisement for another type of job to give you some clues for question 10

```
IDENTIFICATION DIVISION.
PROGRAM-ID.
        COPIER.

ENVIRONMENT DIVISION.
INPUT-OUTPUT SECTION.
FILE CONTROL.
        SELECT LINES-IN-FILE ASSIGN TO PFMS.
        SELECT LINES-OUT-FILE ASSIGN TO TERMINAL.

DATA DIVISION.
FILE SECTION.

FD   LINES-IN-FILE
        LABEL RECORD IS STANDARD
        VALUE OF FILE-ID IS 'EX1IN'.
01   LINE-IN-RECORD              PIC X(80).

FD   LINES_OUT_FILE
        LABEL RECORD IS OMITTED.
01   LINE-OUT-RECORD             PIC X(80).

WORKING-STORAGE-SECTION.

01   OUT-OF-LINES-FLAG           PIC XXX.

PROCEDURE DIVISION.

MAIN-ROUTINE.
        OPEN INPUT LINES-IN-FILE
             OUTPUT LINES-OUT-FILE.

        MOVE 'NO' TO OUT-OF-LINES-FLAG.

        READ LINES-IN-FILE
             AT END MOVE 'YES' TO OUT-OF-LINES-FLAG.

        PERFORM COPY-PARAGRAPH
             UNTIL OUT-OF-LINES-FLAG = 'YES'.

        CLOSE LINES-IN-FILE
              LINES-OUT-FILE.

        STOP RUN.

COPY-PARAGRAPH.
        MOVE LINE-IN-RECORD TO LINE-OUT-RECORD
        WRITE LINE-OUT-RECORD
        READ LINES-IN-FILE
             AT END MOVE 'YES' TO OUT-OF LINES-FLAG.
```

A section of COBOL program

The programmers wrote documentation for each program, so that another programmer could understand the code.

11	**Why might it be necessary for a programmer to read code written by someone else?**

The programmers use a high level language to write the programs. High level languages are designed to be easier for programmers to use. They are similar to the English language in some ways. Sometimes it is possible to read a high level language program and be able to understand what it will do, even if you have never learned the language.

12	**The short program section on the left is written in a high level language called COBOL. See if you can work out what it is supposed to do.**

There are many different high level languages. Usually they are developed to be used in writing programs to solve particular sorts of problems. For example, the language FORTRAN was designed to be good for writing programs to do with maths and science. COBOL was designed for business and commercial programming.

High level languages have to be translated so that they can be understood by the computer. Computers work by following instructions which tell the various parts of the computer what to do and when to do it. These instructions are called machine code instructions. Each type of computer has its own machine code, because the machine code has to be exactly related to the way the computer works. One instruction written in a high level language can be equal to many instructions written in machine code.

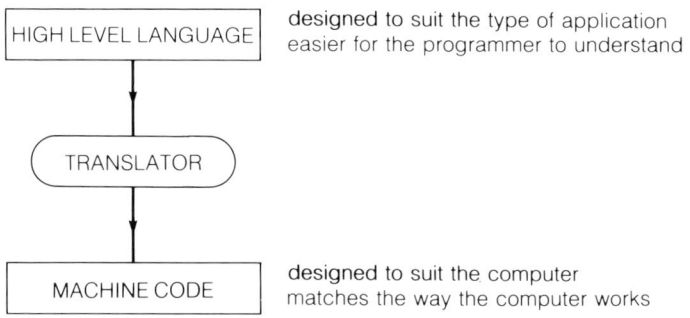

designed to suit the type of application
easier for the programmer to understand

designed to suit the computer
matches the way the computer works

The relationship between high level language and machine code

13	**Many computers can run programs written in a language called BASIC. What sort of program could make it possible to run the same BASIC program on two different computers?**

Translating programs work in one of two different ways. Imagine that you are given a German microscope, and the instructions are all in German. You could ask a German speaking friend to translate the instructions for you. They could do this in different ways.

One way would be for your friend to read the first instruction, translate it to English, then tell you what to do. Then do the same with the next instruction, and all the other instructions.

Another way would be for your friend to translate it all and write down the English translation. Then you could follow the written instructions whenever you wanted to use the microscope.

The first way is quicker the first time, but every time you used the microscope you would need to go through the whole process again with your friend. The second way is slower at first, but works out quicker in the long run.

Computers can translate high level languages in two similar ways. The first way is called interpreting the code. The program is translated one line at a time, and the machine code is lost once it has been used. Every time the program is run, it has to be interpreted.

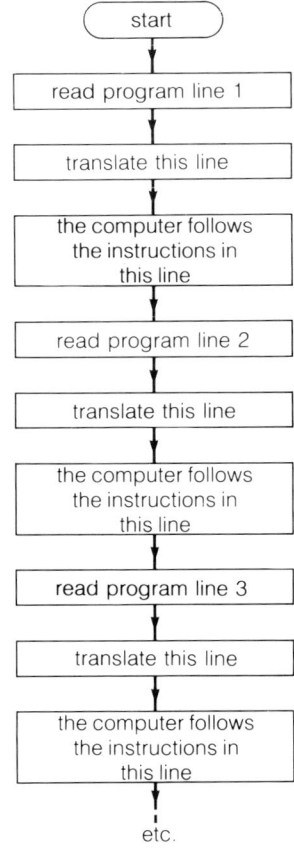

The function of an interpreter

The second way, the whole of the program is changed to machine code, and the machine code is saved. This is called compiling. Every time the program is run, only the compiled code is used. Machine code compiled from code in a high level language is called object code. The code written in the high level language is called source code.

14 Interpreters and compilers are two types of software used to translate high level language programs to machine code. What do you think are the advantages and disadvantages of each type?

15 The programs for the library system could be written so that they could be interpreted or compiled. Which do you think would be best? Why?

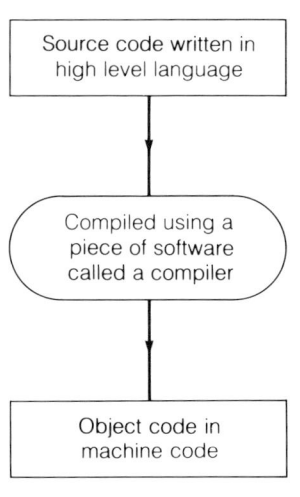

The function of a compiler

Some computer languages are very close to machine code. They are called low level languages. They are easier for people to read than machine code, but not so easy as high level languages. This is an example of some instructions written in a low level language.

```
; section of 8086 code to get MS DOS environment variable
; format of variable: eg PATH=A:\DATA

        mov   ah, 62h            ; load ah register with  62hex
        int   21h               ; MS DOS interrupt 21 call
        mov   ds, bx
        mov   ds, ds:[2ch]
        mov   dx, 0

        sub   si, si
        mov   bx, offset envword ; variable name stored in envword

envloop:
        lodsb
        test al, al             ; test for end of list
        jz    nofind            ; nofind - end of search
        sub   di, di

cmploop:
        cmp   al, '='           ; find the = sign in the string
        jne   notaneq
        sub   al, al

notaneq:
        cmp   al, es:[bx][di]    ; match letters in variable name
        jne   next              ; with this word
        test al, al
        je    foundit
        inc   di
        lodsb
        test al, al
        jne   cmploop
        jmp   envloop

next:
        lodsb
        test al, al
        jne   next
        jmp   envloop

foundit:                        ; found the required variable name
                                ; in the list
```

Low level languages still need to be translated into object code. The programs that do this are called assemblers.

> **16** Can you think of any disadvantages for a programmer who has to write programs in a low level language? Can you think of any advantages?

Any programming team will write and collect program modules that can be used in a number of different programs. For example, there is a program module that takes input data and writes it to a file on magnetic tape. This could be used in a number of different programs. For example, the book issuing program, the book return program, and file updating programs. It would be a waste of time to write this section of program every time it was needed. Programmers make use of 'libraries' of programs, and modules. That way, time is not wasted by rewriting similar programs.

> **17** Can you think of any other programs or modules that might be used frequently? Who would be responsible for the organization and maintenance of a program library? Can you think of any disadvantages in keeping and using a library like this?

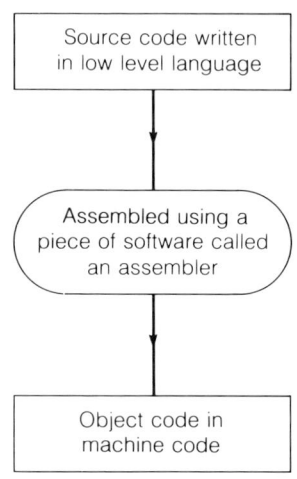

The function of an assembler

▷ Where are the books?

Every day, the LOANS file in the Borough Library is updated. That is, all the loans and returns from the previous day are added to the master LOANS file.

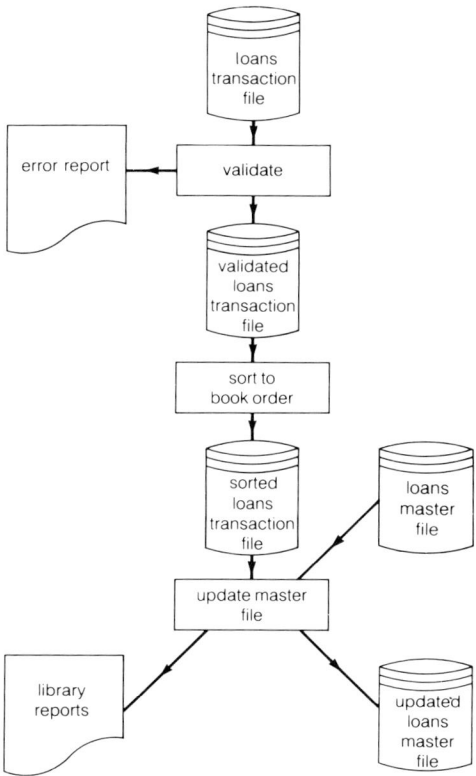

Updating the LOANS file

1 What is the LOANS master file used for? What is the transaction file used for?

2 The LOANS transaction file is on magnetic tape. It is made up from data from each of the branches of the library. How is this data collected at each branch? How is it sent to the library computer centre? How is it combined together to make one transaction file? What fields are included in the file?

3 Validation checks are designed to prevent unreasonable data being input. Describe one validation check that could be used for each field in the transaction file. For each field, give an example of one data item that would be accepted, and one that would not.

4 Data which fails a validation check is output in an error report. Make a design for this error report, showing what it would need to contain.

5 Why is the transaction file sorted to book order?

6 When a book is returned to the library, it needs to be checked against the list of books that have been reserved. This list is called the RESERVED file, and it is kept on magnetic tape. Write down the steps involved in checking returned books against this file. What should be done when a reserved book is returned to the library?

7 Copy the last flow chart onto a sheet of paper. Amend it to show the updating of the RESERVED file.

8 Details of returned reserved books, and of overdue books, are needed so that letters can be sent out. These details are recorded in a temporary file which is produced when the LOANS master file is updated. Show this file on the flow chart.

9 What reports are generated when the master file is updated? Who would use these reports?

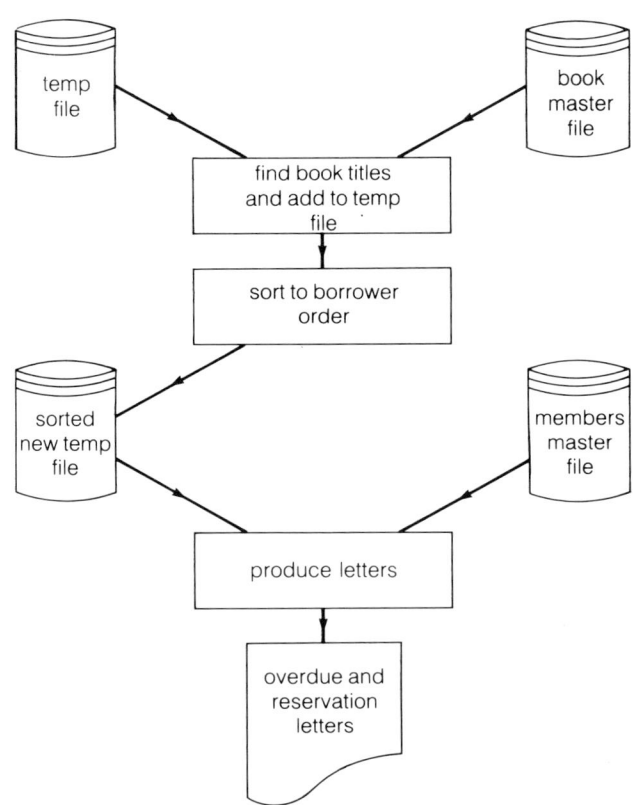

Overdue book reminders. This flow chart shows how the temporary file is used to produce letters for borrowers who have overdue books, and to borrowers who have reserved books which are ready for collection

10 The temporary file does not contain the book titles. These have to be found from the BOOK master file. What does the temporary file contain? Why does the temporary file not need to be sorted before it is processed against the BOOK master file?

The overdue and reservation letters are produced on pre-printed
stationery. That means that some things are already printed on the letters,
and the rest is added by the computer's printer.

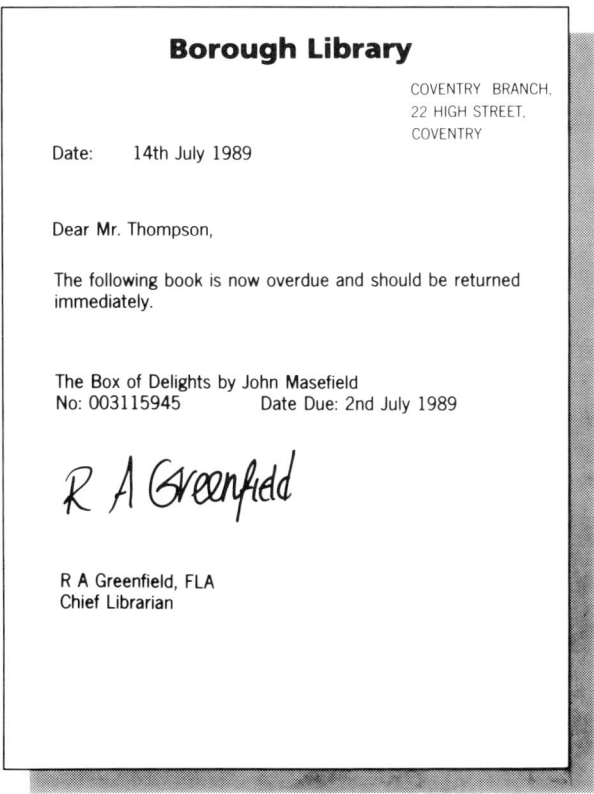

Borough Library

COVENTRY BRANCH,
22 HIGH STREET,
COVENTRY

Date: 14th July 1989

Dear Mr. Thompson,

The following book is now overdue and should be returned
immediately.

The Box of Delights by John Masefield
No: 003115945   Date Due: 2nd July 1989

R A Greenfield

R A Greenfield, FLA
Chief Librarian

An example of an overdue letter

12 Using a word processor, design a pre-printed letter for sending
out to members whose reserved books are ready for collection.
Fill in sample details in a different colour.

Unlike in the manual system, it would be possible to take out more books
than you were entitled to in this library.

13 When would the library system discover that a member had taken
out more books than they were entitled to? What could be done
when over-borrowing is discovered?

It could be disastrous for the library if one of the master files was lost or
destroyed. The library could make back-up copies of the files, but this may
not be necessary. If a master file is lost, it can be re-made by reprocessing
the previous master file with the transaction file. After all, that is how the
latest master file is made in the first place!

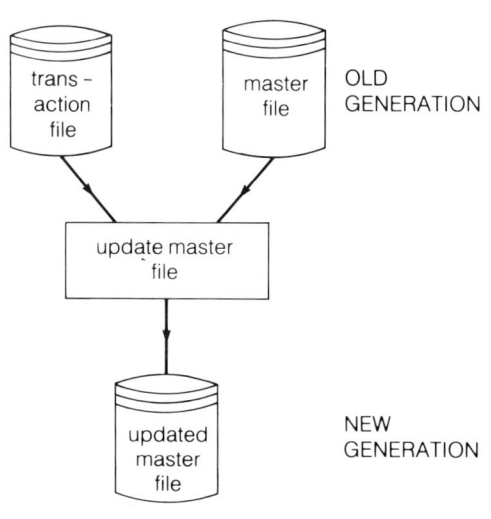

trans-
action
file

master
file

OLD
GENERATION

update master
file

updated
master
file

NEW
GENERATION

The creation of new master file

14 It would not be possible to re-make the master file if either the previous master file, or the transaction file, was lost too. What steps could be taken to prevent files being lost, damaged or destroyed?

▷ Dear Borrower...

The Borough Library's computer is housed in the main Council Offices. All the data files used in the system are sequential files. That means that the data is organized record by record, like this:

    initial record
    record 1
    record 2
    record 3
    termination record

The initial record contains information about the file, for example its name, and how many fields there are in each record. The termination record marks the end of the file. All the processing of the files is done in batch mode. That means that the whole file is processed every time. Items on the file are accessed serially, that means one after another. The cheapest form of magnetic backing store for this type of processing is magnetic tape.

1 Could this file be kept on magnetic disk? Could it still be processed in the same way?

The computer system has a number of tape drives. It also has a number of disk drives, as the programs are stored on disk.

2 Why do you think the programs are kept on disk?

There are also a number of printers for outputting error reports.

3 What other output is produced on the printers?

Dot matrix printers are used because they are fairly inexpensive. And although they cannot produce the very best quality of print, it is good enough for the library's use.
   Look at the examples of print produced by three types of printer:

The following books are now overdue and should be returned **immediately**.

Dot matrix

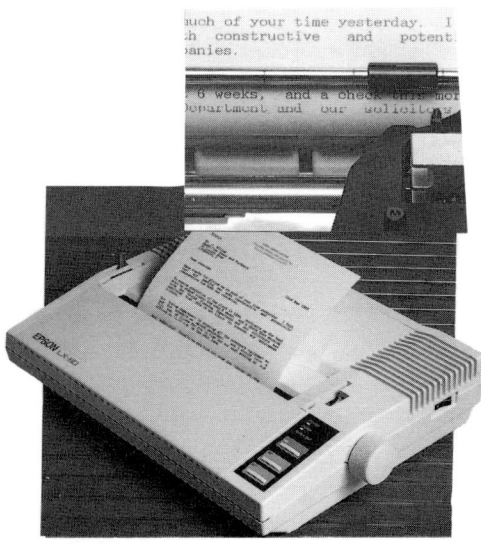

A dot matrix printer forms characters using patterns of dots. The dots are made by fine needles which are 'fired' by electromagnets

```
The  following  books  are  now  overdue  and  should
be  returned  immediately.
```

Daisy wheel

The following books are now overdue and should be returned
immediately.

Laser printer

A daisy wheel printer has a rotating wheel made up of
spokes. Each spoke has a character printed on its end.
The spokes come from a central hub like flower petals
– hence the name

> **4** Which one is the best quality? Find out which one is the most
> expensive. Which one cannot output graphics?

The library branches are not always on-line to the computer. They only link
to the computer when they send their transaction data for processing. If a
library member wants to find out if a particular book is held in the library
they cannot access the BOOK file on the computer to find out. The
branches do not keep catalogues of the books either. It would be very
expensive to produce catalogues on paper, because they would be very
large, and would need to be replaced regularly.

A laser printer uses a laser beam and dry, powdered
ink to produce characters

> **5** Why would the book catalogue need to be replaced regularly?

But the members do need to be able to find out what books are available,
so once a month the computer centre produces the book catalogue on
microfiche. These are pieces of plastic, about the size of a postcard. They
have printed on them a reduced picture of about 100 pages of data. Like
photographic slides, they are read by putting them over a light and a lens
which magnifies them onto a small screen. The device which holds the lens
and the light is called a microfiche reader. The book catalogue on
microfiche is much smaller than it would be on paper, and it is cheaper to
produce new versions every month.

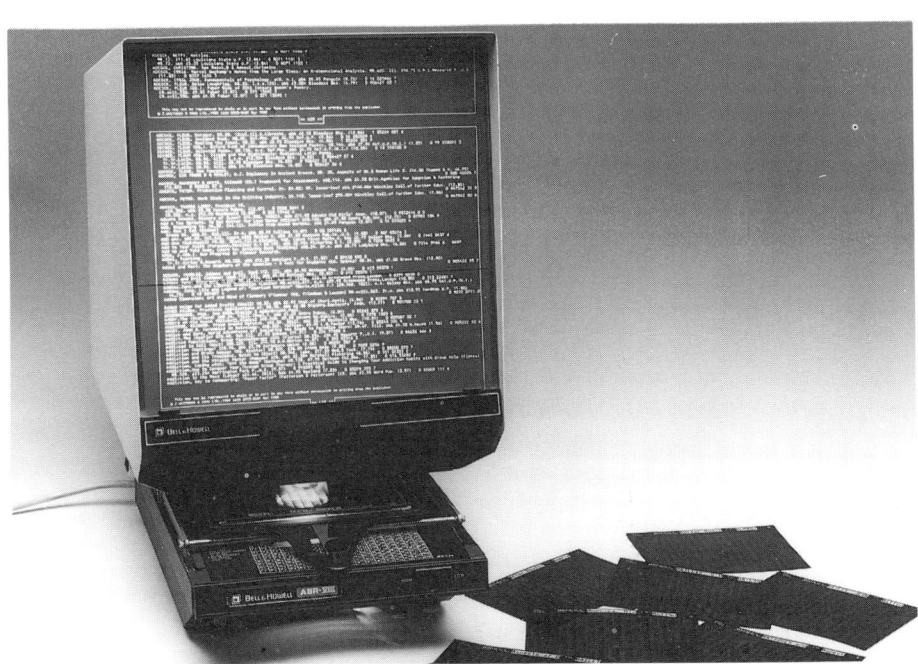

> 7 Can you think of any disadvantages of using microfiche in the
> library?

The computer hardware in the computer system is made up of the Central Processing Unit, and all the peripherals.

> 8 Make a list of all the peripherals that have been mentioned in this
> system. Can you think of any others that are necessary?
>
> 9 Make a list of all the data files that are processed in this system.

From your lists you can see that there is a great deal of organization needed to make the computer work effectively. The use of the peripherals must be planned, and the right files must be available when they are needed. The person who runs the computer system is the computer operator, but they are helped in their job by a piece of software called the operating system.

The computer operator for the library computer is Jenni Abrahams. She has to start up the equipment, and load the programs. She has to keep the printers loaded with paper, and has to put the correct tapes into the tape drives. She watches over and monitors the running of the system. Sometimes she does some cleaning and simple maintenance of the hardware. She has to keep a record (or log) of all the work done by the computer, and of anything that goes wrong. She has to report any faults that she is unable to put right.

> 10 Why do you think it is important for Jenni to keep a written log?

There is a special terminal, called the operator's console. Here Jenni can enter instructions to the computer, and the computer can display any messages that she might need to attend to.

> 11 Can you think of an example of a message that might be output at
> the operator's console?

The operating system is a very important piece of software. Every computer has an operating system. It is really a set of programs which control and co-ordinate all the computer operations. It organizes the programs running on the computer so that they are loaded into memory when they are required. When necessary it transfers control from one program to another. It also ensures that data is read and written to the correct files. It allows files to be copied or erased. It keeps a record of how much space is used up and left over on tapes and disks. If anything goes wrong, the operating system produces an error message at the operator's console.

The operating system controls the way that output is sent to the printers. Printers do not work as quickly as the CPU. They usually have buffers which hold data ready for the printer to print. But the operating system must make sure that too much data is not sent at one time.

There are wires connecting the printer to the computer. Bit patterns for

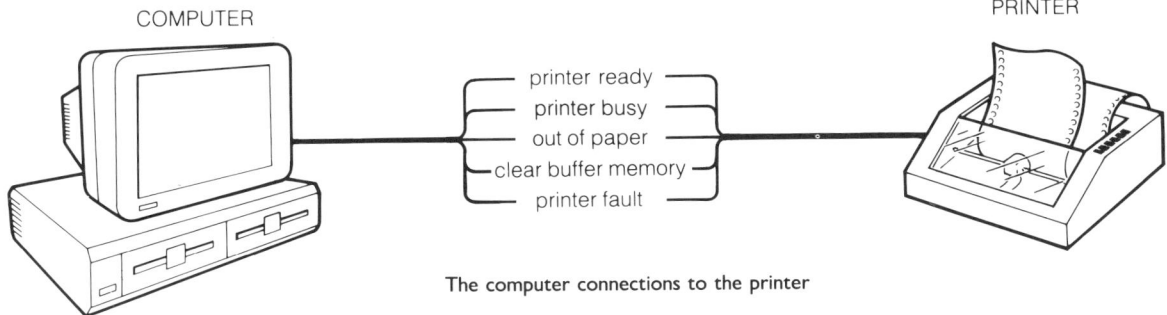

COMPUTER

printer ready
printer busy
out of paper
clear buffer memory
printer fault

PRINTER

The computer connections to the printer

the characters to be printed are carried down these wires. Messages can be sent each way, by switching on a particular wire. Wires are included for each of these messages:

1. to say that a character has been received, and the printer is ready for the next one,
2. to say that the printer is busy,
3. to say that the printer has run out of paper,
4. to say clear buffer memory and get the top page ready so that the printer is ready to start,
5. to say that there is a fault with the printer.

12 Each of these wires carries messages one way, either from the printer to the computer, or from the computer to the printer. For each message, say which way it would be sent.

13 If messages are received at the same time from wires 2, 3 and 5, what do you think has happened?

The operating system would transmit these signals to the operator's console. The operating system also keeps a record of the programs that have been run, and the files that have been processed. It also records all the things that have gone wrong.

14 What is this record of information used for? Why do you think that Jenni and the computer both keep a log?

15 The computers you use in school all have operating systems. Find out the names of the operating system(s), and what they can do. If you have a computer network in school, you will be able to look at quite a complex operating system.

Some of the programs are called utility programs. These are programs which are used over and over again to perform common tasks. For example, there is a Sort utility used in all the file updating processes, and there is a Copy utility which copies a file to another tape or disk. There are also utilities which monitor the performance of the computer.

16 Can you think of any other utility programs?

Jenni has to show her security pass to get into the computer centre. She also has to use a series of passwords to get access to the data files.

17 Why do you think it is important not to let unauthorized people have access to the data files? What harm could be done by letting people look at the files? What harm could be done by letting people amend the files?

Some of the data is personal data, concerning the library members.

18 Which is the personal data?

Many people are worried that personal data is kept on computer files. An Act of Parliament (the Data Protection Act) has been introduced to try to prevent misuses of personal data.

19 How else can personal data be kept? Why are people more worried about it being kept in computer files than in other kinds of files?

▷ At the computer centre

Whatever system is used in a library there are a number of jobs which must always be done. The diagram shows how the same tasks are performed in the school library and the Borough Library. It shows what the librarian needs to do, and what the computer does.

The Borough Library computer system

SCHOOL LIBRARY		BOROUGH LIBRARY	
MANUAL SYSTEM	TASK	COMPUTERIZED SYSTEM	
LIBRARIAN'S ACTIVITY		LIBRARIAN'S ACTIVITY	COMPUTER ACTIVITY
Stamps book. Puts card into borrower's ticket.	BOOK TAKEN OUT FROM LIBRARY	Runs barcode reader over member's and book's barcode. Stamps book.	Light pen reads barcodes. Stores data on cassette tape.
Files book cards and member's tickets into book number order at the end of each day. Labels each day's tickets with return date.	FILING DETAILS OF LOANS	Nothing to do.	All master files updated daily.
A???	BOOKS RETURNED TO LIBRARY	Records book number with barcode readers, puts book to one side.	Removes book number from loans file, checks to see if book is reserved.
B???		C????	D???
	RESERVED BOOK IS RETURNED		
E???	CHECK FOR OVERDUE BOOKS	F????	G???

1 Write down descriptions of all the actions indicated by question marks (A to G).

The two library systems are similar in some ways and different in others.

2 In what ways do you think the school manual system is better than the computerized Borough Library system?

3 In what ways do you think the computerized system is better?

It would be possible to make improvements to the computerized system, if money was available to pay for them. The librarian would like to have an on-line, real-time system. In this type of system, all the library branches would be connected to the computer all the time. When books were taken out or returned, the files would be updated instantly.

4 Why would it be expensive to implement this type of system? What new hardware would be needed? What new software? What extra running costs would there be?

5 How could a real-time system be different from the batch system, in each of the following respects? Would the change be an improvement or not?
a issuing books to borrowers,
b receiving returned books,
c taking reservations for books,
d making sure that borrowers do not take out too many books,
e checking that a borrower is not using a stolen library card,
f sending out overdue letters,
g sending out letters to say that reserved books have been returned.

To enable all the libraries to have immediate access to the computer, they would have to use a multi-access operating system. Most multi-access systems use the method of time-sharing. Each library would think that it was having uninterrupted access to the CPU, but in fact it would have a time-slice. This means that there are very short periods of connection time, with very short gaps in between. During the gap, the CPU would be dealing with another library, or even several different libraries. The CPU would have to have a front-end processor which deals with the communications involved in the system. If the library used more than one terminal, they could use a multiplexer, which allows one communications line to be divided into two or more channels.

6 What extra facilities could the library offer to its members if it had an on-line system?

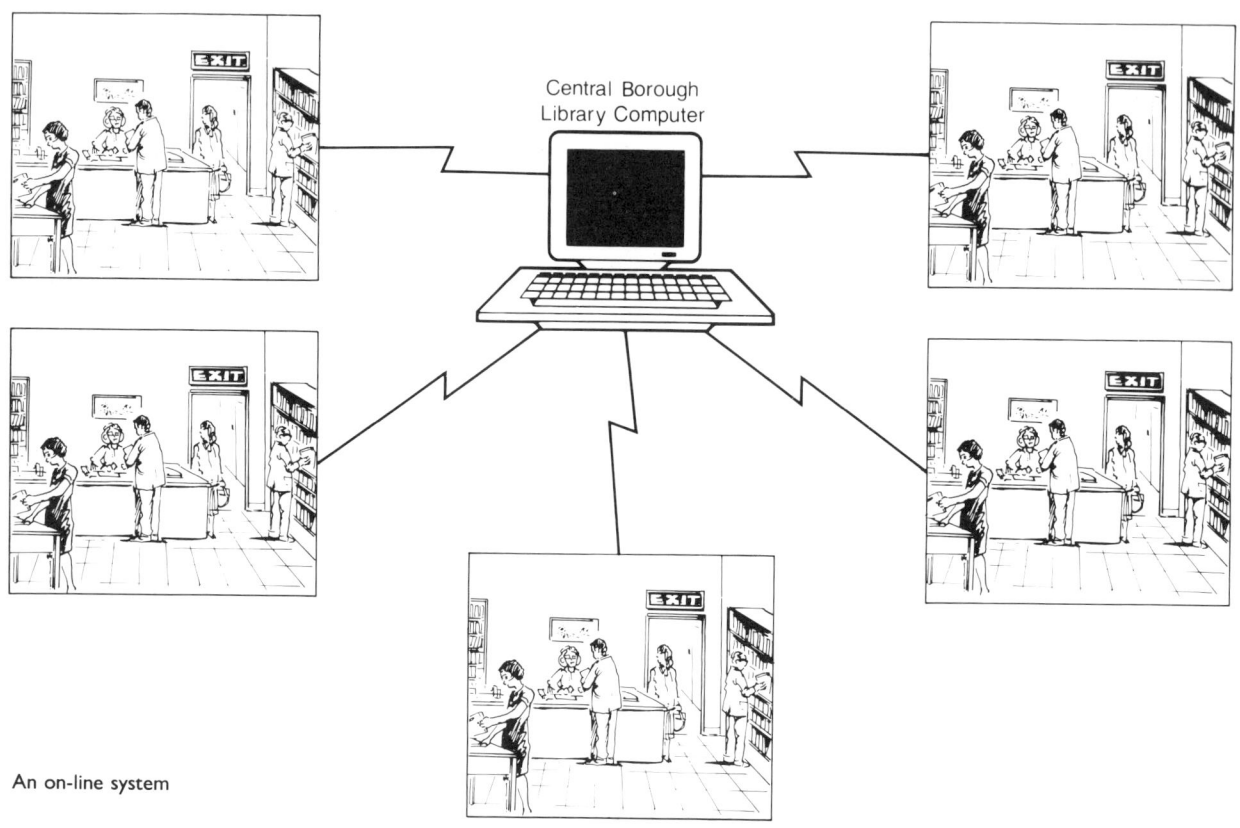

An on-line system

7 What do you think would happen if a fault developed in the
   communication link between the local library and the central
   computer? How would the library keep track of books being
   returned and borrowed? What might the system analysts have
   suggested when they designed the system that would help to cope
   with this problem?

▷ Making the system better

The Borough Librarian sees his job as providing information for the library
members. There is a large reference section of the library where members
can go to look up information. This contains all sorts of books and
magazines, including encyclopaedias, telephone directories, train timetables
and dictionaries.

I What other books and magazines might you find in a reference
   library? Can you think of any information you might not be able to
   find in a reference library?

The librarian has to advise library members where to look to find the information they want. Sometimes this is a very difficult and time consuming task. It can mean looking through many books until you find what you are looking for. And sometimes what you want is not in any of the books you look in. So the librarian wants to make some improvements and looks at ways that a computer system could help.

Chris Stein, the school librarian, has been using a microcomputer to help her find information requested by the children. She finds that her biggest problem is the vast number of leaflets, magazine articles and newspaper cuttings she has accumulated. She has catalogued them all, but often they are about more than one topic, so it's hard to know how best to classify them. She needs to be able to find all the articles a student might need for a particular piece of work.

She decided to use a computer program called SIR, which was specially designed for librarians. She has made a file of information about all the articles. Each record contains the title and author of the article, the name of the magazine or newspaper, etc., and a list of key words which indicate what the article is about. For example, an article on the eating habits of Australian reptiles might have the key words: reptile, Australian, eating.

The files can be searched to find all the articles about a particular key word, or about a combination of key words. Jimmy McDonald wanted to find some articles to help him with his history project on houses. He asked Chris to find him all the articles on houses.

This search (say S1) found that there were 203 articles with house as a key word. This was far too many for Jimmy to look through, so Chris asked him to be more specific in what he wanted.

He said he wanted to know about Roman houses, so Chris did another search (say S2), this time looking for the word Roman. This produced 198 articles.

She then did a search to find all the articles which had Roman AND house as key words. This search, S3, was a combination of S1 AND S2. It resulted in a list of 18 articles. Jimmy was given a printout of the details of the 18 articles, and he could then go and find them.

But then Jimmy remembered that he needed to know about Greek houses too. Chris did another search for the key word Greek (S4). This produced 78 articles. She then did search S5 to find all the articles with key words Greek AND houses, by combining S4 and S1.

Finally, to produce a list of all articles on Roman houses OR Greek houses, Chris combined S5 with S3 to produce the final list, S6.

The librarian does many other tasks in addition to dealing with the loan of books

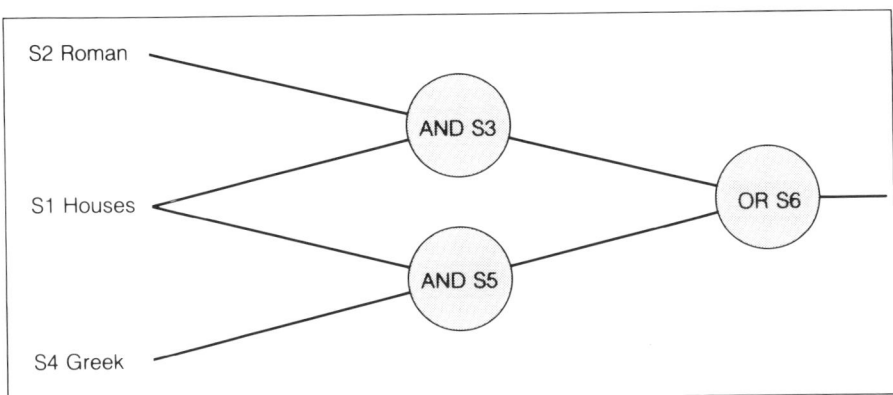

A logic diagram for a Roman houses OR Greek houses search

This type of search can be shown in a logic diagram, or in a truth table.

Truth table for Roman houses OR Greek houses search

Roman	Houses	Greek			
S2	S1	S4	S3	S5	S6
0	0	0	0	0	0
0	0	1		0	0
0	1	1	0	1	1
1	0	0			0
1	0	1	0	0	0
1	1	0			
1	1	1			

2   Copy the table onto paper and fill in the gaps.

Programs like SIR work on files that are structured differently from other sequential files. They are called inverted files. An index is made which contains all the key words. Because each record may have several key words, the index can have more entries than the number of records in the file. Next to each key word is recorded the key field of all the records which included that particular key word. The key field is usually a number which identifies the record.

We can look at some of the records in a small file:

Record number	Key words
2	roman, army
21	greek, egypt, building
23	house, greek, roman
24	house, greek
34	greek, roads
35	towns, house, planning
36	roman, jewellery
43	house, roman, furnishing
71	shop, house, town

When the file is inverted, an index is made, with one entry for every key word. Part of the inverted file would look like this:

Key words	Key fields
house	23,24,35,43,71 . . .
greek	21,23,24,34 . . .
roman	2,23,36,43 . . .

3   Why are inverted files better than other indexed files for this kind of use?

4   In this short example, what are the key fields of the records that would be useful to Jimmy?

Another student, Martina Bonner, is doing a project on reptiles and amphibians. she wants to find out all about their habitats.

5   Design a search to find all the articles that will be useful to Martina.

6   Draw a logic diagram and truth table to show how your search would work.

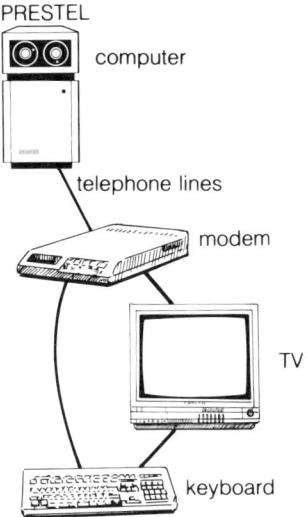

PRESTEL

computer

telephone lines

modem

TV

keyboard

Prestel users can access information on a computer by means of telephone lines, but they have to pay for the use of those lines

The Borough Librarian decides that it would not be possible to implement the same sort of system using the sort of microcomputer that the library could afford. Instead, he buys a less powerful micro to use as a terminal to access remote databases. The British Library's computer has many databases similar to the one in the school library, but much, much bigger. They cover almost all the books and periodicals ever published. By paying a subscription, and buying suitable hardware and software, librarians can gain access to the databases at the British Library.

This system is called Blaise. It allows librarians to find out all the books and periodicals relating to any topic or combination of topics. It works in a similar way to SIR.

In addition to buying a microcomputer, the librarian must also buy a modem to allow it to be connected to the British Library computer via telephone lines.

The library also uses the computer and modem to connect to Prestel. The librarian will only use Prestel to find out things that are not covered by the reference books in the library. The librarian is worried about the cost of using Prestel, and also about the accuracy of the information.

7   Find out how much it costs to use Prestel. There are a number of different charges to take into account. Try to estimate the cost of using Prestel to find out about university courses in Art and Design.

8   You need to find the times of trains to Edinburgh tomorrow morning. Describe three ways of finding this information. For each one estimate the cost of finding out, and the reliability of the information.

9   Prestel can be used for more than just finding out information. What else can be done through Prestel?

Television companies offer information services through systems like CEEFAX and ORACLE. Television sets with special adapters can receive pages of written information, which is sent by the television transmitters. These teletext systems are free, once you have bought a suitable TV set.

Prestel is called an interactive system, because messages can be received and sent by the user. Teletext is not interactive. The user can only receive messages.

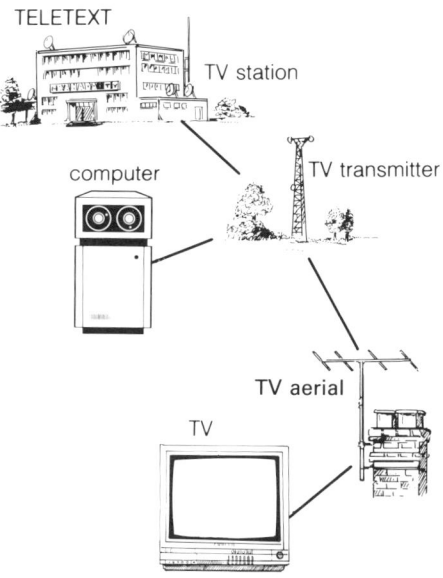

TELETEXT

TV station

computer

TV transmitter

TV aerial

TV

Teletext users access information by means of specially adapted TV sets. Once they have paid for the adapted TV set, these systems are free

10   Make a list of all the differences between Prestel and teletext. Include items such as cost, what they can be used for and how they are transmitted. How useful do you think it is to have Prestel and teletext available in a library? If you had to choose, would you install either of the systems? Which would you have?

11 How useful would it be to have Prestel or teletext at home? If you had to decide, would you have either of them?

Prestel is an example of a viewdata system. It is also possible to have local viewdata systems which are not transmitted, but are just used on one computer, or maybe on a network of computers. The pages of information look just like Prestel pages.

12 Could a local viewdata system be of use in a school library? What could it be used for? Can you think of any other examples of uses for a local viewdata system?

▷ General questions

1 A software company is designing a computerized library system for use in school libraries. They want to sell the system to as many schools as possible. Make a list of all the questions you would ask about the software if you were considering buying it. How could the company make sure that it was able to answer each of the questions?

2 Why is it sometimes useful to code information before inputting it to a computer? What disadvantages might there be in using codes?
A barcode can contain several items of data. For example, in barcodes on items for sale in shops, some bars represent a manufacturer, and some represent the country of origin. Some other codes are faceted this way. A sportswear manufacturer uses her own codes for all the items made in the factory. Every item has a different code number. The factory makes 300 different items. What is the shortest length of code number they could use? In fact the code is 10 figures long. Why do you think this is so? What advantages and disadvantages are there in using long code numbers?

3 What precautions should be taken in storing and using magnetic media? What substances and conditions should be avoided?

4 Home computer owners can generally choose to use either cassette recorders or disk drives as backing storage devices. What are the advantages and disadvantages of each? Which would you prefer?

5 Make a list of all the documentation produced, from the feasibility study to the implementation of a computer system. Give a reason why each piece of documentation is needed.

6 Draw a flow diagram to show how a source program becomes an object program.

7 In many cases, it is disastrous if computer files are lost or destroyed. What can be done to make the risk of disaster as small as possible? If files are lost, what can be done to make it easier to re-create them?

8 Make a list of all the activities involved in the job of computer operator. What sort of qualifications do you think are necessary for this job? Look in some computer magazines for advertisements for computer operators. What qualifications are asked for? Compare these with your list.

9 Make a list of all the tasks that can be carried out by the operating system. Give an example of the use of each task.

10 Describe ten procedures that would be very useful in a general procedure library. Say why you think they would be useful.

11 Local Area Networks (LANs) of computers have many advantages over numbers of separate computers. An LAN consists of several computers connected together so that messages can be sent from computer to computer and the computers can share peripherals. What advantages does a LAN have? The network will require an operating system. What should the operating system do and what features would you expect it to have?

12 Computer programmers have to take great care to make sure that their programs work as they should. Often, during the program writing stage, things can go wrong and the program contains errors called bugs. What diagnostic aids might a programmer use to try to find out what has gone wrong in a program?

▷ *Software activities*

1 Use an information retrieval program to make a file of all your books or records. Use the program to sort the records in different orders, and print out lists of your books in order of author and title and date of publication.

2 Use the SIR program to make a file of articles relating to computers.

3 Use a viewdata program to set up an information file about your school.

4 Use a word processing program to design some of the letters sent out by librarians to borrowers.

Computer Washing

▷ *The story so far . . .*

Wilson must work out how to persuade people to buy Cosmo washing machines instead of other makes

The Cosmo Company makes and sells a range of washing machines. They hope that everyone who wants a washing machine will find a Cosmo machine which suits their needs, at a competitive price.

Wilson Arisa works in the Marketing Division of Cosmo. His job is involved with planning sales and advertising campaigns to help sell more washing machines. He knows, though, that campaigns are not enough. Cosmo must manufacture modern machines that people want to buy. So, another part of his job is finding out what features people want to find in washing machines. Finding out what people want is a very complex activity, because sometimes people don't know what they want until they see it. Because it is so complex, Wilson paid a market research team to do the investigation.

The market research team decided to collect information using a questionnaire. They discussed with Wilson, and other people, the sort of features people might like. They used their ideas as a basis for their survey.

> ### © The Cosmo Company
> # MARKET RESEARCH SURVEY
>
> **1)** When do you do your washing?
> **2)** Is this the most convenient time for you?
> **3)** When would you prefer to do your washing?
> **4)** Why is this more convenient for you?

What other information might you want to find out using a questionnaire?

1 How could computers be used to help in the collection and analysis of data from this questionnaire?

2 Design part of a questionnaire which could be read directly by computer without any need for human input. Is there any data which could not be input in this way?

When the information from the questionnaire had been collected and analysed, the market research team produced a report of their findings. Some of the report is especially interesting to Wilson. Now he can see the sort of features that many people want.

How many people do you think the market research team questioned? Do you think the type of person questioned is important?

63% of people mentioned that they knew from advertisements that washing powder manufacturers now make powders that can be used with warm, instead of hot, water.

A large majority of answers stated that they were worried about the cost of running an automatic washing machine. 28% of the answers were from people who wanted to make more use of night time electricity, since it is cheaper than day time electricity.

A large number of people commented that many of their clothes do not need to be ironed if they are washed carefully.

Many people said that they thought that modern machines were more reliable and safer than older ones because they used computers to control them.

It seems that a machine that is cheap to run would be popular. This type of machine could be made to wash at lower temperatures, therefore using less electricity. If it had a time delay system, it could wash during the night when electricity is cheaper, finishing in the morning so that the clothes did not lie wet in the washing machine, getting creased.

3 The way that the machine operates is obviously important to the customer. What other features might the marketing team think important in helping them to sell a lot of machines?

Now that Wilson knows the sort of features that will help to sell a washing machine, the next stage is to go to the design team. Then Wilson can find out if it is possible to manufacture the sort of machine he wants at a reasonable price. He talks to Sybil Naidu, who is the head of the design department.

Sybil feels sure that her team can design a machine with the features Wilson wants. But more work needs to be put in to see exactly the best way of doing it, and to work out how much the machine will cost.

Sybil tries to explain to Wilson. 'There are several different ways of making an automatic washing machine. The customer may not notice or even care about the way the machine is made, as long as it does what it is supposed to do.'

Sybil continues, 'Automatic washing machines do not have to use any computer technology. They can be just mechanical devices. But often it is cheaper and easier to use micro technology, because the machines will be easier to manufacture and will be more reliable.'

> **4 Why do you think machines are easier to manufacture if they use more micro technology instead of mechanical parts? Why might computerized machines be more reliable?**

Wilson thinks that the machines should always use micro technology. Sybil is not so sure.

> **5 Why do you think Wilson's department is keen on micro technology? Why do you think Sybil is less certain? Why do you think the Marketing and Design teams disagree on what to do?**

Eventually, it is decided that the design team should investigate the possible ways of implementing the Market Department's design features. Then they will report back to Wilson and discuss what to do next.

▷ The washing programmes

Sybil's team has already designed many washing machines. They know that machines should be able to carry out the nine international standard washing programmes. These are put on labels in clothes so that people will know how to wash them. They are coded into numbers and pictures like those shown on the left.

Each washing programme is designed to be used with certain types of clothes and fabrics. Each of the nine programmes uses the best washing process for the fabrics. For example, programme 4 is designed for coloured synthetic fabrics. It washes at a temperature of 50 °C, rinses in cold water, then does a short spin.

> **I Why do you think the washing instructions are written in this coded way?**
>
> **2 How is a washing programme similar to a computer program?**

A simple algorithm for this washing programme could be written as a flow chart.

The international washing codes

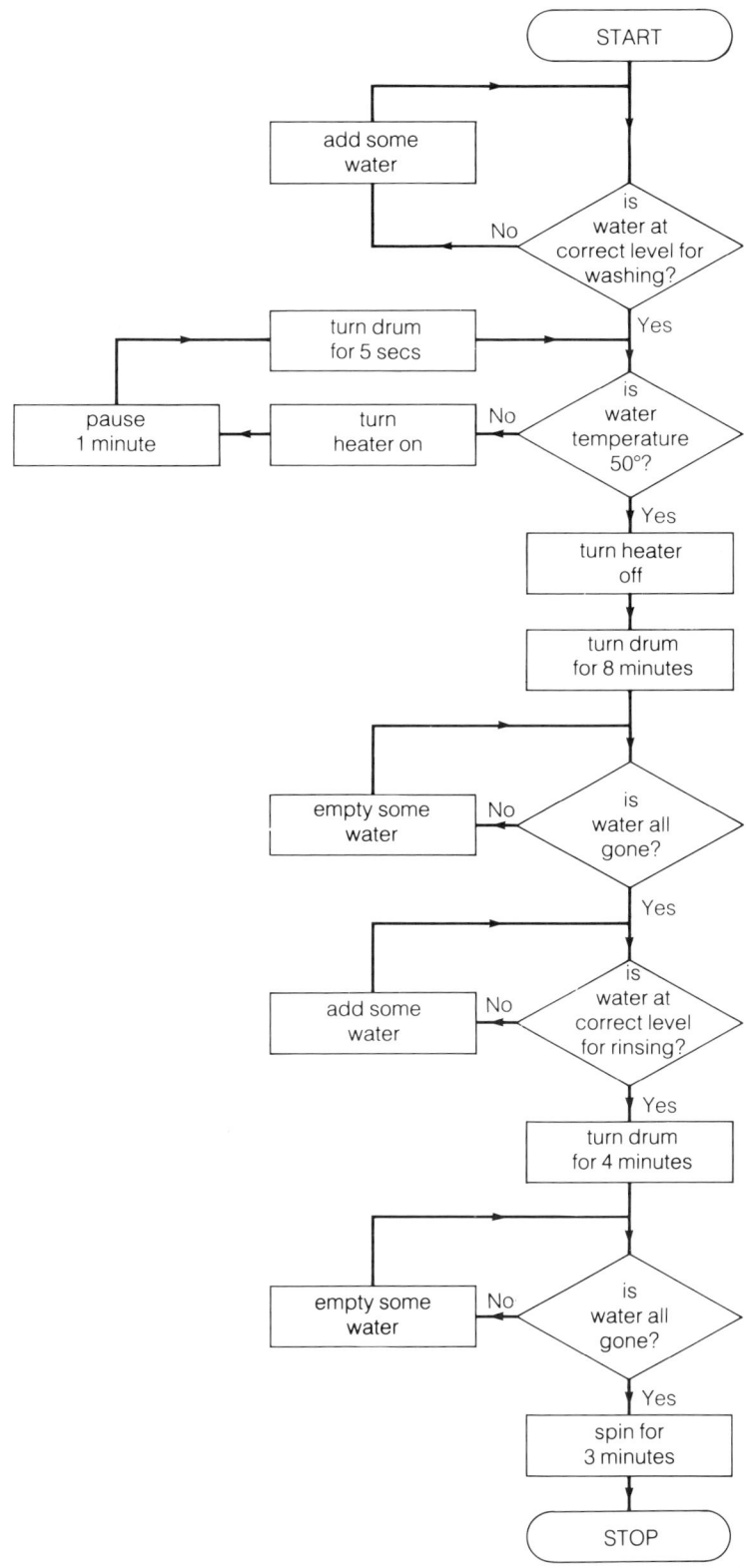

A flow chart for washing programme 4

3 The drum is turned for different reasons. Can you think of three
   different reasons for turning the drum in the wash cycle?

A more sophisticated machine could improve upon this wash. For example, it could wash at two different temperatures. It could wash at 35 °C to take advantage of the detergent in the washing powder, which works best at this temperature. Then it could wash again at 50 °C because the enzymes in the powder work best at this hotter temperature. Also, it could spin the clothes at different speeds. The clothes would be less creased if they were spun first at 400 rpm, then at 600 rpm, then at 800 rpm, with a short rest in between each spin.

> **4   Change the algorithm so that it shows the new improved wash cycle for the more sophisticated machine, with the wash at two temperatures, and the spinning at three different speeds.**

As well as the international standard washing programmes, some machines are able to offer more programme variations. For example, some machines offer a 'half load' option. If you only have a few clothes to wash, this saves time and money, since it only uses half the amount of water. Another option could be a 'quick wash' option. This could be used if clothes are only slightly dirty, and do not need a long, hot wash. Again, this would save time and money by not heating up the water.

> **5   Can you think of any other features that a modern washing machine could offer?**

▷ The design

Sybil, head of the design team, explains to the design team what is needed for the new washing machine. They discuss the different ways that the machine's washing programmes could be controlled.

Keith, one of the designers, thinks that the control should be kept simple. For example, he thinks that the timings for the washing cycles should be done with an electrical mechanical clock. 'Washing machines have been made like this for years and work reliably,' he says.

Alison, also in the design team, does not agree. 'It will be more difficult to control this new machine using switches and timers.' She explains to Keith that a microprocessor would be better able to control the complex processes of this new machine. The basic parts of a microprocessor are the arithmetic and logic unit, and the control unit.

The design team must consider what features a new washing machine should have

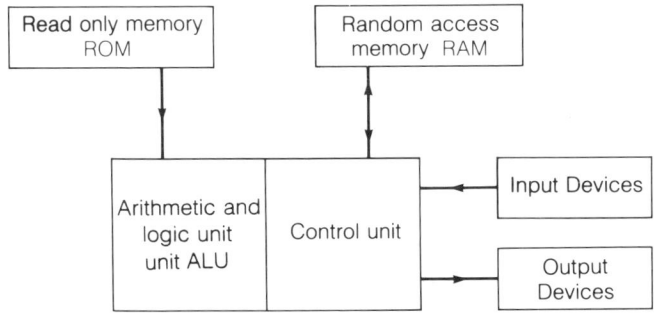

The basic parts of a microprocessor

The microprocessor will also need some extra 'chips' with memory to store and run the computer program. Keith argues with this. He says, 'The microprocessor will have to be programmed to carry out the washing instructions. It will cost more and take longer to develop and produce this more complex machine.'

Alison explains that many household items now have microprocessors or microcontrollers in them. 'For example, you will find them in some food processors, electric drills and clocks. People who buy modern appliances expect them to be "computer-controlled".'

'We could use a microcontroller to control this new washing machine,' Alison says. 'A microcontroller is like a microprocessor but everything is on one chip.'

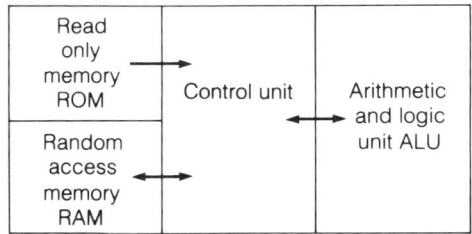

The structure of a microcontroller

What does the customer want? How much will they spend?

| **1** | **What will be the advantage of using a microcontroller rather than a microprocessor?** |

Alison reckons that, 'With the old technology it will be difficult to offer a wide range of washing cycles and good electronic displays. And the machines won't be so reliable.'

'But all these electronic displays will make the machine very expensive,' replies Keith.

Keith and Alison also have different ideas of what the washing machine should look like. Keith sees the new machine looking very much like the last one the company made, the Model 3345. Alison thinks that a new style with better displays for the customer is what is needed.

Model 3345

The design team must decide whether to produce a new style of machine or one which looks like the old model 3345

This shows how big a microcontroller actually is!

They realize that their arguments could go on for a long time. They decide to examine in detail how the washing machine can be made using both of their methods and ideas. Then they can look at the advantages and disadvantages of each.

Alison and Keith draw up a list of advantages and disadvantages for each system and design. The design team can then decide which to recommend to the marketing section.

ADVANTAGES AND DISADVANTAGES OF:

1) **ELECTRO - MECHANICAL CONTROL**

    Simple to contruct for individual features
    Not easy to make complex washing cycles with different features
    Servicing easy and cheap
    The physical size of the controller is large
    It contains some moving parts which may wear out

2) **MICROPROCESSOR / MICROCONTROLLER CONTROL**

    Needs to be developed and programmed
    Will be able to offer a wide range of washing machine cycles
    Changes for future machines can be added easily
    Easy timing displays for overnight use
    Easier to produce clear electronic displays
    No moving parts in the controller so nothing to wear out
    Servicing easy but engineers will have to replace the whole controller if anything fails. It will not be possible to repair the controller.

> 2   Can you think of any more advantages or disadvantages for these two methods of controlling the machine?

Sybil is fairly certain that using a microcontroller is the most likely solution. Before she makes the final choice she asks Alison for more details.

She asks Alison how the microcontroller will work. Alison explains that it will need to be programmed. The program, in other words, the set of instructions, will be stored in ROM. ROM is a type of computer memory. It stands for 'read only memory' and cannot be written to. There is another type of computer memory called RAM. This stands for 'random access memory' and can be read from or written to. It is possible to change anything stored in RAM, but not in ROM. The team will specify what the program will have to do, and then a programmer will write the program. The computer program will then have to be tested, to make sure that it does what it is supposed to do.

The design team consider all the arguments put forward and then make their decision. They decide that a microcontroller will need to be at the heart of the new washing machine. This 'chip' contains a microprocessor together with RAM and ROM. The program to make the washing machine do what is wanted will have to be written by a programmer and put onto this chip. The program will need to stay permanently on the chip.

> 3   Why not load the program into RAM from some form of backing storage?
>
> 4   Where will the program be stored on this 'chip'?

Sybil asks Alison to look at how the microcontroller can be used to detect what is happening in the washing machine; for example, to detect if the door is shut, and to find out the level and temperature of water in the drum of the machine. Alison says that a number of switches have to be placed in different parts of the machine.

These switches act as sensors. They will be connected to the microcontroller, and the microcontroller will be programmed to read the sensors, and make use of the data it reads.

The microcontroller Alison has chosen has four connections to the 'outside world' called Input/Output ports. Alison calls these ports A, B, C and D, so that she knows which is which. She decides that port A will be used for these sensors. She draws a diagram to show how port A will be attached to the sensors.

KEY

S Sensor

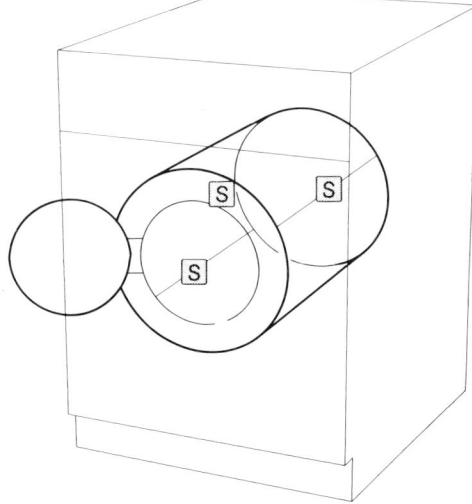

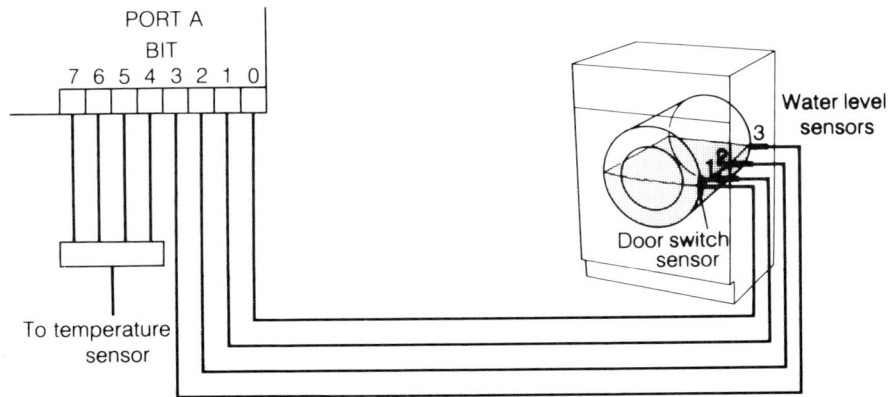

Alison's diagram showing how port A is attached to the sensors. Water level sensor at empty is bit 1, water level sensor at half full level is bit 2 and water level sensor at full level is bit 3

What things must the sensors be able to detect?

A wire connects bit 0 from port A to the door switch, so that when the door is open the computer program reads this as 0 but if it is shut then this bit changes to 1. In a similar way the level of the water can be detected.

---

5 **What will the values of the bits in port A be if the door is shut and the water level is like this:**

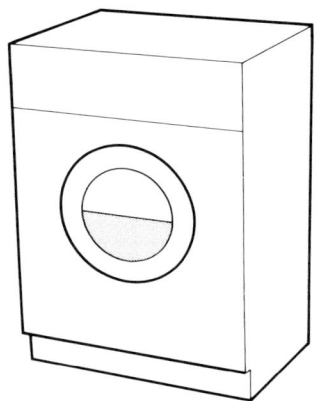

The temperature of the water has to be measured. The heater must be turned off when the water is at the required temperature.

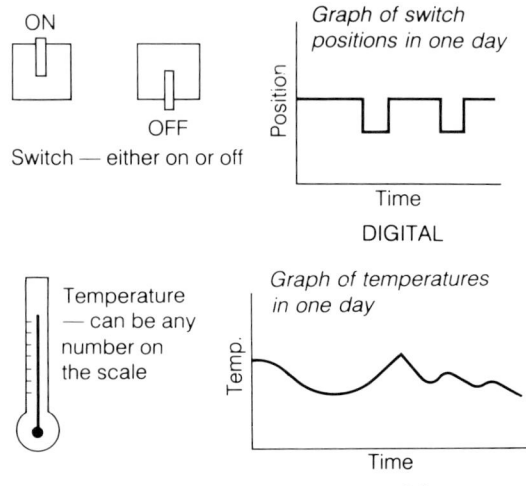

ON
OFF
Switch — either on or off

Graph of switch positions in one day

Position / Time

DIGITAL

Temperature — can be any number on the scale

Graph of temperatures in one day

Temp. / Time

ANALOG

The temperature sensor is not like the door or level sensors. Temperature is not a 'two-state' thing. Temperature is not measured as only on or off. The temperature of the water in the washing machine could be anything between cold and boiling. Because of this, temperature is called an analog measurement. The microcontroller, like most computers, cannot handle analog values. Somehow, this analog measurement has to be changed into a digital form, so that it can be processed by the microcontroller.

ANALOG VALUES → □ → DIGITAL VALUES

> **6** How many different temperatures does the washing machine need to be able to wash at? How many different temperature settings will the machine need to recognize?

Alison thinks that she will have to use only some of the bits from port A. She reckons that using combinations of bits 7, 6, 5 and 4 from port A will be enough. She proposes that different patterns of bits will represent different temperatures. Again, she sketches a diagram to show what she means.

BIT 7	BIT 6	BIT 5	BIT 4		TEMPERATURE
0	0	0	0	⟶	20°
0	0	0	1	⟶	25°
0	0	1	0	⟶	30°
0	0	1	1	⟶	35°
0	1	0	0	⟶	40°
0	1	0	1	⟶	45°
0	1	1	0	⟶	50°
0	1	1	1	⟶	55°
1	0	0	0	⟶	60°
1	0	0	1	⟶	65°
1	0	1	0	⟶	70°
1	0	1	1	⟶	75°
1	1	0	0	⟶	80°
1	1	0	1	⟶	85°
1	1	1	0	⟶	90°
1	1	1	1	⟶	95°

> **7** Using these four bits, how many different temperatures could be recognized by the computer program?

Sybil is still curious about how the analog temperature will be turned into these bit patterns. Alison explains, 'The temperature sensor will be connected to a special device, called an Analog-to-Digital converter.'

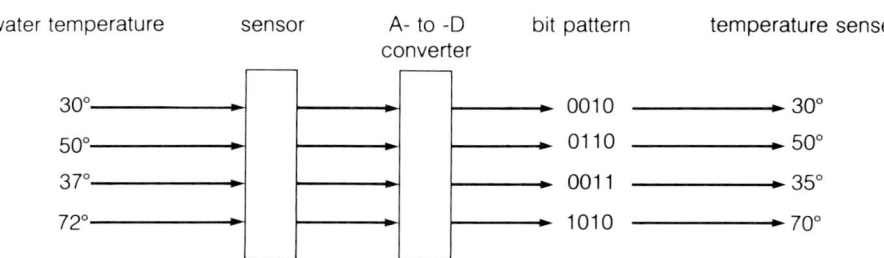

Analog temperatures are changed to bit patterns by the A-to-D converter

Now that they understand how the sensors work, the designers need to think about how the program will be written. They decide to write the program in assembly language and not in a high level language. A high level language would need to be compiled.

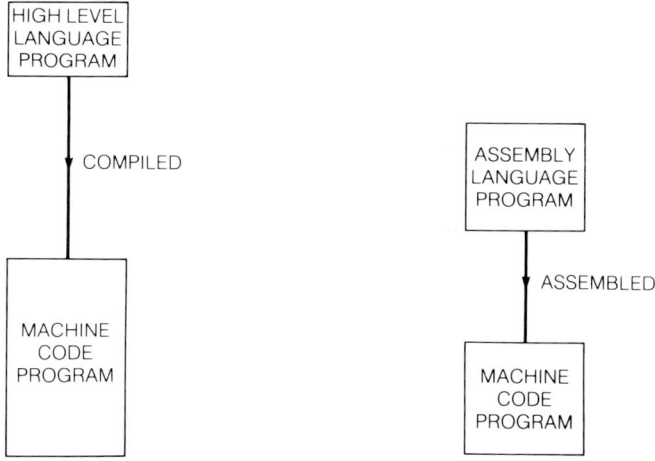

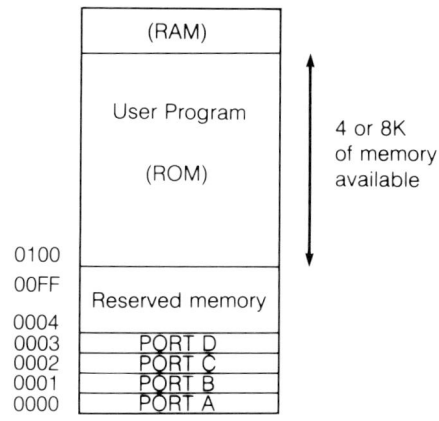

Memory map of a microcontroller

Which ever type of language the program was written in, the program would need to be translated into a machine code object program. The object program will be much shorter if it came from a low level language program. A program written in a high level language will contain extra, unnecessary statements, and may not work as efficiently.

Sally's job in the design team is to write the computer programs. She tries to explain about the different sorts of programs to the design team. To do this, she writes a section of program to show them.

'This section of program looks at the water level and waits until it reaches the top sensor. On Alison's diagram on page 111 the top level sensor is connected to Bit 3. In a high level language the program would look like this:

```
A = 0                   Each port is attached to a place in the memory
                        of the microcontroller.
                        Port A is memory location 0


repeat
     sensors = readport(A);   /* read settings for port A */
     level = bit(sensors, 3); /* find value for bit 3 */
until (level = 1);
```

but when this is compiled it looks like this:'

```
        extrn    .begin, .chl, .swt
        extrn    zsave, zret
        PUBLIC   main_
main_:
        lxi  d,.2
        call zsave
        LXI  H,0
        XCHG
        LXI  H, 6-.2
        DAD  SP
        MOV  M,E
        INX  H
        MOV  m,d
.3:
        LXI  H,6-.2
        DAD  SP
        MOV  E,M
        INX  H
        MOV  D,M
        LXI  H,1
        CALL .ne
        JZ   .4
        LXI  H,0
        PUSH H
        CALL readport_
        POP  D
        XCHG
        LXI  H,6-.2
        DAD  SP
        MOV  M,E
        INX  H
        MOV  M,D
        LXI  H,3
        PUSH H
        LXI  H,8-.2
        DAD  SP
        MOV  E,M
        INX  H
        MOV  D,M
        PUSH D
        CALL bit_
        POP  D
        POP  D
        XCHG
        LXI  H,4-.2
        DAD  SP
        MOV  M,E
        INX  H
        MOV  M,D
        JMP  .3
.4:
        RET
.2      EQU  -4
        extrn    bit_
        extrn    readport_
        extern   .ne
        END
```

'If I write the same program in assembler it looks like this,' Sally says.

```
portA=0                    ; port A is number 0

        lda  £8
wait_level3:
        bit portA
        bne  wait_level3
```

'After assembly it looks like this:'   (Program listed in Hexadecimal (Base sixteen))

```
        A9
        08
        2C
        00
        00
        D0
        FB
```

8 Why do you think the program has to be in machine code when it is run on the microcontroller?

Keith is a bit confused. 'The low level language program is not so easy for people to understand. And the high level language program has fewer instructions. It looks to me as if programming in a high level language is easier than in a low level language. So why do you need to write the program in a low level language?'

9   How do you think Sally can explain to Keith that the program needs to be written in a low level language?

10 Which sort of language do you think is the easiest to program in? Which sort is easiest for finding and debugging the programming errors?

Keith is still not convinced about writing programs in a low level language. 'Can't we buy a microcontroller with an on-board interpreter?' asks Keith. 'I mean one that has got the BASIC interpreter built onto the chip', he adds. 'That way, the programs could be written in BASIC, and stored on the chip in BASIC. When the program is run, the interpreter will translate it one line at a time.'

'We could,' says Sally, 'but for one thing, those chips cost more. And because the program is interpreted it may run too slowly for what we want it to do.'

11 How does the interpreter differ from a compiler in translating Sally's high level program? How would this affect the speed of execution of the program?

Eventually, the design team recommend the use of a microcontroller in the new washing machine. The program for it will be written in a low level language by Sally and her team.

In future years micro-chips will be available with much more ROM at less price.

12 How might this change the decision taken by the design team?

▷ Inside the machine

Sally's section of program to sense the water level has been extended. It now turns on the cold water supply until the water is at the correct level.

```
portA = 0                 ; port A is number 0

turn_on_cold_water:
    lda   8               ; load accumulator with 8
wait_level3:
    bit   portA           ; compare accumulator with memory
                          ; location for portA
    bne   wait_level3     ; if not equal then back to
                          ; previous instruction

turn_off_cold_water:
```

A section of program

The assembler turns this into machine code that will be stored in ROM. The microcontroller will run the machine code program.

Sally looks at the machine code listing for this section of program. 'The numbers on the left,' she explains to Keith, 'are the places in memory that this section of program will go to and read from.'

Memory location	Memory contents
141	A9
142	08
143	2C
144	00
145	00
146	D0
147	FB

Machine code listing

The microcontroller refers to the ports as if they were just memory locations. It refers to port A as memory location 0. The machine code shows that the assembler has translated the instruction LDA 8 into a machine code instruction A9 08. The instruction takes up two memory locations, with the next instruction beginning in location 143.

Legend:

	0
0	BRK Implied 1

— Coded Instruction

— Number of Bytes for Instruction

	0	1	2	3	4	5	6	7
0	BRK Implied 1	ORA (IND. X) 2				ORA ZP 2	ASL ZP 2	RMB0 ZP 2
1	BPL Relative 2	ORA (IND. Y) 2				ORA ZP. X 2	ASL ZP. X 2	RMB1 ZP 2
2	JSR Absolute 3	AND (IND. X) 2			BIT ZP 2	AND ZP 2	ROL ZP 2	RMB2 ZP 2
3	BMI Relative 2	AND (IND. Y) 2				AND ZP. X 2	ROL ZP. X 2	RMB3 ZP 2
4	RTI Implied 1	EOR (IND. X) 2				EOR ZP 2	LSR ZP 2	RMB4 ZP 2
5	BVC Relative 2	EOR (IND. Y) 2				EOR ZP. X 2	LSR ZP. X 2	RMB5 ZP 2
6	RTS Implied 1	ADC (IND. X) 2				ADC ZP 2	ROR ZP 2	RMB6 ZP 2
7	BVS Relative 2	ADC (IND. Y) 2				ADC ZP. X 2	ROR ZP. X 2	RMB7 ZP 2
8		STA (IND. X) 2			STY ZP 2	STA ZP 2	STX ZP 2	SMB0 ZP 2
9	BCC Relative 2	STA (IND. Y) 2			STY ZP. X 2	STA ZP. X 2	STX ZP. Y 2	SMB1 ZP 2
A	LDY IMM 2	LDA (IND. X) 2	LDX IMM 2		LDY ZP 2	LDA ZP 2	LDX ZP 2	SMB2 ZP 2
B	BCS Relative 2	LDA (IND. Y) 2			LDY ZP. X 2	LDA ZP. X 2	LDX ZP. Y 2	SMB3 ZP 2
C	CPY IMM 2	CMP (IND. X) 2			CPY ZP 2	CMP ZP 2	DEC ZP 2	SMB4 ZP 2
D	BNE Relative 2	CMP (IND. Y) 2				CMP ZP. X 2	DEC ZP. X 2	SMB5 ZP 2
E	CPX IMM 2	SBC (IND. X) 2			CPX ZP 2	SBC ZP 2	INC ZP 2	SMB6 ZP 2
F	BEO Relative 2	SBC (IND. X) 2				SBC ZP. X 2	INC ZP. X 2	SMB7 ZP 2

1 Using the instruction code matrix, find out what instruction is stored in location 143. Location 142 shows which bit pattern is to be tested. Which bit pattern would be tested if location 142 contained 4 instead of 8?

e.g.

A9
05 represents LDA 5

CD
04
82 represents CMP 8204

which means

Load the accumulator with the number 5.

which means

Compare the contents of the accumulator with the contents of memory location 8204 to see if they are the same.

8	9	A	B	C	D	E	F	
PHP Implied 1	ORA IMM 2	ASL Accum 1			ORA ABS 3	ASL ABS 3	BBR0 ZP 3	0
CLC Implied 1	ORA ABS. Y 3				ORA ABS. X 3	ASL ABS. X 3	BBR1 ZP 3	1
PLP Implied 1	AND IMM 2	ROL Accum 1		BIT ABS 3	AND ABS 3	ROL ABS 3	BBR2 ZP 3	2
SEC Implied 1	AND ABS. Y 3				AND ABS. X 3	ROL ABS. X 3	BBR3 ZP 3	3
PHA Implied 1	EOR IMM 2	LSR Accum 1		JMP ABS 3	EOR ABS 3	LSR ABS 3	BBR4 ZP 3	4
CLI Implied 1	EOR ABS. Y 3				EOR ABS. X 3	LSR ABS. X 3	BBR5 ZP 3	5
PLA Implied 1	ADC IMM 2	ROR Accum 1		JMP Indirect 3	ADC ABS 3	ROR ABS 3	BBR6 ZP 3	6
SEI Implied 1	ADC ABS. Y 3				ADC ABS. X 3	ROR ABS. X 3	BBR7 ZP 3	7
DEY Implied 1		TXA Implied 1		STY ABS 3	STA ABS 3	STX ABS 3	BBS0 ZP 3	8
TYA Implied 1	STA ABS. Y 3	TXS Implied 1			STA ABS. X 3		BBS1 ZP 3	9
TAY Implied 1	LDA IMM 2	TAX Implied 1		LDY ABS 3	LDA ABS 3	LDX ABS 3	BBS2 ZP 3	A
CLV Implied 1	LDA ABS. Y 3	TSX Implied 1		LDY ABS. X 3	LDA ABS. X 3	LDX ABS. X 3	BBS3 ZP 3	B
INY Implied 1	CMP IMM 2	DEX Implied 1		CPY ABS 3	CMP ABS 3	DEC ABS 3	BBS4 ZP 3	C
CLD Implied 1	CMP ABS. Y 3				CMP ABS. X 3	DEC ABS. X 3	BBS5 ZP 3	D
INX Implied 1	SBC IMM 2	NOP Implied 1		CPX ABS 3	SBC ABS 3	INC ABS 3	BBS6 ZP 3	E
SED Implied 1	SBC ABS. Y 3				SBC ABS. X 3	INC ABS. X 3	BBS7 ZP 3	F
8	9	A	B	C	D	E	F	

Instruction code matrix

1 READ ONLY MEMORY
2 RANDOM ACCESS MEMORY
3 CONTROL DECODE
4 ARITHMETIC LOGIC UNIT
5 CLOCK
6 INPUT/OUTPUT DECODE

0.2 inch

This shows the relative positions of different parts of a microcontroller

When the program runs and Sally's section of program is executed, the cold water supply will have been turned on. The program will continue to look at port A, testing bit 3, until the value is 1, showing the correct water level has been reached.

The program counter will contain the location of the next instruction in memory to execute.

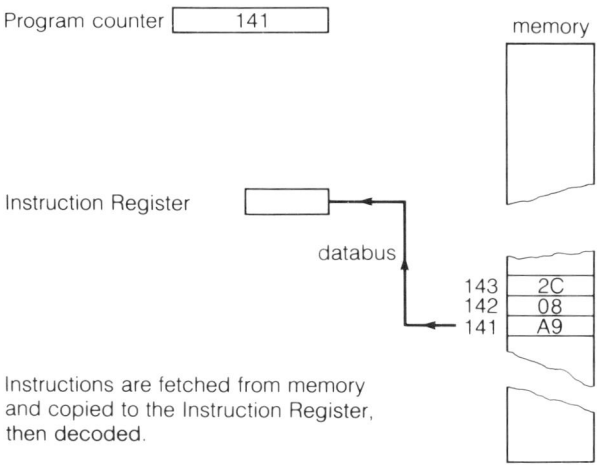

Instructions are fetched from memory and copied to the Instruction Register, then decoded.

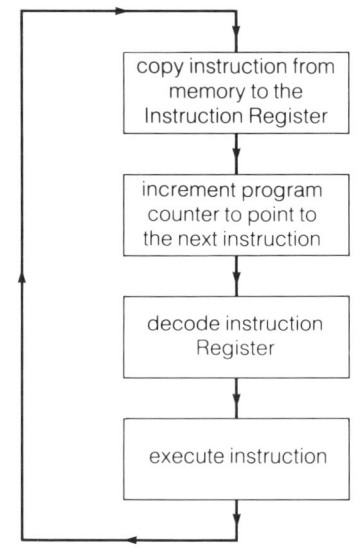

The control unit of the microcontroller FETCHES this instruction, A9, and copies it into the program instruction register. Here the instruction is decoded, so that the microcontroller knows what instruction is to be carried out. The location 142 is examined to see which number should be copied into the accumulator. Before the instruction is carried out the program counter is changed to point to the next instruction. This cycle is shown in the flow diagram on the left.

2 What will the contents of the program counter be now?

This ends the FETCH part of the program execution. The microcontroller now carries out the decoded instruction. This is called the EXECUTE part of the program execution. This process is repeated again and again, each time the next instruction is FETCHED, the program counter changed, and then the instruction carried out, as shown in the flow diagram on the left.

Sally has written another short piece of program. It has been assembled to machine code.

Memory location	Memory contents
121	A9
122	00
123	CD
124	01100000B
125	30
126	FA

An extract of machine code

3 Use the instruction code matrix to find out what the machine code instructions mean.

4 What does the instruction in memory location 121 do?

5 What is this section of Sally's program used for?

▷ What's going on?

The marketing team are impressed with the work done by the design team and suggest that a prototype microcontroller-based new machine be built. The first and most important job of the microcontroller is to control the washing machine mechanism. But it can also be used to indicate on a display panel what is happening. It is important that users of this new model of washing machine know what the machine is doing and what stage in the wash it has reached.

1 Why is it important for users to know where the machine is up to in the wash cycle?

Michael is a member of the design team who works mainly on the hardware side of the design. He has suggested that a series of lights on the front of the machine could tell the users all they need to know.

Jane, one of Michael's colleagues is not happy with this solution and proposes that the new machine should have a fuller, graphics display showing what the machine is doing.

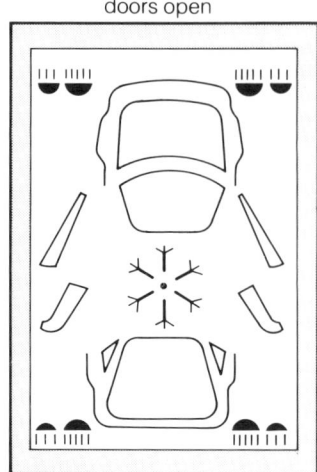

doors closed   doors open

A display from the dashboard of a Ford car

'My Ford car has got a good display system. It shows when a door is open, or if one of the lights is not working, or if the road is icy,' she explains to Michael.
'A switch is attached to each door which is turned on if the door is open. When the switch is turned on the picture on the display changes.'

Jane takes Michael to see the car display. 'If you open one of the doors that door switch will be turned "ON" and the display controller will change the display.'
She suggests that a similar fluorescent display is designed by the team for the new washing machine.

The fluorescent display is not like a TV screen. It is a number of drawings using several colours. Each part of the display can be turned on or off, with as many parts switched on as needed. The pictures are fixed when the display is made and each area of the screen can have only one picture.

2   What are the advantages of using Michael's suggestion of a series of lights?

3   What are the advantages of using pictures rather than words and lights to display information?

The team decide that a fluorescent display will be a good idea in this new machine.

4   Design the fluorescent display that could be used with the washing machine. Your design should include pictures to show which wash cycle has been chosen, and what stage of the wash it has reached.

The number of possible pictures to be displayed is too many to be controlled by individual bits from one of the ports of the microcontroller.

5   How many pictures could be turned on or off using both ports C and D?

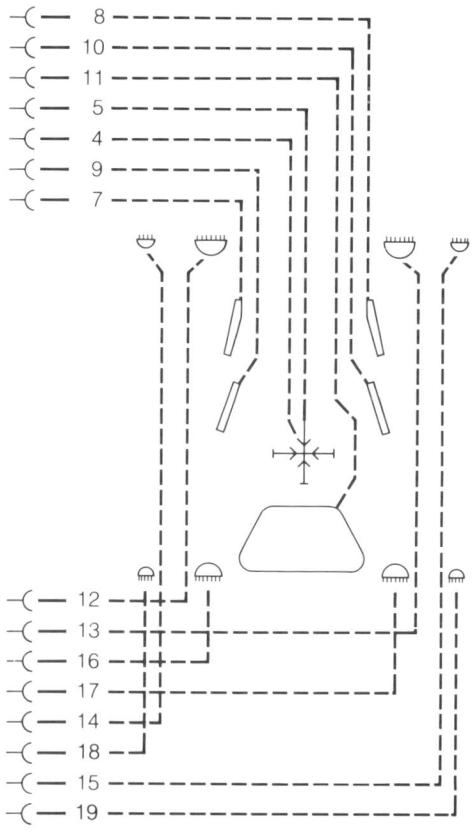

Wiring to the Ford flourescent display

Michael suggests that the display has its own display processor. The data from port D will be input to this processor, as a sequence of instructions. 'Combinations of bits from port D will be used to represent different instructions, like in a computer program,' he explains. 'We need to have a list of the things that the display could show. For each of these, we need a different bit pattern. Depending on the bit pattern it gets from port D, the display processor would switch on a different part of the display. Sending a zero could turn all of the display off.'

6 This is the start of a table of pictures to be displayed. Finish the table by adding all the other pictures that you think need to be displayed.

0	clear display
1	wash programme 1
2	2
3	
4	
5	
6	
.	
.	
21	
.	half load
.	

All the pictures that could be displayed on the washing machine panel

7 How many different pictures will be needed?

Each picture must be represented by a different bit pattern. Each pattern will be made up of six 0s and 1s, for example, 000000, 010101, 110011 etc.

8 How many different bit patterns could be sent from port D?

The fluorescent display will be receiving data sent in this serial form. It will need a serial interface to allow it to receive and decode serial data.

The design team are anxious that messages sent from the washing machine controller to the display are received correctly. They decide to use bit 5 as a parity bit. Using even parity will mean that if port D sends the five bits

11101

then a sixth bit, a 0, will be added so that there is an even number of 1s sent in the six bits. With even parity, there should always be an even number of 1s. After the six bits have been sent, they will be checked. If there is an odd number of bits, then something has gone wrong during the transmission.

9 If the first five bits are all 1s, what will the sixth bit be?

10 Will parity checks discover all the transmission errors?

11 If the display received 011010 from the microcontroller followed
by 100100, which message has been corrupted?

In the microcontroller that the design team are using, port D, shown below,
is a serial port. This means that instead of a number of separate wires
coming out from the port there is only one. The six values for the bits at
the port are sent down this wire one after another, starting with bit 0 and
finishing with bit 5.

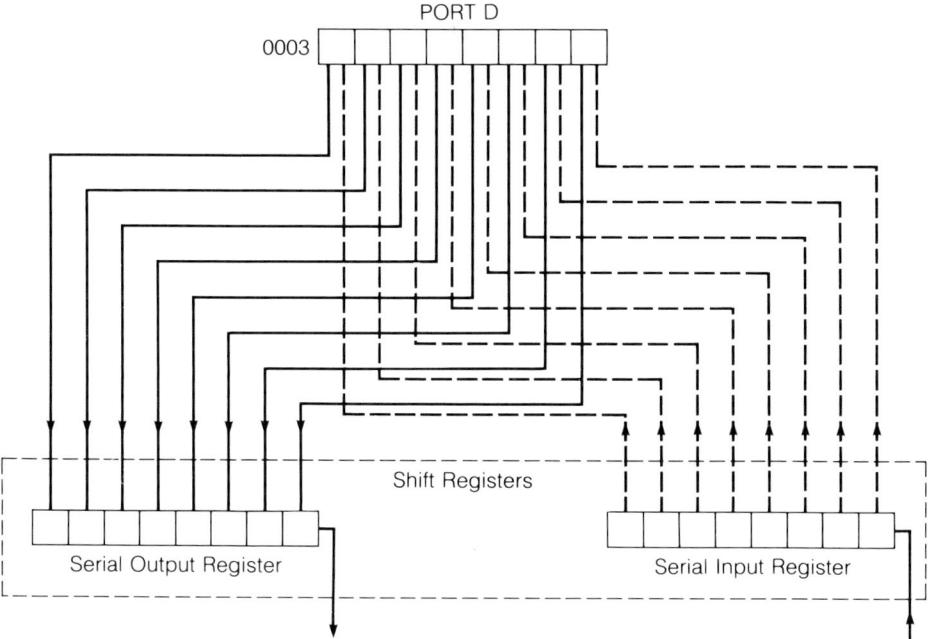

So that the display processor knows when a new message is being sent
and when the message is completed, extra bits are sent, in addition to the
data and parity bits. One start bit will be sent before the five data bits,
then the parity bit, followed by two stop bits indicating the end of this
instruction.

e.g.	1 start bit	i.e. 1
	5 data bits representing 21	i.e. 10101
	1 parity bit, even parity	i.e. 1
	2 stop bits	i.e. 11

Because five data bits are used for each signal, the processor is said to
process 5-bit words. The message sent down the wire from port D will
look like a train of pulses representing the 1s and 0s.

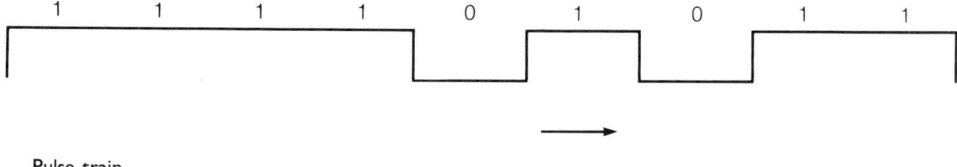

Pulse train

The number of stop bits can be 1 or 2. The sending and receiving devices must agree upon this. They also need to agree on word length and parity setting.

The use of a parity bit to check that the data has been received correctly is very important because problems of data corruption can be quite common in electrically operated machines. Mains voltage devices such as motors can cause electrical interference.

Port D and the display processor also need to agree upon the rate at which port D will send these bit patterns. This speed is called the baud rate. The baud rate is the number of bits that can be sent every second.

BAUD RATES

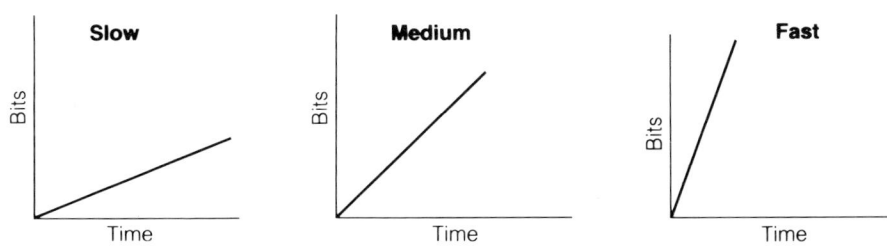

Graphical representation of Baud rate

---

12 What will be the effect of using a slower rate of transfer between the microcontroller and the display processor?

13 What sequence of data values needs to be sent to display the following at the same time: Programme 6, half load, short spin?

▷ Getting it clean – removing the bugs

The program developed by Sally and her team has been tested during the programming stages. Sally is the systems programmer and project leader. She has divided up the programming tasks between her small team of programmers. Each programmer is responsible for testing their own sections of program.

1 What else should be done to make sure that the program does not contain any bugs?

2 How can the marketing team know that the new machine will do what they expected of it?

When the marketing team see what this new machine can do they are impressed. But seeing their ideas put into practice gives them some more ideas. They suggest a number of possible changes and improvements to the new machine. Wilson, from the marketing team, is very pleased with the fluorescent display. 'I can think of other things that could be shown on this sort of display. Could you change it?' he asks.

> **3 What do you think Sally will say to this suggestion?**
>
> **4 Why will it be so difficult to add extra pictures to the display?**

The prototype machine will be tested for many hours using each possible wash cycle and all the special features. They must test all of the paths through the computer program.

When the design team are happy that the computer program works properly, they will then have many copies of the microcontroller made. These chips will be made with the computer program in the chip's ROM.

> **5 What might happen if a bug is discovered after the chips have been made?**

▷ What could go wrong?

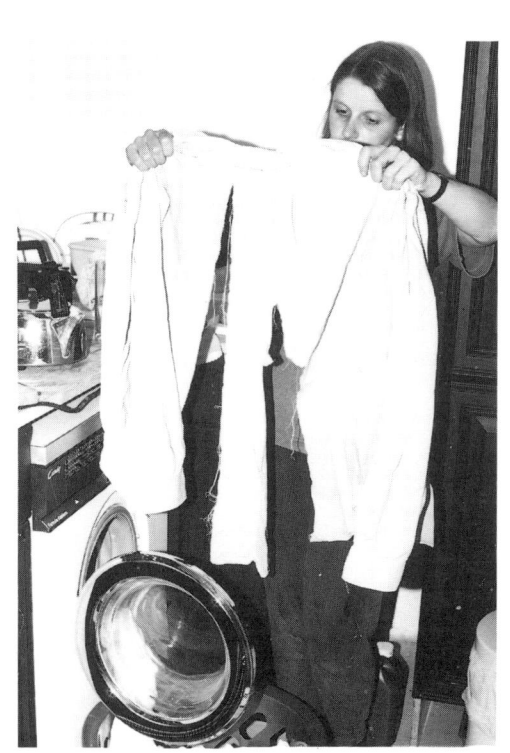

Can you think of any way sensors could prevent damage to clothes?

Washing machines need to be reliable. Their owners need to use them regularly, and get very annoyed if they don't work properly. A fault in a washing machine could cause more than inconvenience. If a machine does not work properly, it could cause damage to the clothes.

Micro-electronic components are usually very reliable, but they are not perfect. There is always a small chance that a component could fail, or operate incorrectly. The design department must bear this in mind when they design a washing machine. Even if a component goes wrong, they must take precautions so that no harm is done to the clothes, or to anyone using the machine.

A lot of these precautions involve the use of sensors in the machine. There are different types of sensor in a washing machine, for example:

▶ temperature sensors to check on the water temperature,

▶ water level sensors, to check on the amount of water in the machine,

▶ a sensor to check on whether or not the door is shut.

The sensors have to be fixed in place in the machine.

Data from each sensor is read by the microcontroller, so each sensor needs to be connected to the microcontroller. Each sensor can only detect two different conditions. Each sensor can output two different signals. One indicates one condition, the other indicates another condition. For example, a water level sensor indicates whether water has reached a certain level, or not. A temperature sensor indicates whether or not a certain temperature has been reached.

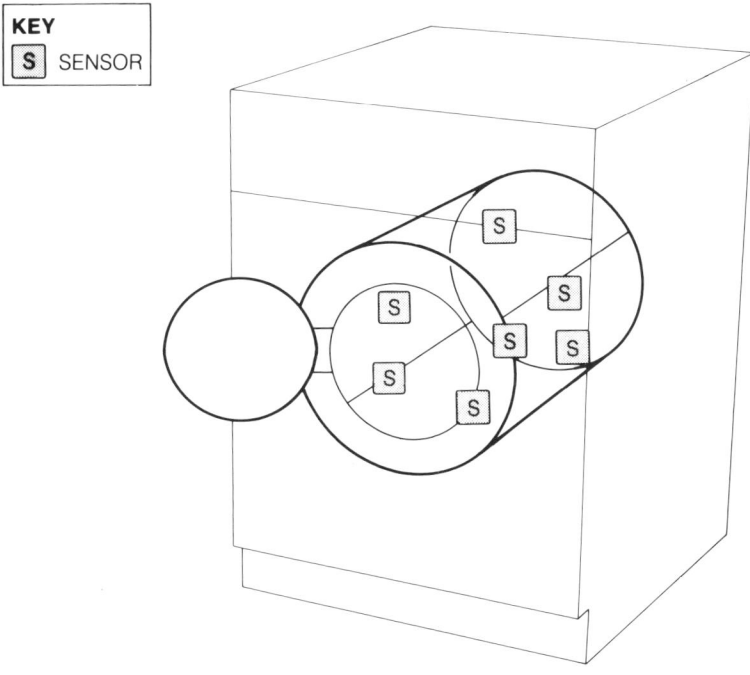

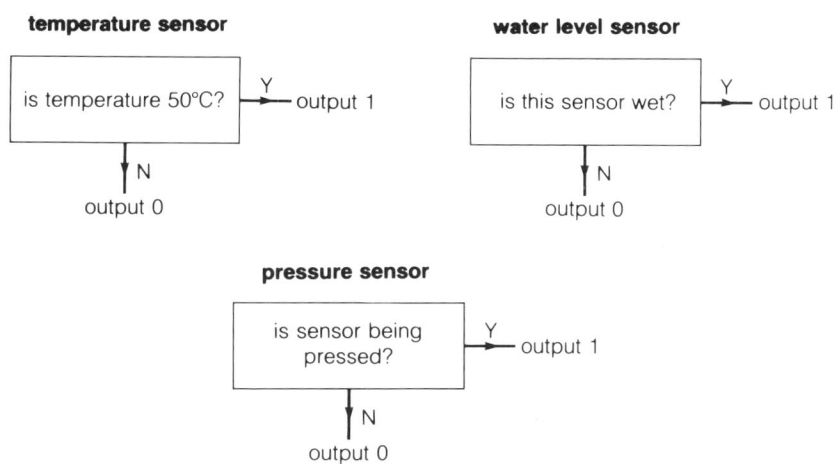

temperature sensor

is temperature 50°C? —Y→ output 1

↓N
output 0

water level sensor

is this sensor wet? —Y→ output 1

↓N
output 0

pressure sensor

is sensor being pressed? —Y→ output 1

↓N
output 0

---

1   What two conditions does a door sensor indicate?

Sybil has to try and think of all the things that could go wrong with a machine. Then she has to try to think of ways of solving the problem. Here is an example.

Suppose a washing machine had a water level sensor. Water comes into the machine until the water level sensor detects the correct level. Then the heater is switched on. But the temperature sensor does not work. It does not detect that the water has reached the correct temperature.

---

2   What would happen in this case? What effect would that have on the clothes?

Sybil thinks of two different ways of solving this one. Firstly, there could be several temperature sensors. If all of them were read, it would be easy to detect that one was faulty.

3   Why would it be easy to tell if one sensor was faulty?

Another solution would be to use a timer. She could work out the maximum amount of time that it would take to heat cold water to the required temperature. The timer could wait for this length of time. If, at the end of this time, the sensor still has not detected the correct temperature, then it could be assumed that something was faulty.

4   What should happen in the machine if either of these methods detects a fault?

Sybil thinks of another example of a fault. Suppose the water level sensor goes wrong. Suppose it always shows that the correct water level has been reached. Some clothes are put in the machine, and the machine is switched on. The water level sensor immediately detects the correct water level. The heater is then switched on.

5   What would happen to the clothes in this situation?

6   How could this problem be overcome?

Other sorts of faults are possible, too. The microcontroller receives signals from the sensors as electrical pulses. Electrical interference from the motor could cause a switch to receive a signal that has not been sent from the microcontroller. For example, the pump could accidentally be switched on in the middle of a wash. This would cause all the water to be emptied before the washing was finished. Sybil's solution for this is to switch off devices that should not be on, at regular intervals. That way, even if something is switched on by mistake, it will soon be switched off again.

7   Can you think of another example where switching something off could prevent an accident?

Mechanical and electrical components can fail too. For example, the pump motor could break down. This means that even when the 'switch on' signal is sent, nothing happens. The water will stay in the machine. This would be a nuisance, but it could also cause damage to the machine if it tried to spin the clothes while the drum is full of water.

A flow chart showing the stages from rinsing the clothes to spinning them dry is shown on the right.

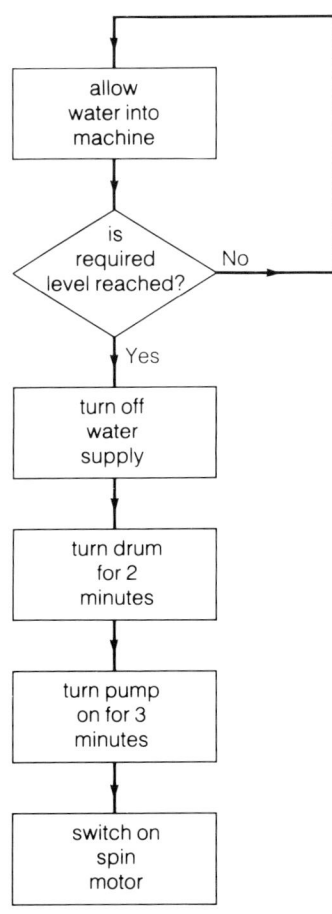

8 **Change this flow chart to show the extra steps needed to detect whether or not it is safe to start spinning the clothes.**

Suppose that there is a leak in the washing machine. Water can escape at the same rate as the water coming in to the machine. This flow chart below shows what will happen.

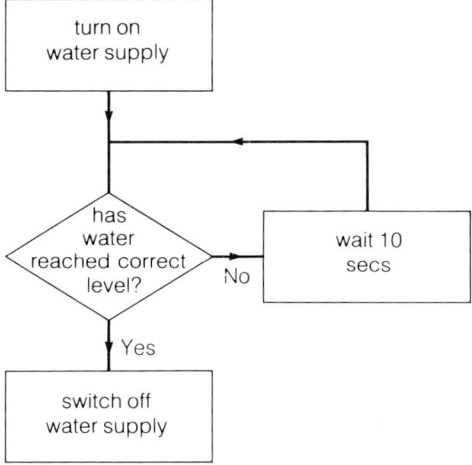

9 **When would the water reach the correct level? What would happen then? What would be the effects of this malfunction?**

10 **How else might this sort of accident happen, even if the machine did not have a leak? What could be done to prevent it?**

11 **Can you think of any other faults that might occur? How would you deal with them if you were designing a washing machine?**

A micro-electronically controlled machine can have some disadvantages compared to an electro-mechanical machine. Suppose, for example, that there is a power cut in the middle of a wash. When the power is restored the machine needs to carry on from the point at which it was stopped. This is no problem for the electro-mechanical machine. It would still be set at the point in the wash cycle it had reached when the power was cut. This would not necessarily be true for a micro-controlled machine.

12 **Why is it likely that the machine is not able to recall where it had got to?**

Washing machines in laundrettes are used by many different people. Do they need to be specially designed because of this? What features will be most important?

One solution would be to have a battery operated back-up memory, which saves data on the current position in the wash cycle.

13 Can you think of any other solutions to this problem?

A lot of potential problems can be detected, and solutions can be suggested for them. But Sybil finds that she is not able to implement them all, because each one will increase the cost of the machine.

14 What sort of problems are most important to avoid?

Some problems will be caused not by the machine, but by the people using it. For example, someone might use the wrong sort of washing powder, which results in masses of soap suds all over the place.

15 Can you think of any other problems that could be caused by the machine's operator? Do you think that the manufacturer should produce machines which are designed to minimize the effects of customer's mistakes? How could mistakes by the customer be avoided, or at least reduced?

▷ General questions

1 Computer technology can be used to control devices in many applications. In each of the following examples, say what input the microprocessor would receive, and what sort of output is needed.

a A greenhouse which has its temperature monitored and controlled by computer.

b A robot arm in a car factory. The arm holds a welding torch for welding seams in the cars' bodies.

c   In a biology experiment, monitoring the growth of a seedling.

d   A microprocessor-controlled burglar alarm system installed in a house.

e   A computer-controlled level-crossing gate.

f   A computer-controlled toy car.

g   Monitoring the blood pressure and pulse of a patient in hospital.

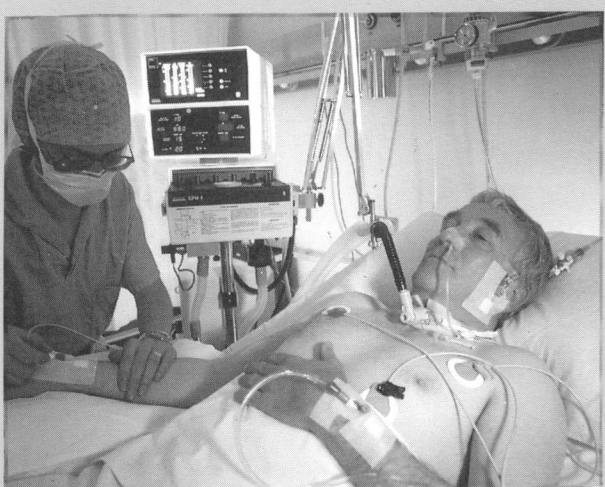

2   A computer designer is working on a new machine. She needs to work out how many different characters the computer should be able to recognize and process. Then she can work out how many bits she must use to store each character.

If she allows only 1 bit to store a character, then the computer will only be able to cope with two characters.

1st character represented by 0
2nd character represented by 1

If she allows 2 bits, then four different characters can be represented.

1st character represented by 00
2nd character represented by 01
3rd character represented by 10
4th character represented by 11

If she uses 3 bits, list all the bit patterns she could use. How many different characters could be represented?

If she uses 4 bits, how many different characters could be represented?

How many different characters could be represented using 5 bits? 6 bits? 7 bits? 8 bits?

The designer must work out how many characters she needs to be able to use. She needs:
► all the letters of the English alphabet (capital and small letters),
► all the different digits,
► all the different punctuation marks.
What other sorts of characters should be included? How many different characters are there altogether?

What is the smallest number of bits that can be used for each character, if each character is to have a different bit pattern?

The computer designer is also designing machines which will process characters from the alphabets of other languages. How many characters does each of these languages have in its alphabet? How many bits would be needed to represent each of these alphabets?

Gujerati	Urdu
Japanese	Arabic
Greek	French

3   A microprocessor is like the central processing unit (CPU) of a computer. But in most computers, the CPU occupies more than one chip.

Apart from the CPU, what other devices would be needed to make up a simple computer configuration? Draw a diagram showing how the other parts are used with the CPU. Use arrows to show where data flow from one device to another.

In a small business, one person has the job of making out the customers' bills. This person gets the details of the customers' orders in their in-tray. Other information about the customers is found in the filing cabinet. The person uses a calculator to work out the bills, and then writes the bills out by hand on pre-printed stationery.

This job could be done using a computer. Match up the part of the computer that would take the place of each thing in the manual system, by pairing one item from each of these two lists:

manual system	computer system
filing cabinet	arithmetic and logic unit
in-tray	printer
person	magnetic disks
calculator	keyboard
person's pen	control unit

4 The process of canning baked beans in a factory is to become part of a computer controlled system. Before designing and programming the process, the algorithm for the bean canning production line must be carefully recorded. The designers and programmers will use this algorithm in the work.

For each can of beans, the correct weight of beans must be poured into an empty can. The full can then moves along the line. A metal lid is placed on top of the can, and welded in place. The can then moves along to the next stage, where it is heated to a temperature which will kill all bacteria. When the can has cooled down, a label is stuck on it.

Draw up an algorithm to show the bean canning process. Include any extra stages and checks you think might be necessary.

5 The fluorescent light display of the Ford car is an example of a simulation. The display is a model of the car. The model is used because it is easier for the driver to see. The driver can look at the display instead of looking at each door and light in the car.

Computers are often used to model or simulate situations. Sometimes things are modelled because they are too dangerous to do in real life, like a dangerous chemical experiment. Some things are modelled because in real life they happen too slowly, or too quickly, for human beings to see, for example, the growth of a plant. Sometimes it is just too difficult or expensive to set up and watch the real thing. For example, in designing a bridge to cross over a river, the designer may want to try out the bridge to see if it is strong enough before it is built.

Why do you think situations need to be simulated? What sort of information can be found from a simulation?

Here is a list of simulations. For each one say why you think it needs to be simulated on a computer.

a A simulation of a nuclear power station's safety measures.
b A simulation of the actions that could be taken to clear up an accidental oil spillage in the sea.
c A simulation of the queues of people in a bank.
d A simulation of a Grand Prix car race.
e A simulation to test the strength of a new building material.
f A simulation of the effects of a nuclear bomb.
g A simulation of a space craft landing on the moon.
h A simulation of the traffic flow at a junction where traffic lights are to be installed.
i A simulation of the activities in the Earth's atmosphere.
j A simulation of the behaviour of human lungs.
k A simulation of the control of a plane.

▷ Software activities

1 Have a look at some simulation programs. Try to discover what they are simulating, and the purpose of the simulation.

2 Use a painting package to produce a design for a new kitchen appliance.

3 Use an integrated software package to design and cost the layout of a kitchen. Use the painting part of the package to produce the design. Use the spreadsheet part to produce a costing for the kitchen units, appliances and fitting. Use the word processing part of the package to write a letter to a potential customer giving them the details of the costs and fitting arrangements for their new kitchen.

Computer Disks

The directors of the Dolfin Record Company decided that the company was not making enough use of computers in the running of the business. Some departments have used computers quite a lot, and for some time. For example, there is an IBM mainframe used in the finance department, and there is a small data processing department which includes two programmers and two clerks.

1　The finance department is responsible for working out and paying the salaries for all the Dolfin employees. Why do you think the finance department was the first to use computers?

2　The directors know very little about computers and what computers can do. Why do you think they have decided to make more use of computers?

The directors decided to appoint a new member of staff. The job involves investigating what computers are already used for in the company, and finding out what else they can be used for. The successful candidate for the job was Wayne, and he has worked at Dolfin Records for about 6 months now.

Before joining Dolfin, Wayne worked in the USA with the American Federation of Musicians. He has had a lot of experience in designing computer systems. He does not have any detailed knowledge of computer programming, or of exactly how the 'insides' of computers work.

3　Do you think that Wayne has the right qualifications for the job? Do you think that his lack of programming knowledge is important? Are there other people in the company who do know a lot about programming?

Wayne's first task when he started at Dolfin was to find out exactly what was going on! He had to find out who was using computers, and what they used them for. He also had to find out all about the way the company was run, so that he could see where else computers might be useful.

4 How could Wayne find out all the information he needed? Can you think of any problems he might have?

Wayne discovered that there were four main sections to the company: Making, Selling, Finance and International. Each section was made up of a number of different departments.

Making	Selling	Finance	International
A&R Dept signing groups recording songs deciding on records *Production* sleeve designs record pressing	*Marketing* advertising picture discs, etc. *Promotion* TV appearances radio *Press* newspaper interviews magazine features *Sales Force* record shops	*Salaries* Dolfin staff *Legal* contracts *Accounts* income from sales expenditure	Linking with Dolfin's 17 companies in other countries

Although the company is successful, Wayne discovered that some tasks could be done more efficiently, and that some tasks were sometimes done more than once.

5 If Wayne gets more computers, will the company automatically become more efficient? Make a list of all the things Wayne must do before buying any new computers.

6 Why is it important that work is done efficiently without wasting too much time, or employing too many people?

7 Most of the people who work at Dolfin are very happy with their jobs. They are worried that computers will make them change the way they work. Do you think that they need to be worried?

Wayne also discovered that some of Dolfin's work was done outside the company; for example, calculating how much money an artist should receive from sales of his or her record. This data was processed by a computer bureau, who did the same job for other record companies too.

8 What are the advantages to Dolfin of having this data processed by a computer bureau? Can you think of any disadvantages?

Once an album has sold 100 000 copies, the artists are awarded a gold disk like this one

So far, Wayne has spent most of his time finding out about the company and its activities, and planning future computer use. In the end, Wayne would like the company to have an integrated computer system for every department to use. But some departments cannot wait for this; they need computers straight away.

9   Why do you think Wayne wants to have one system for the whole company, rather than a separate one for each department?

10   Will it be possible for Wayne to satisfy the departments that need computers immediately? What must he bear in mind when planning for these departments?

▷ Can computers help?

It is very important that all the departments work together when a record is released. This diagram shows all the different activities carried out by each department when a record is released. Some things have to be done before the record is released, and some afterwards. For most things, the timing is very important. For example, if shops do not have copies of a record they cannot sell them. In the same way, it is not always useful to advertise a record before it is available in the shops.

RECORD MAKING

— Record the record.

— Arrange for master copies of the record to be ready on time

— Book time at the manufacturers for the records to be pressed

— Prepare record sleeve design

— Arrange for record sleeves to be printed

— Arrange for record sleeves to be sent to record manufacturers for assembly.

RECORD SELLING

Marketing:

— Organise advertising campaign. Adverts can be on TV, radio, newspapers, magazines or posters.

— Design and make adverts.

— Decide on any special arrangements, for example 7 and 12 inch records, picture discs, free gifts and competitions.

Promotion:

— Aim to get record played on radio stations and on TV programmes.

— Try to get artist as a guest on suitable radio and TV programmes.

Press:

— Try to persuade newspapers and magazines to write articles about the artist.

— Get journalists to review the record.

Also, the record company may try to release the record while the group are touring, so that they can advertise it when they play. They will try not to release the record when the group are on holiday, or are busy recording new songs. They also try to release records at different times over the year, so that they don't have too many records out at one time. That way, they have time to work on each record properly without being too rushed.

The Heads of all the departments (called HODs) meet together once a week. At one of their meetings they all listened to a tape of the new single from a new band, Diwana. The HODs liked the song, but were not very happy with the recording. They thought that the vocals were too quiet compared to the backing. Reluctantly, they decided that the song would have to be 're-mixed' to bring the vocals forward.

This could take some time to do, and will mean that it will not be possible to release the record on schedule. A number of activities now have to be reorganized.

The manufacture of the records will have to be delayed by at least a week. The manufacturing company is very busy, and will not be able to make a start on the Diwana's record for at least two weeks. The printing of the record sleeves can proceed as originally arranged, but the sleeves will have to be stored until they are needed.

The promotion department had fixed up some radio and TV appearances for the group, to publicise their record, and these will have to be rearranged now.

| 1 | Why do these appearances need to be rearranged? |

The press department will also have to rearrange some interviews they had set up with journalists from some daily papers and music magazines.

| 2 | Why will these interviews need to be changed? |

Wayne asks the HODs whether a computer would help to reorganize some of these things.

3 How could the computer help in this case? What sort of things would the computer be unable to do? Who would decide on how computers could be used in this case?

The aim of the promotions department is to increase people's knowledge about records and artists, and therefore increase sales. Some activities seem to help increase sales for some artists, but don't work well for others. For example, some artists are entertaining on chat shows, while others do better sticking to singing and playing!

All promotional activities cost money. For an artist to appear on a TV show could involve spending money on hiring equipment, transport, rehearsal studios, clothes, and the time of members of the promotions department.

The Managing Director asks the Head of Promotion, Nick, which promotional activities work best. Nick is unable to say precisely. Firstly, he doesn't know the exact cost of the activities. Secondly, he does not know exactly how effective each one is.

4 What information would help Nick to work out the cost of each promotional activity? What information would help Nick to see how effective each one is?

Wayne thinks that the computer could help in this case. He thinks that a spreadsheet program would be suitable. It could be used to calculate the total expense of an activity, and the change in sales immediately after it.

5 What data would need to be input to the spreadsheet? How could it produce the desired results?

6 What output is needed from the spreadsheet? Many people find it difficult to understand tables of figures. Design the output from the spreadsheet so that the results are clear and easy to read.

Nick is still not entirely happy with the idea of a spreadsheet. And he and Wayne both realize that other factors influence the sales of records, apart from the promotions department's work. Wayne decides that he will try to design a program that all the selling departments can use, and which will produce more attractive output.

7 What other factors can influence the sales of a record?

8 What input will be needed for this program? Who do you think should input the data?

9 Wayne suggests that the output could be in the form of graphs. They will show all the things that have been done to increase the sales, and they will also show the actual daily sales. Make your own design for this output screen.

10 The output could be produced only on the screen, or it could be output onto paper too. What sort of devices would you consider for producing this hard copy? What sort of device do you think Wayne should recommend?

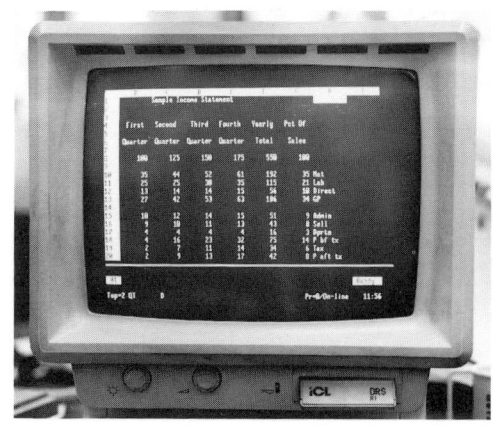
Spreadsheets are good for doing 'what if?' calculations

Before Dolfin make and sell records for the new band, Diwana, a contract is signed by both the company and the group. This legal document sets out what Dolfin will do for the band and what money the band will get in return for sales of records. Here is part of the contract for another band, the Comstars, as an example.

DOLFIN RECORDS
Recording Contract

Made with ``The Comstars"
on April 20th 1989

Conditions

1　The above named group to make **6** albums for release by the above named record company.
2　For each record sold the group will receive a royalty of **10%** of the wholesale price.
3　The group will receive a cash advance of **£900,000,** payable in **6** installments from which recording costs must be paid.

Comstars' contract with Dolfin Records

Every artist with Dolfin will have a similar contract, with some changes depending upon the circumstances of the band.

> **I　What changes would have to be made to this contract before the Diwanas sign it?**

Michael, who works in the legal department, has the job of preparing copies of the contracts which are to be signed this week.

> **2　What computer software package would be of most use to Michael in preparing contracts for artists?**

Because all contracts are similar, with only a few differences between artists, Wayne suggests that Dolfin write their own computer program to produce contracts. He knows that this program must be easy to operate with the minimum of keyboard work. Much thought must go into the wording of messages on the screen so that they are clear but can be quickly read.

3 Design the input screen for this program that will allow Michael to produce different contracts. The screen should prompt for the changes from the standard contract.

It is very important that no mistakes are made when entering the data. Wayne suggests that the inputs should be filled in by hand on a form first, then typed in at the keyboard.

4 After typing in the data, the user is asked to verify that it is correct. How could the data capture form help in verifying the data? Using a word processing package, design a suitable data capture form.

5 Wayne and Michael want to make the program easy to use, even for people who cannot type very well. How can Wayne make some of the data easier to input?

Wayne wants to make sure that users of the program will not input invalid data into the computer. Each input will be validated to see that it is of the right type, e.g. a valid date Day/Month/Year, a number, or words.

6 For each input say what sort of keyboard characters are acceptable.

Michael uses the computer for other things. He uses it to produce letters and other documents, and thinks that he knows quite a lot about computers. He asks Wayne why a special program needs to be written for producing contracts when they could use one of the commercial packages that came 'free' with the machine. He and his colleagues in the legal department already know how to use some of these programs.

7 What arguments might Wayne use to convince Michael that learning to use this new program will be better than using one of the 'free' packages, like the word processing package?

8 Why are these 'free' packages not really free?

The contract is signed, and a copy kept by both Dolfin and the Diwanas. Wayne sees that this is just one stage in the process of the legal department's dealings with the band during the next two years. Hopefully the new record will sell well and Dolfin will then have to pay the Diwanas their percentage as agreed in the contract. The Diwanas hope to sell 500 000 copies of the record.

9 If they end up selling 100 000 copies how much money will Dolfin have to pay them?

The legal department is responsible for working out these amounts for each artist regularly. The amount paid to each artist depends upon the figure agreed in the contract and how many copies have been sold. The agreed figure to be paid for each sale may also be a different value for sales in different countries.

Signing the contract

The sales and amounts to be paid to the artists could be set out to look like this:

Payment Table

Date May 1989

Product	Artist	Sales	Royalty	Total
DOL126	Crash	12 500	0.12	1500.00
SAB002	Sabello Manyati	21 000	0.34	7140.00
DOL134	Eileen O'Hare	9 200	0.30	2760.00

A payments table for artists

A spreadsheet package could be used to do these calculations.

10 Use a spreadsheet package to design a spreadsheet to do this job.

At present all these calculations are done using a computer program developed by a computer bureau that Dolfin uses. The bureau processes Dolfin's data too. Dolfin supply their sales figures for each record to the company together with the necessary contract details. The bureau's computer does all the necessary calculations to produce statements of how much money is to be paid to each musician. The bureau does this job for Dolfin and other companies in the record business every three months.

Wayne investigates the different ways that this data could be processed. He produces a list of all these methods. They range from keeping the same system without any changes, to writing all the programs at Dolfin and running them on their own computer. In between these two are a range of other options.

11 What other options do you think there could be? What are the advantages and disadvantages of each option?

Wayne suggests that the long-term solution would be to do the whole process in-house.

12 Why do you think Wayne makes this suggestion? What reasons can you think of for delaying this move to total in-house work? Why might they *gradually* take the work on within the Dolfin organization?

Some of the data which is needed for calculating royalties is included in singers' and musicians' contracts. Wayne has suggested that the program to produce artists' contracts could access a common database which could also be used by the program to calculate payments.

Wayne suggests that there could be a number of related files, all linked together. The two main files will be:

▶ the artist's file, which contains the name of the artist and a unique identifying number.

▶ the product file, which contains just the unique code number for every Dolfin record.

These files could be linked together, as shown below.

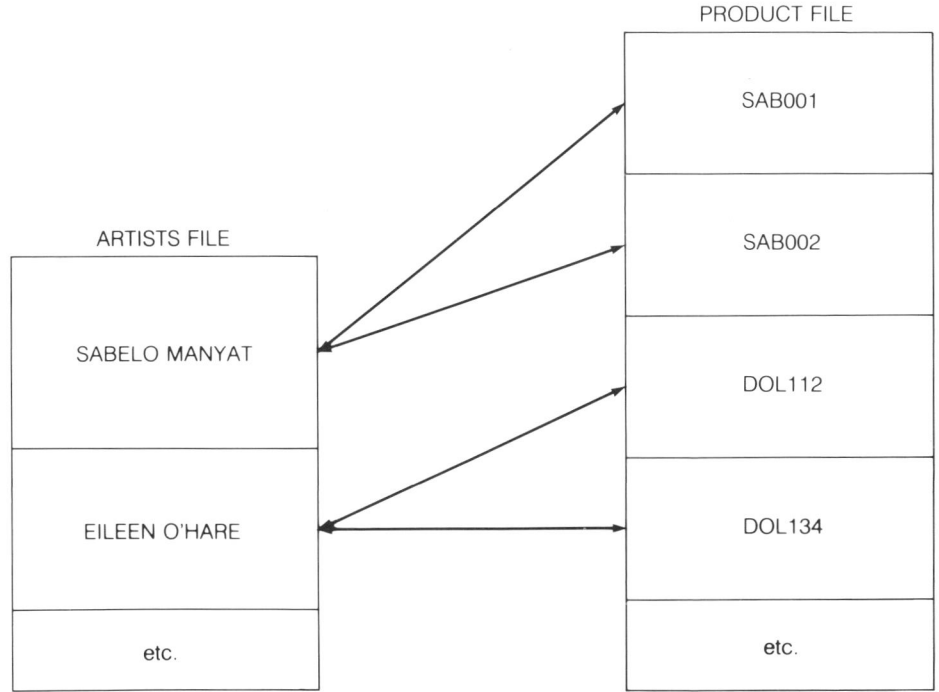

To calculate royalty payments, these other files would need to be accessed:

▶ artist file

▶ product file

▶ contracts file

▶ sales file

▶ artist expenses file

13 For each of these files, give a reason why it needs to be accessed when royalty payments are being calculated.

Michael has been told that it will be easy to use this new system but he is concerned that if it is easy to use, it will be easy for anyone to make changes to the information held on the computer.

14 What safeguards will Wayne need to build into the system specifications to ensure that only those working in the legal department can make necessary alterations, and that once a contract has been signed changes cannot be made to the information held on the computer?

The program will need to use information held in different computer files in the system. The number of records sold and the royalty per record to be paid will be required.

15 List the files and fields that will be read and the operations which must be performed for the program to produce the royalty payments for artists.

16 Draw a flow chart to show the steps involved in calculating the royalty payments.

Wayne has to decide what is the most appropriate programming language to use to write this program. There is a wide range of different languages available for use on the computer system, some of these are shown in the table below.

Language	Description
BASIC	Specifically designed for beginners. Usually interpreted especially on microcomputers
ALGOL	A high level language for mathematical and scientific application
COBOL	Used for business data processing
FORTRAN	Used for programming in scientific applications
LOGO	Has list processing features. Widely known for its 'turtle graphics'
PROLOG	Based on mathematical logic. Used in information retrieval applications
APL	Has a specially designed character set. Used in advanced mathematical applications
Pascal	Designed to encourage structured programming
Assembly language	A low-level programming language
Machine code	A language which can be executed without any translation. Relates to specific machine operation

17 What language features will be necessary? Wayne intends that many different users in the company will be able to access the artists' datafiles at the same time. Will this influence the choice of computer language used? What computer language would you advise Wayne to choose?

18 Why would some of these languages *not* be appropriate for this sort of program?

▷ Records around the world

Dolfin Records is a UK company, but it has many other companies in other countries. These companies release and sell records made by the UK company. They also make and release records made by local artists. Some of these records may also be released in Britain. Each foreign company does its own marketing, press and promotion, and so on.

There is a department in the UK company which co-ordinates all the foreign companies. It is called the international department. It makes sure that all the companies know in advance what records are being recorded and released in the UK.

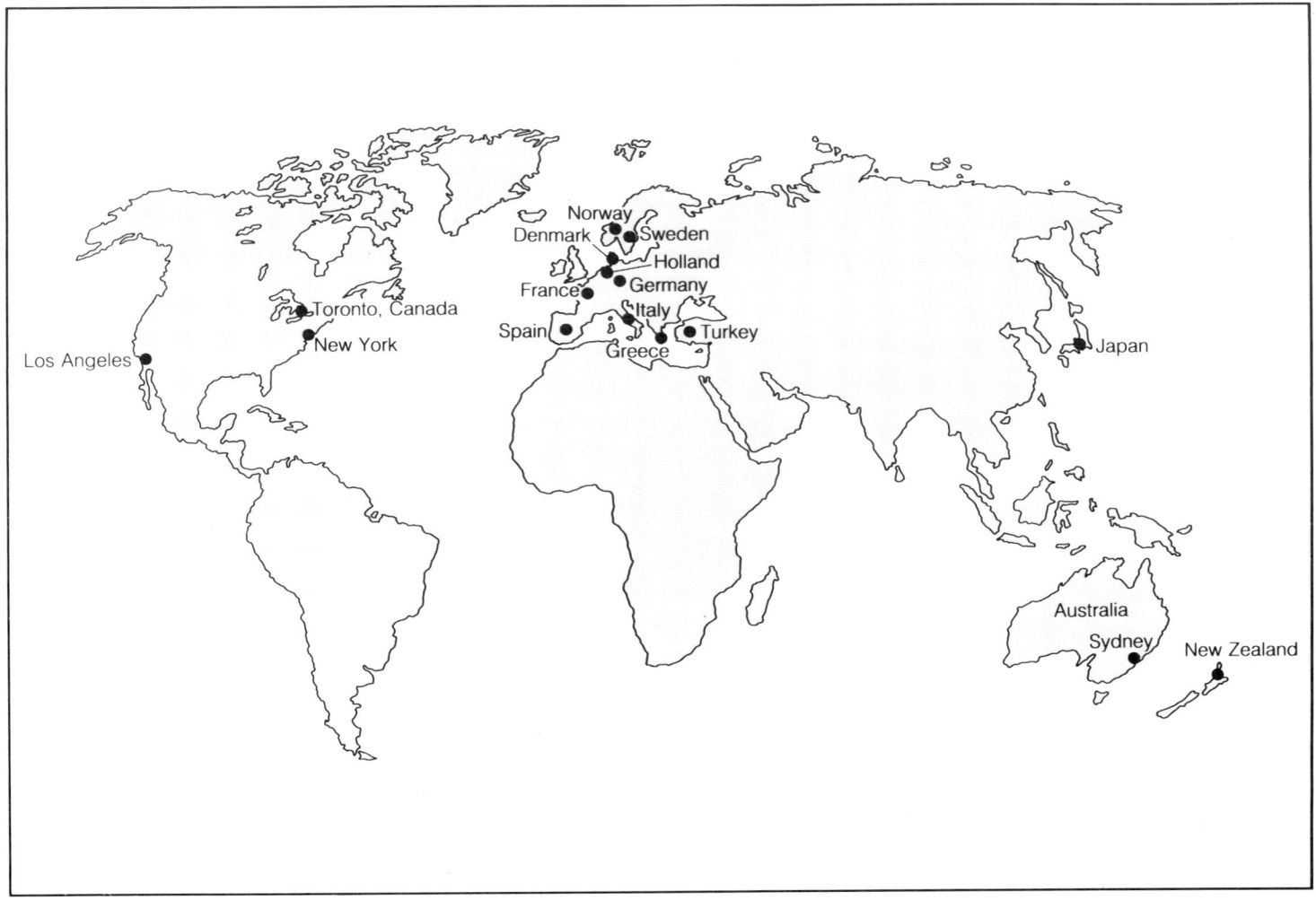

Dolfin Records' companies are spread all over the world. What are the advantages and disadvantages of this?

It also provides the materials needed by the companies if they are going to sell a UK record. Sometimes records are manufactured in the UK then sent abroad. At other times, a copy of the master tape and artwork for the record sleeves will be sent, so that the overseas companies can manufacture their own records. The product shipping department is responsible for sending these items to other countries.

1   How do you think it is decided whether to send finished records, or master tape and sleeve artwork?

2   What information is needed by the foreign companies about the artists and records in the UK? Can you think of any other information they might need from the UK company?

3   What information does the international department need from each of the foreign companies?

4   What different ways of communicating can be used between companies in different countries?

Wayne is considering whether or not it would be feasible to design an international computer system, with each company having a computer linked to a central computer and database in the UK.

5 What advantages would this computer system have over other communication methods? What disadvantages would it have? How could Wayne decide whether or not to go ahead with an international computer system?

Next, Wayne needs to decide if a computer system can benefit the work of the product shipping department. This department seems to work smoothly, using the manual system that has been developed over the years. Wayne knows that the department is responsible for sending all the product items all over the world. If a record is to be sold in Australia then they will need to make the arrangements to send what is required to Australia.

The department works closely with the international department, arranging the marketing of the products all over the world. If a few records are needed for sale in Greece then it may be most economical to send them direct from England. The Chain Gang's new record has been selling well in Great Britain and sales on the Continent are expected to be high. Copies of the record will not be sent from England, as this would be expensive in shipping costs. A copy of the master record for pressing, together with copies of the artwork for the album cover, are sent and the records are then made locally.

Wayne needs to find out in detail what members of this department do and what information they need to do their job and who within the company they give information to. Wayne spends several days discovering what the department does.

6 How can Wayne find out in detail what the department does?

He will need to communicate what he has discovered to other people.

7 Who will he need to communicate with? How should he do this? What forms should his communications be in? For example, should they be written reports, diagrams, flow charts, etc.? Give reasons for your choice or choices.

8 If it is decided to computerize some of the activities of the department, Wayne may suggest some changes in the way the department works. What problems might he have to face in doing this?

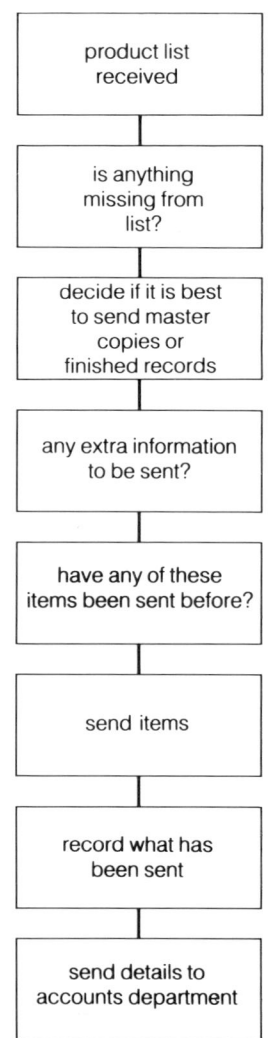

product list received

is anything missing from list?

decide if it is best to send master copies or finished records

any extra information to be sent?

have any of these items been sent before?

send items

record what has been sent

send details to accounts department

Wayne draws up the diagram on the left to show what the department does in sending the necessary stock items to another country for them to produce a record.

Narendra, who works in this department, looks at the chart and explains that they check orders from international divisions to make sure that the goods have not been sent previously and that all the necesary items have been requested.

'Look,' he says. 'The following parts were asked for from Japan last week so that they could produce albums there.'

Part no.	Description
012310	Domino; Chain Gang; Master side A
012312	Domino; Chain Gang; Master sleeve insert
012313	Domino; Chain Gang; Master sleeve

9 Can you see what they forgot to order?

Narendra saw the mistake and corrected it.

10 How could a computer help to do that sort of job?

Narendra explains another problem that they had: 'The German company asked for the masters of a record. When we checked the files we discovered that we sent them copies over a year ago!'

11 How could the computer recognize that and stop unnecessary copies of masters being sent around the world?

12 What changes will have to be made to Wayne's charts before they show accurately what the department does?

Eventually Wayne decides that using a computer will make some of the tasks that the department do easier. Next he must decide exactly how the computer system can be used by the department. He puts his ideas down in writing as the International Department's Computerisation Proposals.

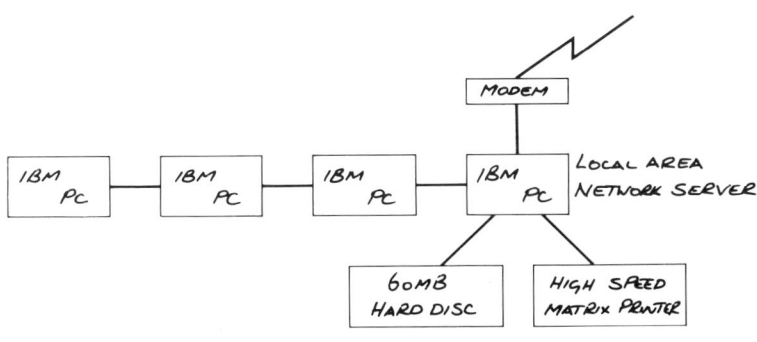

The International Department's computerization proposals

Wayne's departmental proposal includes the specific hardware and software.

> 13 Give a reason why you think Wayne suggested each of these purchases.
>
> 14 Using a computer will change some jobs. What sort of changes might be made? How should these changes be made?

Staff in the department are worried that using a computer will make their jobs more difficult and that errors will occur.

> 15 What can Wayne do to reassure the staff? What else should Wayne do to ensure that there is a smooth transition to using the computer?
>
> 16 What would you suggest that the department should do to help make the introduction of the computer system as smooth as possible?

Look at the space taken up by the large number of filing cabinets needed to store this information

The implementation of the computer system may not be as smooth a process as was hoped by Wayne.

> 17 What could go wrong? As members of the department are trained to use the system, what possible problems could arise? Whose fault is it when errors occur in using the new computer system?

Narendra is concerned that if errors occur then the computer system might 'lose' important information. After all, the information would previously have been kept safely in one of their numerous filing cabinets.

> 18 What can be done to prevent this? What if the computer system doesn't work properly at first and there are faults: how can the department continue to operate?

The department will computerize the task of keeping records of shippings of stock items and test this for the next three months. Then if all is well other parts of the system will be computerized.

> 19 What advantages are there in not computerizing all the tasks in one stage?

Wayne could look for an applications package to buy to do this task. Instead he has proposed that the task of record keeping of shipments is done by using the commercially produced database system called 'dBase III+'. This system is available for the computer system Wayne proposes.

dBASE III PLUS
The data management standard.

dBASE III® PLUS has all the features that made dBASE III the number one selling database management system — *plus* more capability without programming, more power for programming, *and* built-in local area networking as well as stand-alone PC capability. dBASE III PLUS fully addresses the needs of beginning as well as experienced personal computer users. It's the one data management system that grows with you as your needs grow. dBASE III PLUS can store, edit, retrieve, and print information quickly and easily across a broad range of applications: from mailing lists and labels to entire accounting systems . . . from invoicing and personnel records to sophisticated inventory management systems.

20 Wayne could have got the programmers to write a program to do this task in a high level language like BASIC or COBOL. Why do you think Wayne does not do this?

The database system will still require a programmer to write the appropriate routines to carry out the necessary tasks defined by Wayne's charts for the shipping department. Some of the utility programs in the program library could be used or adapted for this purpose.

21 Can you think of any utility programs that might be used here?

22 When the programmer has written the new routines Wayne will insist that they are tested. He will also want the whole package tested. How will this be done? Much thought will go into choosing the data to test this program. What is the purpose of this?

23 The department will need to see and try out the computer system during its development. The people who work in the international department know very little about computers and nothing about programming. So how can they help in the process of the system development?

When the system is complete it will be used by the department for a trial period. They will probably suggest some changes or possible extra features.
   It is possible that programmers involved in writing these routines might leave Dolfin at some point to go and work elsewhere. The programs would then have to be maintained and developed by another programmer.

24 Wayne wants to make sure that the programs are easy to understand by new programmers. What should be done to make sure that this is so?

▷ *Sharing information*

Some departments need to use information about singers and musicians. The promotion department needs to know when they will be on tour, or recording new songs, then they can see when they are available for TV appearances, for example. They decide to make a computer file to keep the information they need. Wayne can see that other departments would need the same information, and he persuades the departments to have one central data file which they can all access via their terminals.

1 Why do you think Wayne encourages them to have one central data file?

2 Make a list of all the data you think would need to be stored about Dolfin's singers and musicians. For each item, say which departments would need it.

One of the disadvantages of having one central file is that some data might need to be restricted to certain departments, or certain people within departments. For example, a famous singer might not want everyone in the company to know her ex-directory telephone number.

3 Can you think of any other data which should be restricted?

Wayne sees that some parts of every record need to be restricted to certain employees. Some data should be restricted so that it can be seen but not amended by some people.

4 Suggest ways that would prevent unauthorized users seeing some of the data. How could some users be prevented from amending the data they can see?

Some information should not be seen by anyone who does not work for Dolfin.

5 What information should be kept secure from outside viewing? Suggest ways of making sure that sensitive data remains within the company.

6 Design the file and record structure for this data file.

The data kept in this file needs to be kept up-to-date. Certain people will be permitted to update the file when they find it necessary. They should not have to wait until the end of the day to do this; amendments should be made straight away. Wayne's system will use a method of record locking to allow this to happen. This means that while a record is being amended, no-one else will be able to access it, but they will be able to access the rest of the file.

7 How could this record-locking be done?

8 Can you think of any problems that could arise from record locking? Suggest ways in which the problems could be overcome.

The Data Protection Act makes it illegal for inaccurate data about people to be kept on a computer file. Anyone with personal data included in a computer file has a right to see what is stored about them, to ensure that it is accurate.

9 Do you think that singers and musicians would be surprised at any of the information that is recorded about them? Do you think that the company will avoid storing some data on computer because of this?

▷ *Developing the system*

Dolfin have used a variety of computing facilities in the past, ranging from their powerful in-house mini computer to the one-off personal computers. Wayne has drawn up two charts showing the computers used by the company when he started to work there.

	Configuration of equipment
Stand-alone PCs	10 PCs, some one-offs, some the same. All have printers, but all printers are different.
IBM mini computer	55/20 with 12 terminals spread around various departments. There are two network printers. One is in the legal department, but they share it with International. All the other users share the other printer.
Local area networks	Taurus Icon network of 6 PCs with one network printer.
IBM mainframe	This is quite an old computer. It is slow, with relatively small amount of memory.

Data Protection Act 1984

CHAPTER 35

ARRANGEMENT OF SECTIONS

Part I

Preliminary

Section
1. Definition of " data " and related expressions.
2. The data protection principles.
3. The Registrar and the Tribunal.

Part II

Registration and Supervision of Data Users and Computer Bureaux

Registration

4. Registration of data users and computer bureaux.
5. Prohibition of unregistered holding etc. of personal data.
6. Applications for registration and for amendment of registered particulars.
7. Acceptance and refusal of applications.
8. Duration and renewal of registration.
9. Inspection etc. of registered particulars.

Supervision

10. Enforcement notices.
11. De-registration notices.
12. Transfer prohibition notices.

Appeals

13. Rights of appeal.
14. Determination of appeals.

A

Wayne's breakdown of Dolfin's computers by system type

Department	Equipment	Usage (software)
Record Making		
A&R	3 IBM terminals 1 IBM XT PC	Word processing only Information storage and retrieval
Production	2 terminals linked by telecom to the manufacturer's computer 1 Olivetti PC	For accessing stock levels Word processing only
Record Selling		
Marketing	2 IBM terminals	Word processing only
Promotion	1 Olivetti M24 PC	Word processing and information storing and retrieval
	1 IBM AT PC	Word processing and information storing and retrieval Producing mailing lists
Press	4 IBM terminals 1 Walters PC	Word processing only Word processing only
Sales	1 IBM terminal	Word processing only
Finance		
Salaries	IBM Mainframe	Payroll
Legal	2 IBM terminals 1 printer	 Word processing only
Accounts	Taurus Icon Network	Using a standard accounts application package
	1 Minolta PC	Word processing only
International		
	1 Compaq PC	Word processing only

Wayne's breakdown of Dolfin's computers by department

1 **Every type of computer is used with a different word processing package. How many different word processing packages are used in the company? What problems do you think this range of software causes, for example, in staff training, or when someone moves from one department to another?**

Wayne recommends that the company standardizes on both hardware and software.

2 **Why do you think Wayne makes this recommendation?**

Much of the work is done using stand-alone PCs. But different departments need access to the same information in many cases. Also, the same data is often input by more than one department. It is important for information to be kept up-to-date.

3 Wayne suggests that the company links a large number of machines together. Why do you think this is better than only using stand-alone machines?

In Wayne's view it is important that information is only input once. He also thinks that data should only be stored in one file (not including back-up copies), which can be accessed by all authorized staff.

4 Are there any disadvantages in this type of system?

5 What kind of security measures will need to be taken to stop unauthorized staff reading the data? How can the system stop unauthorized people from making changes to the data?

Wayne needs to recommend the hardware that Dolfin should buy. He has looked at the needs of the company and the way the company operates. He has decided on the systems that need to be implemented, so now he need to find out about suitable hardware. He has to investigate the range of computer hardware available from the computer manufacturers. If possible, Wayne would also like to make use of the computers that Dolfin is already using.

Wayne proposes a system based on a powerful IBM mini computer, which can serve many of the needs of the various departments.

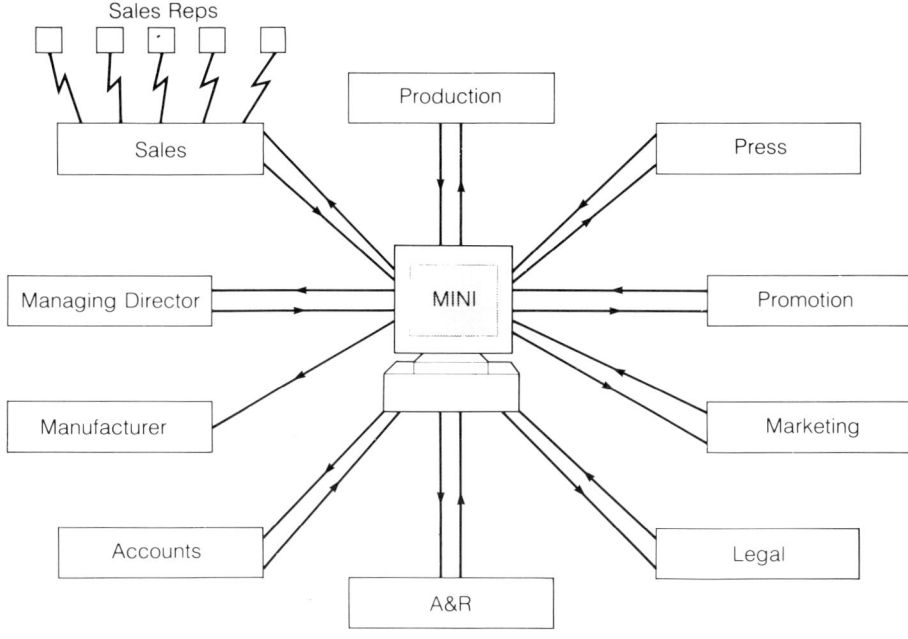

The proposed computer system for Dolfin Records

This system will allow departments to share information, and to pass information from one department to another. For example, the production team can produce the text to go on an album cover. They can find out the names of the musicians from the data input by the finance department into the contracts file. Using a high quality printer, they can output the text in a form which can be used on the album cover.

Can you think of any other job where you might use a hand-held computer?

6 What types of printers could be suitable for this output?

The sales reps visit shops to persuade them to stock Dolfin records. With this system, they would be able to enter details of orders into portable hand-held computers. The orders could then be transmitted via telephone lines to the sales department's network.

7 What use is the sales information to the production department? How could they find out details about the sales?

Some of the machines linked in to this system will be computers. Others will be terminals. A terminal consists of a screen and a keyboard. The terminal is not a computer. The terminal sends messages to the main computer which docs all the processing.

Wayne has discussions with each department so that they can decide how many computers and how many terminals they need. The mini uses a time-sharing operating system for the terminals' work. Each terminal is allocated a small amount of procesing time in rotation.

8 Why do you think terminals will be used instead of computers in some departments?

9 What are the advantages and disadvantages of a time-sharing system? Do you think that Wayne has made the best choice? Could you make any other suggestions?

Some computing activities take a lot of CPU activity to perform. Other tasks require little use of the CPU. Some require immediate response to the user, while for others a few seconds delay in responding to the user is acceptable. Using a personal computer to do some tasks locally will ease the problem of tasks that are very greedy on CPU time. These PCs can still be on the same system as the terminals, communicating with the main computer, but they will not require the main CPU to run programs in the PC's memory.

The CPU time is the amount of processing time taken to do a task, but this gives little indication of how long it might take to do a task in a time-sharing system. This is because lots of other users could be sharing the CPU time as well. Sometimes users have to wait a short while for a response. For example, they may press a key on the keyboard, but it will not show the screen immediately. This delay is called the response time. For many tasks, slight delays are acceptable.

10 Intelligent terminals are able to do a small amount of procesing. They can also hold data in a buffer memory. Would intelligent terminals help to improve response times?

Here are some tasks that the computer could be required to perform. Each one would have different requirements in terms of CPU time and hardware.

A spreadsheet package is used to keep records of sales figures with promotion costings. For example, the spreadsheet could be used to calculate the costs of promotional activities for a particular record. The output would be required both as a printed table, and as a graph.

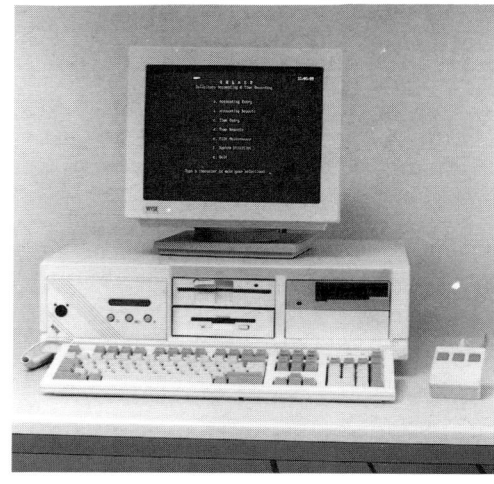

Microcomputer system showing monitor, disc drive and mouse

> 11 Would this need a very fast response time? Would it use a lot of CPU time? What part of the proposed hardware system should be used for this task? What peripherals would be needed?

A word processing package is used to write a letter to a group outlining the details of a television appearance. Word processing involves fast manual input of data at the keyboard. A quick response rate is required as each key is pressed. It could help if a mouse was available for input, too. The output will need to be in good quality print on headed notepaper.

> 12 Would this need a very fast response time? Would it use a lot of CPU time? What part of the proposed hardware system should be used for this task? What peripherals would be needed? A mouse would give a slower response time than a keyboard, so what advantages are there in using a mouse?

The payroll run for employees is done every month. The salary for each employee is calculated. The tax and other deductions are also worked out. A payslip is produced for each employee on pre-printed stationery.

22 York Road,
London W13 3DE

COMPANY Dolfin Records				EMPLOYEE DO23003 Walden Jane D	
CUMULATIVE TO DATE					
DATE 11.12.89	GROSS 13294.97	GROSS TAXABLE 13294.97	TAX 2710.80	NI CONTRIBS. 877.50	
	TAX CODE	PREVIOUS EMPLOYMENT			
PERIOD 09	BASIC 0650H	GROSS	TAX		ANALYSIS 023 00
GROSS PAY Basic 1458.33 Bonus 800.00		DEDUCTIONS TAX 514.50 N.I. 87.50		HOURS OVERTIME RATE HOLIDAYS EMPLOYERS CONTRIBS. N.I. 113.21	
TOTAL PAY 2259.33		TOTAL DEDUCTIONS 612.00		NET PAY 1646.33	

> 13 Would this need a very fast response time? Would it use a lot of CPU time? What part of the proposed hardware system should be used for this task? What peripherals would be needed?

The company that actually presses Dolfin's records telephones the accounts department. They want to know why they have been paid less than they had asked for on their last invoice. The accounts department need to access the file with details of the bill and its payment.

> **14** Would this need a very fast response time? Would it use a lot of CPU time? What part of the proposed hardware system should be used for this task? Will any hard copy output be required? What peripherals would be needed?

▷ Compiling the Charts

Every week a chart showing record sales in the UK is produced. It is produced by a market research company, and is paid for by the BBC, the record companies and the music industry's trade magazine.

This chart is immensely important to record companies. Firstly, it shows them how successful they are in relation to other record companies. Secondly, and more importantly, it increases some record sales. Some people only find out about records when they get into the top 40. Other people buy records just because they are in the charts. So it is very important to record companies to get their records sales shown in the charts.

The charts are based on the records that are sold in shops, not on the number of records sold to shops by the record companies. But the record companies need to persuade the shops to stock their records, or else they won't be able to sell them and they won't get into the chart.

Two methods have been used to measure the number of records sold each week. Neither of them tried to find out which records had been sold in every record shop. There are just too many. Instead, both of them relied on choosing a selection of shops and hoping that their sales gave an accurate picture of national sales.

The old system

A small number of record shops were selected in different parts of the country. The identity of the shops was supposed to be secret, but in fact it was quite easy to find out which they were.

The record 'Do they know it's Christmas?' produced by Band Aid raised millions of pounds for charity when it shot to number one in the charts in Christmas 1984. This Live Aid concert raised yet more money in July 1985

As well as music charts, there are also weekly charts for the most popular TV programs. How do you think these are worked out?

Every record has a code number. Every time a record was sold, the assistant wrote the code number down on a form like this:

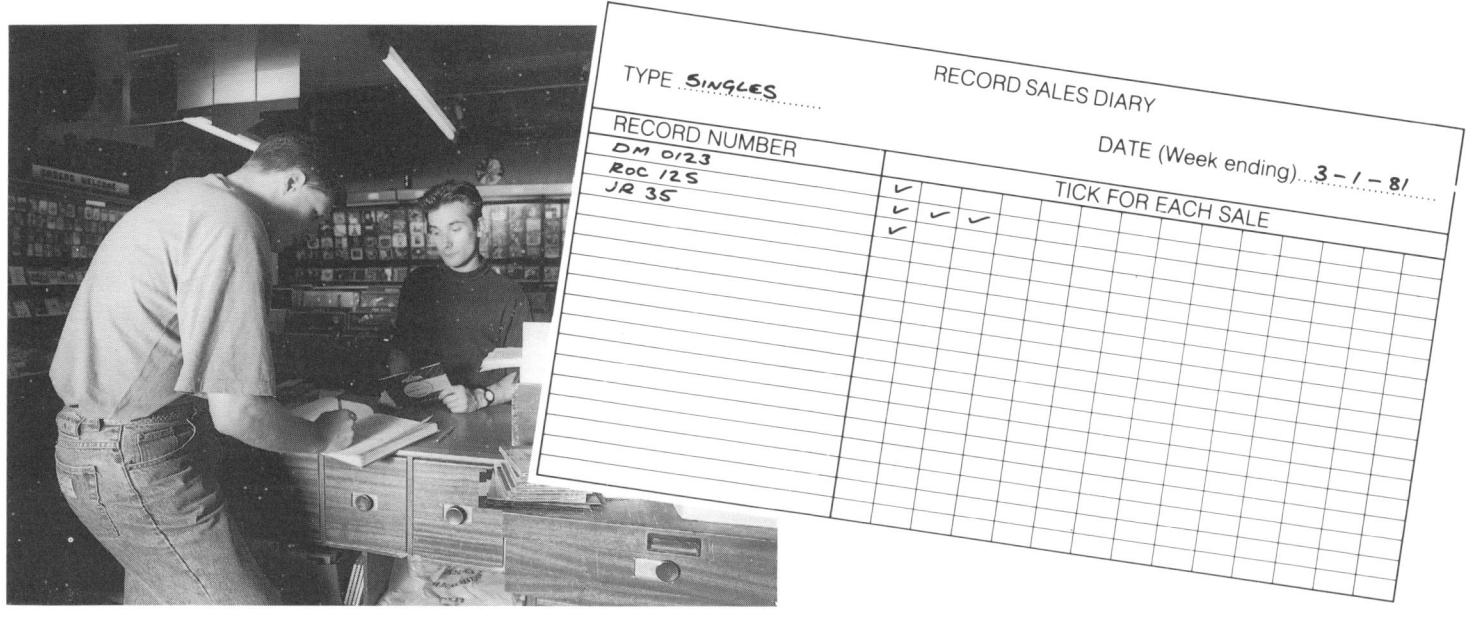

TYPE *Singles*	RECORD SALES DIARY					
RECORD NUMBER			DATE (Week ending) *3-1-81*			
DM 0123			TICK FOR EACH SALE			
ROC 125	✓	✓	✓			
JR 35	✓					
	✓					

At the end of Friday's trading, the shop posted its forms to the market research company. The forms were not sent at the end of Saturday's trading because the last post on Saturday is at lunch time. It was thought that Saturday's sales would be too out-of-date for including in the following week, so Saturday's sales were excluded completely. The chart was produced by manually processing the information. It was ready by lunchtime on Tuesday.

> **1 What disadvantages are there in this system? How might unscrupulous record companies try to make it appear that their records were selling more?**

The new system

The new system is based on computers and modern communications. More shops were selected to be on the chart panel, although not all of them have their sales included every week.

Keeping track of the records sold using a data recorder

Each shop has a data recorder. Every time a record is sold, the assistant keys in the record's code number. This is recorded on a magnetic tape, together with the date and time. The name of the shop is included at the beginning of each tape.

At various times during the week, the data on the cassette tape is transmitted over the telephone lines to the market researcher's computer. The data is processed and examined for irregularities. Eventually the chart is issued at about 4 p.m. Sunday afternoon. It is put onto Prestel pages the next day, and also printed in *Music Week*, the trade magazine.

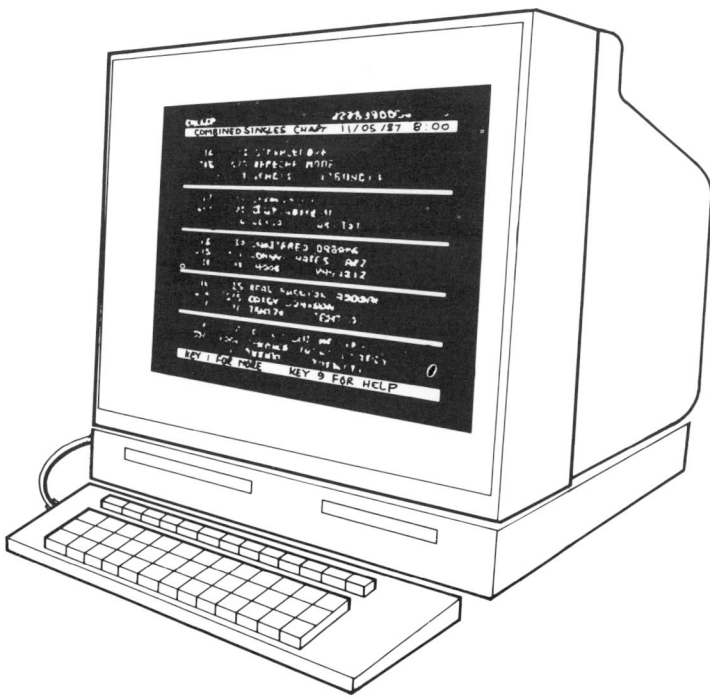

The up-to-date singles chart on PRESTEL

2   Why is the data collected at different times?

3   When do you think *Music Week* becomes available? Why do you
    think the chart is put onto Prestel?

In addition to the main chart, a 'mid-week' chart is produced on Friday, to
help the record companies keep up-to-date with their records' progress.

4   It would be possible to produce a chart every day with this system.
    What would be the advantages and disadvantages of issuing a new
    chart every day?

5   In the new system it is more difficult for a record shop to keep it
    secret that they are on the chart panel. Why?

6   Can you think of ways that might be used to make it appear that
    some records are selling faster than they actually are?

7   What advantages does the new system have over the old one?

8   What sort of irregularities could it detect? How could it check and
    deal with these?

9   Can you think of ways in which this system could be improved?

In what ways could a modern record shop benefit from using computers?

Record sleeves are now printed with barcodes, which include their unique identity code. Many record shops are using POS terminals instead of ordinary cash registers. Some shops use computers for their stock control.

10 Using all this information, design the best possible system for collecting data and producing the charts.

▷ *General questions*

1 The managing director of an international company wants to hold a meeting for the heads of all of the company's foreign branches. Make a list of all the different ways that this invitation could be sent. For each one, say whether or not there would be hard copy of the invitation. Give the advantages and disadvantages of each method.

2 Problem Solvers plc are a company who help organizations to decide whether or not to use information technology in their businesses. They employ a number of systems analysts. These systems analysts have to recommend the sort of help that computers could give to an organization. Problem Solvers' personnel officer, Louis Cohen, has been told that the company needs to employ another systems analyst. He puts an advertisement in a computer journal, and many people write to him to ask for further details of the job. Imagine that you are in Louis' position, and write a description of the job of a systems analyst.

3 These two systems flow charts show two different methods of updating a computer file. One shows the batch updating of a file of data relating to the employees at a factory. The other one shows the on-line updating of a file of data for booking theatre seats. What parts of the system are common to both applications? Which parts are different? Work out which flow chart belongs to each application, and give as many reasons as you can for your decision.

4 Rosie Dean is an author. She thinks that a computer might help her with her writing, and also with organizing the information she collects and keeps for her writing. She also thinks that a computer might help her to keep a record of her income and expenses. What items of computer hardware and software would she need to buy? Include in your list a suitable form of backing store, and all the necessary peripherals. Give reasons for each item.

5 Some organizations use computers, but do not have computers of their own. They have their data processed by a computer bureau. There are advantages and disadvantages in using computer bureaux. Here is a list of computer users. For each one, say what the main advantages and disadvantages would be for them using a computer bureau. Say whether or not you would recommend the use of a bureau for each example.
   a A doctor wants to keep information about her patients on computer file. She thinks it will be a more efficient method of record keeping, and that it will help her to keep up-to-date.
   b A manager of a small manufacturing company wants to use a computer to process the company's payroll. It must calculate how much each person has earned each month, and keep records of how much they have been paid, and what tax and National Insurance contributions they have made.
   c A theatre wants to use a computer to help organize the booking office. They want the computer to keep a record of which seats are available for each performance.
   d A chemical works wants to use a computer to monitor the chemical processes. The computer must be able to control the apparatus, so that, for example, it can reduce the temperature if necessary.
   e A small record and cassette library wants to use a computer to help keep track of the records and tapes, and the people who borrow them. The librarian wants to be able to know who has borrowed each record and tape.

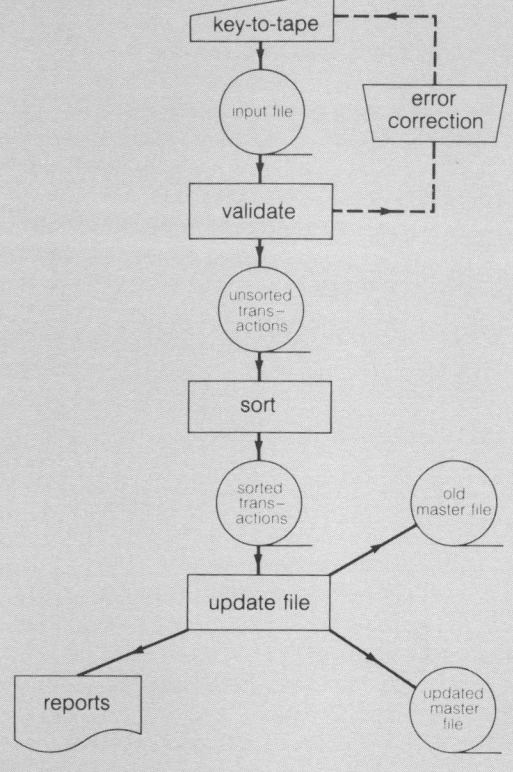

Flow chart 1

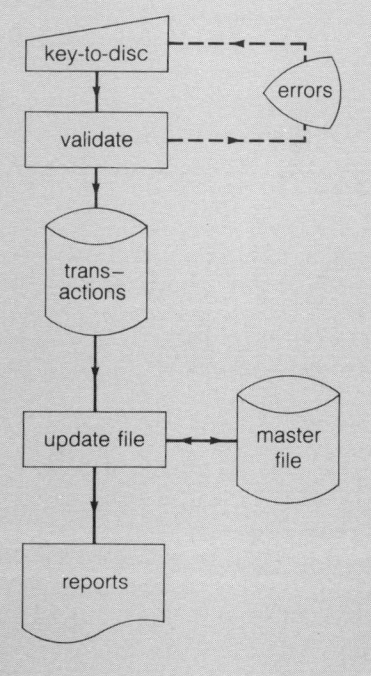

Flow chart 2

6 Some people say that the increasing use of computers has caused unemployment. It is also said that increased use of computers has changed the way that some people work.

Give examples of jobs that have become redundant because of the use of computers. In general, what type of jobs are disappearing?

Give examples of jobs that have been created. In general, what kind of jobs have been created?

Give examples of jobs that have changed a lot because they are now involved with computers. In general, what are the major changes?

What advice would you give to someone who was undecided about the sort of career they should try for?

7 Some people say that detection of crime would be made easier if personal details, including fingerprints, of everyone in the country were kept in a central computer databank. Some people also think that the police should have access to other files of information such as those held by the Inland Revenue, banks and credit card agencies.

What arguments are there both for and against this availability of information? Find out how the Data Protection Act protects personal information.

8 Diwana are going on tour to promote their new record. They want to make sure that everything goes well, and that their live shows will encourage people to buy their records. They want to make sure that they look good on stage, and take a lot of care with their clothes. They also consider the arrangement of their equipment on stage, and the stage lighting. They will be appearing on many different sized stages during their tour. How could a computer help with the design of the stage set?

It is possible to use stage lighting which is controlled by computer. The lighting can be linked to the music, so that certain lights are switched on or off when the sound reaches a certain volume. Patterns of lights can be programmed to achieve special effects.

How else might Diwana make use of computer technology on their tour? What aspects of the tour organization could not be helped by using computers?

9 An applications package is a program, or a set of programs designed to do a particular task. Examples of applications packages are programs to do jobs like payroll, theatre seat booking and stock control.

Zelda Software House produces applications packages for its customers. The manager at Zelda Software House wants to write a set of guidelines for their programmers and analysts. He thinks that there are some points that should be considered when writing any applications package. What do you think he should include in his list of guidelines?

▷ Software activities

1 A group's fan club receives a lot of requests for information from fans. They have to write back to each club member, giving them the information that they need. Use a word processing package to produce an example of one of these letters. How else might a fan club make use of a word processor?

2 Use a viewdata package to produce an information display about a group or singer.

WDK are a company who organize concert tours for different sorts of acts, from orchestras and groups to ~icians and hypnotists. They need to keep a lot of information about venues that are available for putting on shows. For example, they need to know the size of the stage, the capacity of the hall and the cost of hiring it.

Use an information retrieval package to create a file of information about a number of venues. Use the package to select suitable venues for acts. For example, for a magician who performs close-up magic to small audiences, or for a world famous group who need a very large stage to accommodate their lighting rig and speakers.

4 Use a painting program to design an album or single sleeve for a group.

Understanding the Words

This section gives some extra help with the meanings of words.

Words are often easier to understand when you see how they are used. This section gives some examples of where to look in the book to find the word used in context.

algorithm – a set of instructions. *See Ch 1 – Following instructions, Ch 3 – The Money Program and Ch 5 – Getting it Clean—removing the bugs.*

ALU – stands for arithmetic and logic unit.

analog – analog data is continuous and can take any value within certain limits. This is not easy to understand, so here is an example. An analog watch has hands which move smoothly around the clock face. The hands are always moving and the watch always shows the exact time.

An alternative type of watch would be a digital watch. The time displayed stays the same for a second before changing, so you cannot tell when it is, say, 33½ seconds after 1 p.m. *See Ch 4 – The story so far . . . and Ch 5 – The design.*

analog to digital converter – a device which changes analog data to the sort of data that computers can work with – digital data. *See Ch 5 – The design.*

applications package – a computer program that does something useful, such as a word processing package or a stock control program. *See Ch 6 – Developing the system.*

arithmetic and logic unit – the 'heart' of a computer's central processor unit. It is the part that compares and adds data. *See Ch 5 – The design.*

ASCII – sounds like 'askey'. It is a common set of codes for letters, numbers and other characters. *See Ch 4 – The story so far . . .*

assembler – a computer program. It translates computer programs written in assembly language into a form that a computer can work with. *See Ch 4 – Deciding on the system and Ch 5 – The design.*

assembly language – a computer programming language. It is close to the way a computer works and is an example of a low level language. *See Ch 5 – The design.*

automatic re-ordering – a way in which a shop can obtain extra stock. When the number of items in stock becomes low, the computer system places an order for more items. *See Ch 1 – Taking stock.*

back-up memory – a means of saving data even when the power to the computer is switched off. *See Ch 5 – What could go wrong?*

barcodes – patterns of two-coloured stripes which represent numbers. *See Ch 1 – The story so far . . . , and Coding Information.*

BASIC – a computer language. It is an example of a high level language. *See Ch 4 – Deciding on the system and Ch 6 – Records around the world.*

batch processing – one way in which a computer system can work. Programs and data are collected together and processed in one go. *See Ch 1 – The story so far . . . and Taking stock.*

baud rate – the speed at which data moves from one device to another. *See Ch 4 – The story so far . . . and Ch 5 – What's going on?*

binary – in a set of two. In a binary number system there are only two digits. Computers perform arithmetic using a binary number system. See **bit**.

bit – a binary digit 0 or 1. *See Ch 4 – The story so far . . . and Ch 5 – The design and Inside the machine.*

bubble memory – a type of computer memory. Data is stored by magnetizing very small elements called bubbles. Bubble memory can store vast amounts of data in very small spaces. *See Ch 1 – Putting the stock on file.*

buffer – a temporary storage place for data. For example, a printer works more slowly than a computer processor. The processor sends data to the printer faster than the printer can cope with. So the printer has a buffer to store the data which is waiting to be printed. *See Ch 4 – Dear Borrower . . .*

bug – a mistake in a computer program. *See Ch 5 – Getting it clean – removing the bugs.*

byte – a pattern of bits. Often, one byte is the code for one character. *See Ch 4 – The story so far . . .*

CEEFAX – a teletext system. It is broadcast with BBC television pictures and can be received by some television sets. *See Ch 4 – Making the system better.*

central processor unit – the 'nerve centre' of a computer. It controls and co-ordinates the other parts of the computer. *See Ch 5 – General questions 4.*

character set – a complete set of characters for a computer. *See Ch 4 – The story so far . . .*

check digit – an extra digit used to find errors in data later on. *See Ch 1 – Coding information.*

chip – a common and popular name for an integrated circuit. *See Ch 5 – The washing programmes.*

COBOL – a computer language. It is an example of a high level language. *See Ch 4 – Deciding on the system and Ch 6 – Records around the world.*

coded information – representing information in a different way. It is usually done to make information simpler and shorter. *See Ch 2 – The Camberwell incident.*

compiler – a computer program. It translates computer programs written in a high level language into a form that a computer can work with. It translates the whole program before following any of the program's instructions. *See Ch 4 – Deciding on the system.*

computer bureau – an organization which processes other organizations' computer data. *See Ch 6 – The story so far... and Paying the musicians.*

computer configuration – the collection of computer hardware that makes up a particular computer system. *See Ch 6 – Developing the system and General questions.*

content addressable file store – a way of storing and quickly locating data. *See Ch 2 – Patterns of incidents.*

control unit – the part of the central processor unit (CPU) that co-ordinates the various parts of the computer when a program is run. *See Ch 5 – The design.*

CPU – stand for central processor unit.

daisy wheel printer – a printer with the character set arranged on a plastic wheel. The wheel hits a ribbon which makes the printed mark on the paper. These printers give good quality print, like typewriters, but they cannot print graphics. *See Ch 4 – Dear Borrower...*

Data Protection Act – *See Ch 6 – Sharing information.*

database – a collection of data arranged in a particular format. *See Ch 6 – Paying the musicians and Records around the world.*

data capture – collecting data for a particular computer use. *See Ch 6 – Paying the musicians and Ch 1 – Putting the stock on file.*

digital – digital data can be exactly represented by numbers. See also **analog**. *See Ch 5 – The design.*

direct access – storing or retrieving data without the need to read any other stored data first. Also called random access. *See Ch 1 – Keeping track.*

disk controller – hardware designed to make efficient use of disks and disk drives. *See Ch 5 – What's going on?*

display processor – a device which controls and operates a display. *See Ch 5 – What's going on?*

documentation – the written comments and illustrations accompanying a program or system. *See Ch 1 – Designing the system and Ch 4 – Deciding on the system.*

dot matrix printer – a printer which can print characters and graphics made up from patterns of dots. *See Ch 4 – Dear Borrower...*

EFT – stands for electronic funds transfer.

EFTPOS – stands for electronic funds transfer at point of sale.

electronic funds transfer – the transfer of money between banks and other organizations, using a direct computer link. *See Ch 2 – Lock up your data!*

electronic funds transfer at point of sale – where goods can be paid for in shops etc., by the direct transfer of money from the buyer's bank to the seller's bank via a direct computer link. *See Ch 2 – Lock up your data!*

error message – where the computer lets the user know that a mistake has been found. Sometimes the cause of the error is also given. *See Ch 4 – Dear Borrower...*

feasibility study – a study of an organization to find whether, and how, a computer may be of use. *See Ch 1 – Designing the system and Ch 4 – General questions.*

fetch–execute cycle – what happens in the CPU in order to carry out a program instruction. *See Ch 5 – Inside the machine.*

field – a part of every record in a file. For example, a file containing information about cars could have one record for each car. One field in each record could be the colour of the car. *See Ch 1 – Keeping track, Ch 4 – The story so far... and Deciding on the system.*

file – an organized collection of related data. *See Ch 1 – The story so far..., Keeping track and Ch 2 – Helping with inquiries.*

flowchart – a diagram showing a series of events. Sometimes called a flow diagram. *See Ch 1 – Following instructions and Ch 5 – What could go wrong?*

FORTRAN – a computer language. It is an example of a high level language. *See Ch 4 – Deciding on the system and Ch 6 – Records around the world.*

front-end processor – a small computer which receives data from a number of input devices, organizes it and transmits it to a more powerful computer for processing. *See Ch 4 – At the computer centre.*

hard copy – computer output on paper or similar media. *See Ch 6 – Can computers help?*

hardware – computer equipment.

high level language – a computer programming language designed to be used with particular types of applications and problems, and which can usually be used on a number of different computers. *See Ch 5 – The design.*

implementation – if it is decided that an organization could make good use of a computer system, and the computer system has been decided on, the next stage is the implementation of the system. This stage includes the installation of the system, and the training of the staff. *See Ch 1 – Designing the system and Ch 6 – Records around the world.*

indexing – a method of looking up records in a file very quickly. *See Ch 2 – Pattern of incidents and Ch 4 – Making the system better.*

instruction register – a special place in the CPU which stores the next programming instruction to be carried out. *See Ch 5 – Inside the machine.*

instruction set – the complete set of commands that the CPU can carry out. *See Ch 5 – Inside the machine.*

intelligent terminal – a computer terminal which is able to perform some processing. *See Ch 6 – Developing the system.*

interactive system – allows two-way communication between system and user. *See Ch 3 – Banking on TV and General questions and Ch 4 – Making the system better.*

interactive video – a combination of an interaction computer system with a video system. *See Ch 4 – Making the system better.*

interblock gap – space on magnetic tape between blocks of records. *See Ch 4 – The story so far...*

interpreter – a computer program which translates a program written in high level language into a form that a computer can work with. It translates the program one line at a time, and carries out each instruction before translating the next one. *See Ch 4 – Deciding on the system.*

inverted file – a way of structuring a file to allow fast access to the data. *See Ch 4 – Making the system better.*

key-field – every file has a key-field which is used to identify each record. *See Ch 1 – Keeping track.*

keyword – important words which can be searched for in a database. *See Ch 4 – Making the system better.*

kilobyte – 1024 bytes. See **byte**.

Kimball tags – small cards with punched holes sometimes found attached to goods (especially clothes) in shops. *See Ch 1 – Taking stock.*

LAN – stands for local area network.

laser printer – a printer which produces high quality text and graphics. *See Ch 4 – Dear Borrower...*

laser scanner – a device which uses a laser to read machine readable codes such as barcodes. *See Ch 1 – The story so far...*

LED – stands for light emitting diode. These are small coloured lights used, for example, to indicate when a disk drive is being used. *See Ch 5 – What's going on?*

local area network – a number of computers and peripherals linked together by direct cables. Local area networks do not use telecommunication links. *See Ch 1 – Putting the stock on file.*

low level language – a computer programming language which is designed to be used on a particular computer, and which is closely linked to the way in which the computer works. See also **assembly language**. *See Ch 4 – Deciding on the system.*

machine code – a program in machine code is a set of instructions which can be carried out by a computer without the need for any translation. *See Ch 4 – Deciding on the system.*

magnetic storage – data can be stored on a range of magnetic media e.g. card, disk and tape. *See Ch 1 – Keeping track, Putting the stock on file and Taking stock.*

mainframe – a computer with a large amount of memory and a very fast processor. *See Ch 1 – Designing the system.*

mark sense forms – special forms on which marks can be made in specific places. These marks can then be read by a device in a computer system. *See Ch 1 – Taking stock.*

master file – a file of data which is the main source of information for a job. *See Ch 4 – Where are the books?*

memory map – this shows the different ways in which the computer's memory is used. *See Ch 5 – The design.*

memory location – a particular place in a computer's memory. *See Ch 5 – Inside the machine.*

MICR – stands for magnetic ink character recognition. This is a system which uses specially shaped characters printed with magnetized ink. These characters are machine-readable. A common example of this system is the writing found along the bottom of cheques. *See Ch 3 – Clearing the cheque.*

microcontroller – is a computer system dedicated to a particular task, and which contains a microprocessor and memory. *See Ch 5 – The design.*

microfiche – small plastic sheets containing many pages of very small text and drawings. Microfiche are read by projecting the image onto a screen. *See Ch 4 – Dear Borrower...*

microprocessor – one chip that does the work of a central processor unit. *See Ch 5 – The washing programmes.*

mini-computer – a computer with large amount of memory and a fast processor. *See Ch 6 – Developing the system.*

modem – a device that converts computer data into a form that can be transmitted over telephone lines. *See Ch 4 – The story so far...*

modulo check – a validity check used to detect errors in data which is transmitted from one device to another. *See Ch 2 – Helping with inquiries.*

mouse – an input device used to point to and select items on the computer screen. *See Ch 6 – Developing the system.*

multi-access – a computer system with which several users can use the computer apparently at the same time. *See Ch 4 – At the computer centre.*

multiplexor – a device which allows several users to share a single communications channel. *See Ch 4 – At the computer centre.*

network – a number of computers linked together and sharing facilities. *See Ch 1 – Putting the stock on file.*

non-volatile memory – computer memory which does not lose its contents when the computer is switched off. *See Ch 1 – Putting the stock on file.*

object code – the program output from an assembler or compiler. *See Ch 4 – Deciding on the system.*

OCR – stands for optical character recognition.

off-line – part of a computer system which is not under the control of the CPU. For example, a printer may be switched off-line so that paper can be loaded. *See Ch 1 – Keeping track and Ch 4 – At the computer centre.*

OMR – stands for optical mark recognition.

on-line – part of a computer system which is under the control of the CPU. *See Ch 1 – Keeping track and Ch 4 – At the computer centre.*

operating system – a computer program that controls the parts of a computer system, making sure that the system works efficiently. *See Ch 3 – Cash around the clock and Ch 4 – Dear Borrower...*

operator – the person who operates the computer, receiving and acting on instructions from the operating system and computer users. *See Ch 4 – Dear Borrower...*

operator's console – a terminal used by the computer operator. *See Ch 4 – Dear Borrower...*

optical character recognition – a system which uses specially shaped characters. These characters are machine-readable. *See Ch 1 – Taking stock.*

optical mark recognition – a system where marks printed on paper can be read with a special device. *See Ch 1 – Taking stock.*

ORACLE – a teletext system. It is broadcast with ITV television pictures and can be received by some television sets. *See Ch 4 – Making the system better.*

package – a software package is a complete, ready to use piece of software. *See Ch 6 – Paying the musicians.*

packet switching – the routing of a 'message' through a network system of computers to a particular destination. *See Ch 3 – Banking on TV.*

parallel running – using two systems at the same time in case one does not work properly. *See Ch 1 – The story so far...*

parity – the use of an extra binary digit for the purpose of checking the accuracy of data. *See Ch 4 – The story so far...*

parity bit – the extra binary digit added to a set of bits for later detection of errors. *See Ch 5 – What's going on?*

peripherals – devices attached to the CPU of a computer, for example, printer, disk drive, mouse.

pilot study – a small scale test of a system to see how it will work. *See Ch 1 – The story so far...*

PIN – stands for personal identification number. A PIN is used as a password to gain access to an on-line computer system. *See Ch 3 – Cash around the clock, The money program.*

port – the point at which signals enter and leave the CPU. *See Ch 5 – The design and Inside the machine.*

Prestel – an interactive teletext system. The user is connected to a remote computer via telecommunications lines. *See Ch 3 – Banking on TV and Ch 4 – Making the system better.*

price look-up (PLU) – the means of finding the price of an item of stock in a shop from a computer file. *See Ch 1 – Putting the stock on file.*

procedure – a set of computer instructions which carry out a specific task. *See Ch 3 – The money program.*

program – a complete set of program instructions or procedures. *See Ch 1 – Designing the system, Ch 2 – Traffic incident and Ch 4 – Deciding on the system.*

program counter – a register in a computer's memory which holds the address of the next program instruction to be carried out. *See Ch 5 – Inside the machine.*

program library – a collection of programs and/or procedures. *See Ch 6 – The story so far . . . and – Records around the world.*

pseudo-code – an algorithm set out as a set of instructions resembling a programming language. *See Ch 3 – The money program.*

POS terminal – stands for point of sale terminal. This is a device used to record the details of goods sold in a shop and to process the transactions. *See Ch 1 – The story so far . . .*

pulse train – a sequence of binary pulses. *See Ch 5 – What's going on?*

RAM – stands for random access memory. This is memory which can be read from and written to. *See Ch 5 – The design.*

ROM – stands for read only memory. This cannot be written to, so data cannot be added to, changed or deleted. *See Ch 5 – The design and Inside the machine.*

real time – where processing is of a comparable speed to events in the system. *See Ch 1 – The story so far . . .*

record locking – a process which ensures that records are correctly updated in a system where several users may be reading and writing to the same file at the same time. *See Ch 6 – Sharing information.*

record – part of a file consisting of related items of data and treated as a unit. For example, in a file of information about trees, each tree will have its own record. *See Ch 2 – Helping with inquiries.*

register – a special place in a computer's memory. See, for example, **instruction register**. *See Ch 5 – Inside the machine.*

security of data – *See Ch 6 – Paying the musicians, Sharing Information and Developing the system.*

sensors – input devices which detect changes in the environment, for example, temperature, light and movement. *See Ch 5 – The design and What could go wrong?*

server – the central controlling component of a network of computers. *See Ch 1 – Putting the stock on file.*

software – computer programs.

source code – a program written in a high or low level language. *See Ch 4 – Deciding on the system.*

spreadsheet – a software package in which data is stored in rows and columns. It allows the user to investigate what might happen to the data under certain conditions. *See Ch 3 – General questions.*

stand-alone – a single computer system, not networked to any others. *See Ch 6 – Developing the system.*

systems analysis – investigating the workings of an organization with a view to recommending a computerized system for it. *See Ch 4 – Deciding on the system and Ch 6 – General questions.*

systems analyst – a person who carries out a systems analysis. *See Ch 3 – What the customer sees and Ch 4 – Deciding on the system.*

systems diagram – a diagram showing the way an organization works and the flow of information through it. *See Ch 6 – General questions.*

teletext – a computer-based information retrieval system containing pages of information. Teletext systems can be either broadcast with TV signals (like CEEFAX and ORACLE) or (like Prestel) transmitted via telecommunication lines. *See Ch 2 – Lock up your data!, Ch 3 – Banking on TV and Ch 4 – Making the system better.*

terminal – a device which is part of a computer system, and where data can be input and output. *See Ch 1 – The story so far . . ., Putting the stock on file, Ch 2 – The Camberwell incident, Spreading the word and Ch 3 – Cash around the clock, What the customer sees.*

time-sharing – a way of allowing **multi-access** to a computer system. Each user is allowed, in turn, very short periods of the computer's time. The time between each period is so short that it appears that each user has continuous use of the system. *See Ch 3 – Cash around the clock and Ch 6 – Developing the system.*

time-slice – the name given to each short period of time allocated to each user in a time-sharing system. *See Ch 3 – Cash around the clock and Ch 4 – At the computer centre.*

transaction file – a collection of records used to update a master file. *See Ch 4 – Where are the books?*

translator – a computer program used to convert programs from one programming language to another. *See Ch 4 – Deciding on the system.*

transmission errors – faults that are found in data after it has been sent from one device to another. *See Ch 4 – The story so far . . .*

truth tables – are used to work out the consequences of different **binary** inputs to a system. *See Ch 1 – Following instructions.*

turn-around document – a computer produced form on which data is entered. The form is then returned and becomes an input document. *See Ch 3 – Checking for mistakes.*

updating – the process of making changes to a file. *See Ch 1 – Putting the stock on file, Ch 4 – Where are the books? and Ch 6 – Sharing information, General questions.*

user-interface – the link between the user and the computer program. It includes things like the screen display, and methods of input. *See Ch 3 – What the customer sees and General questions.*

utility programs – are programs which carry out processes on files such as copying, moving, printing or sorting. *See Ch 4 – Dear Borrower . . . and Ch 6 – Records around the world.*

VDU – stands for visual display unit, which is a computer screen or monitor. *See Ch 1 – The story so far . . . and Putting the stock on file.*

validation – a process of checking for errors in data. It is used to find errors which make the data incomplete or unreasonable, such as where a character has been left off, or a date is entered as 45/11/89. *See Ch 1 – Keeping track, Putting the stock on file and Ch 6 – Paying the musicians.*

verification – a process of checking for errors in data. It is carried out after data has been transferred from one medium or device to another. For example, after typing in data from a printed page, or after data is read from a disk. *See Ch 1 – Putting the stock on file, Ch 3 – Clearing the cheque and Ch 6 – Paying the musicians.*

volatile memory – a type of computer memory that loses its contents when the power is switched off. *See Ch 1 – Putting the stock on file.*

voice synthesizer – a device which produces sounds which sound like the human voice. *See Ch 1 – The story so far . . .*

word processor – a computer system used to produce formatted documents. *See Ch 6 – Paying the musicians and Developing the system.*